BORGES BEYOND THE VISIBLE

BORGES BEYOND

THE VISIBLE

Max Ubelaker Andrade

THE PENNSYLVANIA STATE UNIVERSITY PRESS

University Park, Pennsylvania

Library of Congress Cataloging-in-Publication Data

Names: Ubelaker Andrade, Max, 1979– author.
Title: Borges beyond the visible / Max Ubelaker
    Andrade.
Description: University Park, Pennsylvania : The
    Pennsylvania State University Press, [2019] |
    Includes bibliographical references and index.
Summary: "Presents a new approach to Jorge Luis
    Borges' work, exploring dimensions of his literary
    project involving theology, blindness, literary
    imagination, gender, sexuality, and suicide"—
    Provided by publisher.
Identifiers: LCCN 2018061597 | ISBN 9780271083544
    (cloth : alk. paper)
Subjects: LCSH: Borges, Jorge Luis, 1899–1986—
    Criticism and interpretation. | Visualization in
    literature. | Sex in literature. | Suicide in literature.
Classification: LCC PQ7797.B635 Z941327 2019 |
    DDC 868/.6209—dc23
LC record available at https://lccn.loc.gov
    /2018061597

Published by The Pennsylvania State University Press,
University Park, PA 16802-1003

The Pennsylvania State University Press is a member
of the Association of University Presses.

It is the policy of The Pennsylvania State University
Press to use acid-free paper. Publications on uncoated
stock satisfy the minimum requirements of American
National Standard for Information Sciences—
Permanence of Paper for Printed Library Material,
ANSI Z39.48–1992.

For Samantha.

For my family.

For my teachers.

Contents

Illustrations

Acknowledgments

I am tremendously grateful for the guidance, friendship, and support of Alicia Borinsky; I hope that her influence and example can be seen throughout this book. I also want to express my gratitude to Ilán Stavans, who not only provided invaluable recommendations at an early stage of the project, but also helped steer me toward literary studies not so long ago. Many conversations, with students, friends, colleagues, and teachers have shaped this book. I wish to offer a special thank you to Julio Crespo, Hugo Beccacece, and Aravinda Bhat. Thank you also to the international *Blind Creations* conference hosted by Royal Holloway, University of London in 2015 and Boston University's *Writing in the Americas Program*, which—led by Alicia Borinsky in Boston and in Buenos Aires—allowed unique conversations about Borges and his work to take place between scholars, writers, and students.

A number of individuals and institutions offered their help in providing images for this book. I would like to thank Harvard Art Museums, the Maritime Museum (Stockholm), and Björn Larsson for their generosity, as well as Germán Álvarez for the opportunity to photograph the interior halls of the old building of Argentina's Biblioteca Nacional. The Harry Ransom Center at The University of Texas at Austin was extraordinarily helpful in providing access to unique archival material and I am grateful for their warm welcome.

Thank you to Pennsylvania State University Press—to Patrick Alexander, Kendra Boileau, and Alex Vose for helping bring this project into existence, to Regina Starace for the wonderful cover design, to Alex Ramos and Laura Reed-Morrisson for their editing expertise, and to the manuscript's reviewers for their insightful suggestions. I would also like to thank and acknowledge my colleagues at the University of Massachusetts Lowell for their continued support.

My deepest gratitude is to my family. To Samantha, to my mother and my father, to Lisa and Nico and Olivia. This project was built on a foundation of love, honesty, humor and dedication that you created over many years and strengthen every day. Thank you.

Introduction

In the prologue to María Esther Vázquez's *Los nombres de la muerte*, Borges writes a sentence directed to his readers, and hers:

> Ya que el lector de nuestro tiempo es también un crítico, un hombre que conoce, y prevé, los artificios literarios, el cuento deberá constar de dos argumentos; uno, falso, que vagamente se indica, y otro, el auténtico, que se mantendrá secreto hasta el fin. (4:161)[1]

> Now that the reader of our time is also a critic, someone who knows and foresees literary techniques, the story should contain two arguments; one, false, which is vaguely suggested, and another, the authentic one, which will be kept secret until the end.

Even if we hold this binary lightly, allowing for the possibility of multiple levels of meaning and more than one authentic reading, we are still left with a powerful idea: that a story's more accessible interpretations should be approached with a degree of skepticism, that one of their functions might in fact be to misdirect or mislead. Before we leap, as readers, to the solutions and insights that are readily available to us, embracing the most conspicuous explanations and approaches, Borges suggests that it is important to cultivate a sense of independence and even disobedience as we intuit the way forward.

We do not know when or if "the end" will arrive with its promised revelations, but we do know that there will be tempting, less-than-true solutions available along the way. Sometimes the story that we see is not the story in its fullest form.

To read Borges is, in this sense, to learn how to mistrust the authority of his characters and narrators, to sense peculiar oversights in the text, small contradictions and shifts in tone that can suggest other possibilities, patterns, and voices. As Sylvia Molloy writes, his stories, when read closely, often reveal themselves to be fragmentary, unstable fictions riddled with "breaks that mark" the page and "hint" at uncanniness; she writes of "gaps," "ambiguities," and "quirks" that, together, refuse the "promise of a flowing text" (*Signs of Borges*, 1–2). Paradoxes, omissions, and subtle ironies form part of the internal logic of Borges's literary work. His stories insinuate that these irregularities correspond to one another in a meaningful yet difficult-to-perceive order, while also providing sets of references and allusions (to specific texts, names, places, and objects) that allow the game of interpretation to begin.

The possibilities of interpretation emerge through a sense of the tension between the explicit material that Borges's characters and narrators offer us and the more obscured patterns that emerge obliquely, gaining strength after multiple readings, sustained research, and a cautious evaluation of the acquired evidence. Sometimes, as Borges suggests above, the hidden dimensions of his stories overturn their most visible, easily accessible attractions: the original balance is upset, and we have to contend with a new understanding of what is "true" and "false." The promise of an "authentic" reading, a secret coherence, adds urgency to the desire to find a way toward deeper truths in the midst of all the suspect explanations that are handed to us.[2]

Reading in this way inevitably involves turning to other books, to the encyclopedias and works of theology, history, literature, and philosophy that overlap with Borges's fiction. These are texts with different degrees of verifiable separation from Borges; some are directly cited by him, others are alluded to, and a few represent only speculative possibilities of influence. Yet it is important to note that this outward turn toward extraliterary concepts and discourses implies a shift in perspective that does not, as one might expect, lead to a predictable sense of stability and scholarly familiarity. We are, in these moments of investigation, reading everything through an emphatically literary framework, through a fictive logic born of Borges's provisional, imaginary reality.[3] Alicia Borinsky writes that encountering such texts without forgetting the original literary contexts that they form part of requires a special destabilizing lens, a mode of interpretation designed to guide us toward an understanding of risks, doubts, or possibilities that lie, in fiction, beyond the simple dichotomy of the true and the counterfeit.[4]

It is important, in other words, not to lose sight of the idiosyncratic literary logic that Borges's references and allusions are bound up in, despite the temptation to find refuge in the familiarity of their original disciplines. While the borrowed orders of history, philosophy, or theology can promise to lend a sense of rigor and control to one's interpretations (as can, of course, works of literary theory), each may, in the process, effectively mask the capacity of Borges's stories to reorder reality in their own unique terms. Fiction, according to this understanding, is both a lens and an object of study; as the tension builds between these two functions it can also become a means of disruption and transformation.

This, I believe, is one of Borges's foundational insights: the way in which fiction can transform one's relationship with the deepest underpinnings of reality, memory, and identity without offering a new orthodoxy in its place. By insisting on provisionality, by starting over again at every story, his work, interlaced with irony and humor, evokes and disrupts illusions of stability without abandoning the lucidity of language.[5] Borges, like his friend and mentor Macedonio Fernández, takes seriously the notion that in the moment of reading we can undergo an important change—through our invention of a different, fictional reality we, guided by language, memory, and imagination, are potentially reshaped as well, alongside our sense of the real. As disbelief is suspended (or revealed, or contorted), space opens for the cultivation of a new kind of experience and different, perpetually shifting conditions of perception, thought, and feeling.

This book describes how Borges attempted to use this process of transformation in contexts of serious personal difficulty that defied simple or simplistic approaches.[6] I show how Borges, working with his relationships with blindness, sexuality, and suicide, created literary contexts in which each struggle was altered to such a degree—through the destabilizing, literary engagement with reframed texts, individuals, objects, and concepts—that it could open up (for him and for us) into new forms of experience and perception. Not unsurprisingly, this practice—which was both personal and strongly connected with the development of the author's strategies of representation—was not displayed to the reader in a manner that allowed for it to be easily seen. Neither, however, was it completely erased from his work.

Visuality, sexuality, and suicide each involved different challenges for Borges, and the work that he did to engage with them differs accordingly. The three chapters of this book thus work independently from one another, corresponding to the specific conditions of each context's literary transformation and the constellation of texts, concepts, and histories that Borges reframes within his fiction. In all of them, however, we are asked to question the ways in which Borges creates and undermines a sense of palpable reality, combining sensory evocations with trace reminders of the presence of the reader, of literary artificiality, and of the unavoidable centrality of the active, world-creating imagination. They work at once with a sense of intimacy and distance, offering alluring displays of imagination and insight while also suggesting that there might be something else operating just out of view.

The first chapter of the book describes how Borges created characters and narrators who were able to turn their attention to the nature of their own literary existence and contemplate it—even challenge it—using tools borrowed from religion. I show that the prohibitions of visual representation associated with Islam (its aniconicity and iconoclasm), combined, in Borges's mind, with its focus on divine text (via the Qur'an), to make it an ideal template for a literary theology that could question the primacy of the visual in fiction while elevating language to a place of central importance. In stories such as "Tlön, Uqbar, Orbis Tertius," "El Aleph," and "El Zahir," this double gesture (an elevation of textuality alongside a strategic devaluation of visuality) forms part of a practice that asks us to reconsider our relationship with the visual and its allure, especially within the context of literary interpretation. This set of reflections takes on additional significance when it is understood through the author's own relationship with blindness. I suggest that, for Borges, literary existence was marked, optimistically, as a space within which imagination wins out over sight.

The second chapter describes how Borges represented sex and sexuality in his stories in a way that carefully combined public and private levels of meaning. It positions "Emma Zunz" as a central text, arguing that the story secretly restages a traumatic, isolating experience of sexual coercion that Borges went through as a young man. Together with "La intrusa," it both expresses and obscures anger, shame, and pain while suggesting a unique kind of intimacy that upends traditional gender binaries. In "El jardín de senderos que se bifurcan," "Las ruinas circulares," and "La secta del fénix," I propose that Borges delves deeper into sexuality, procreation, and the conceptual limits of family in a way that crisscrosses between his personal life and his literary life as an author and reader. Together, the chapter offers these stories as Borges's most subtle and misunderstood meditations on the nature of time, family, and belonging.

The final chapter is an encounter with Borges's strategies for representing and transforming the limit of death in his fiction as it relates, specifically, to suicide. Taking "La otra muerte" as its first example, the chapter begins with a description of how Borges reframes the idea of suicide as an act of crossing the divide between an everyday mindset and the radical freedoms associated with literary imagination. In the story, I show that Borges offers a kind of literary death to the reader, one that must be taken on voluntarily, received as a gift, in order to approach its central riddle. This approach is contrasted with Borges's efforts to grapple with suicide in a more personal register that, accordingly, is far more hidden from view. In "La salvación por las obras," I demonstrate that Borges is grappling with the violent suicide of one of his actual readers in a way that implicates himself in the act of self-destruction—for complex personal reasons, he cannot help but understand that he and his reader are beginning to travel a similar path. The story gives voice to Borges's anger as well as to his capacity for cruelty. Yet it also suggests that literature is a relatively safe arena for these impulses. Fiction, it seems, allows him to die without dying, to be cruel without violence, to live multiple lives parallel to his own: it both liberates and transforms.

The epilogue of this book is built around "Místicos del Islam," one of Borges's unpublished essay drafts housed within the archives of the Harry Ransom Center at the University of Texas at Austin. I believe that this manuscript points to a crucial undercurrent present in all three chapters of this book: the idea that Borges's faith in fiction was ultimately based on a profound respect for its irreverence, its capacity for rebellion, disruption, and idiosyncratic resistance. If Borges sought out literature as a path of freedom, liberation, or even salvation, I suggest that it was precisely because of the ways it could open into countless acts of irony, disobedience, and iconoclastic transformation.

It should go without saying that the interpretations offered here are not necessarily intended to contradict or invalidate other approaches and readings. Different interpretations can and should coexist when there are no conflicts between their respective uses of evidence, logic, and analysis. As much as Borges might sound above as though he is offering a single, secret, coherent truth at the center of his stories, his statement applies just as well to stories that communicate multiple truths, on different levels, amidst the counterfeit ideas, explanations, and theories that the stories themselves are fully complicit in suggesting. On the other hand, meaningful conflicts between incompatible interpretations do arise and should ideally provide opportunities for critical conversations about Borges's work as well as different methods and styles of interpretation.

It may be useful to point out that while there is a tradition of evoking open-endedness when working with Borges's texts, this book places a strong emphasis on fiction's capacity for communicating specific, complex meaning in multiple (visible and less visible) registers. At times, as Jaime Alazraki has noted, evoking ambiguity can simply be a way to describe the experience of encountering overlapping discourses that have not yet been identified, understood, or approached in a clear or coherent way.[7] One can, in this sense, see the potential danger that accompanies the practice of celebrating indeterminacy in one's conclusions: doing so risks foreclosing fiction's capacity for expression instead of pointing in the direction of new possibilities of investigation. Alicia Borinsky cautions that "it has become far too easy to find that literature and art celebrate their incapacity to render univocal meanings. In a sense, undecidability is the new happy ending of literary interpretation, a demagogy that relativizes individual interpretations of a given work even as it privileges critical discourse over 'literature'" (*Theoretical Fables*, xi).

While there are many aspects of Borges's stories that, for me, continue to hover in a state of undecidability, I find that it is most helpful to allow for the strong possibility that this ambiguity is the result of my own inability to perceive the discourses and ideas in play, that it is not the intended or actual end point of any particular story's capacity for communication.

On a related note, I believe that it is also worth mentioning that the guiding principle in the preparation of this book has been a sense of appreciation for the moments in which I have been emphatically aware of not understanding key aspects of Borges's stories, poems, and essays. Leaving these spaces of not knowing open—not allowing them to be immediately filled in by the various explanations that the mind inevitably offers—was central to the development of the project. As Sylvia Molloy has written, the "gaps" or "interruptions" in the flow of one's reading can easily be sidestepped in favor of what is more easily seen and understood.[8] Given that doing so often involves a (somewhat) satisfying return to a sense of control, authority, and certainty, it can be difficult to resist. Yet when the mind is able to be aware of—and momentarily step out of—its tendency to impose and project its own proliferation of internal patterns on the uncertain or the unknown, it is able to then perceive invaluable difficulties that cannot be easily resolved. This book has been built on a foundation of these doubts, questions, and confusions. To emphatically not know is different, of course, from celebrating the indeterminacy of a story in that it is, quite simply, a beginning instead of an ending: it is an invitation to investigate and explore. In this spirit, I hope that this book is unambiguously read as a similar invitation, as another beginning, one that I offer with gratitude for those who have invited me, countless times, to follow in their footsteps by walking a different path.

Borges's Literary Theology
Fiction and the Visible

Quienes han fatigado su entendimiento con doctrinas
teológicas, pero sin aplicarlas a la vida, eligen lugares
rocosos y viven entre montones de piedras.

Those who have exhausted their minds in theological
doctrines without applying them to life choose rocky
landscapes and live among piles of stones.

—**Emanuel Swedenborg**, *De Coelo et Inferno* (from Borges
and Bioy Casares, *Libro del cielo y del infierno*, 24)

In Jorge Luis Borges and Adolfo Bioy Casares's short story "Un pincel
nuestro: Tafas" (1967), the narrator describes the short life of José
Enrique Tafas, a painter with a Muslim background who decides to
abstain from representing living beings in his art in order to comply
with a theological principle. Tafas tells the narrator that "en el Alcorán
de Mahoma [. . .] queda formalmente prohibida la pintura de caras, de
personas, de facciones, de pájaros, de becerros y de otros seres vivos"
(In Muhammad's Qur'an [. . .] it is formally prohibited to paint faces,
people, features, birds, young bulls, and other living beings).[1] The
artist's solution to his crisis of representation is unusual. He purchases
postcards of landmarks—such as the Café Tortoni—and uses them

to create paintings of astounding realism. Tafas then washes the paint off of the canvases before covering them in shoe polish so that they are completely black. On the gallery wall, each black canvas is then labeled with the appropriate textual description of the previously painted scene (*Café Tortoni*, for example). While his public cannot see his work, they can imagine it for themselves. The narrator suggests that while Tafas's paintings are often confused with those of certain "abstract" painters, his project is more of a theologically considered "Islamic" realism.[2]

The story of Tafas is perhaps the most distilled example of a strategy that Borges uses throughout his career. It is based on two simple gestures but, as we will see, is applied in diverse ways to push readers to reconsider the unique tension between everyday experience and the act of reading fiction. These gestures are associated, in Borges's stories, with appropriated, transfigured theologies that often involve Islam but can also extend to include Gnosticism, Judaism, and Christianity.

The first gesture is the erasure, occlusion, or destruction (symbolic or otherwise) of an emphasized visual field. The second gesture is the elevation of a text. With these two moves, Borges is able to cue and interrupt our expectations with regard to conventionally alluring strategies of visual description and provide us, instead, with a moment of emphasized textuality designed to inspire curiosity about what we are, in fact, actually doing: reading words on a page, mentally fashioning a reality for ourselves to observe, experience, or even inhabit. Within the internal context of Borges's stories, the pleasure of passively enjoying visual delights is thus often contrasted with the more challenging project of imagining them into existence (and, further, contemplating the nature of the process of imagination).

In the case of Tafas's art, after the erasure of the original scene and the shoe polish blackout of the canvas, the diminutive label of the painting is the *only* thing that can guide the imagination of the painting's viewer. The simple task of observing a familiar, even clichéd image is replaced with the more arduous project of its mental imagination. If we picture for a moment the viewers of these canvases in the artist's gallery, they must read the text and, looking at the black canvas, project their imaginations into the framed void.[3] Their ability to "see" the canvas will depend on their ability to read and (more importantly) to imagine.

While "Un pincel nuestro: Tafas" is structured as a joke, its two gestures are enough to create a simple allegory for the uniqueness of literary experience that, in Borges's earlier stories, is expressed in far more complex ways. Such stories include "El Aleph" (1945), "El tintorero enmascarado Hákim de Merv" (1935), "El espejo de tinta" (1933), "Tlön, Uqbar, Orbis Tertius" (1940), "La busca de Averroes" (1947), and "El Zahir" (1949).[4] Read closely, these stories point to one of Borges's fundamental projects: the creation of an invented theology that allows his characters to question the nature of visuality within literature and come closer to understanding its textual and imaginative foundations. Motivated by the literary ideas that he discussed with his friend and mentor Macedonio Fernández and, also, I believe, by his impending blindness, this obscured project shows Borges grappling with both his relationship with fiction and his understanding of his own physical limits.

The story that represents the clearest amplification of the gestures highlighted above in "Un pincel nuestro: Tafas" is also Borges's most famous text: "El Aleph." It begins with the narrator (whose name is "Borges") recalling his thoughts about a woman named Beatriz Viterbo on the morning of her death in 1929. We read that when she was alive, Beatriz Viterbo had been frustrated by his devotion just as "Borges" had been humiliated by her rejection.[5] He remembers how, on that morning of her death, he had resolved to visit her family on her birthday to pay his respects and had done so every year since. Their home, he writes, was crowded with portraits of Beatriz. This initial visit is how "Borges" came to know Carlos Argentino Daneri, her cousin. He is portrayed as a pompous, energetic, and foolish man. "Borges" describes him, in 1941, reciting a "vindication of modern man" that proclaims how, due to the wonders of technology, such an individual no longer has to travel: the world comes to him. Soon we learn that he is creating a poem related to these ideas titled "La Tierra" (The Earth). Daneri reads verses and then proceeds to explain their brilliance; he is then mocked mercilessly in the story.

In October, Daneri calls "Borges," profoundly upset. His landlords have decided to demolish his house in order to build a sweetshop. Daneri tells him that he needs the house to finish his poem because it has an Aleph that he discovered in the basement as a child. An Aleph, he says, is one of the points in space that contains within it all points. One can, he explains, look into it and see, without confusion, every place in the universe from every possible perspective. "Borges" agrees to come to the house and see the Aleph, certain that Daneri has gone insane. At the house, he follows Daneri's instructions despite his wariness about his acquaintance's mental state and, unexpectedly, sees what was promised. It is portrayed in the story as a sphere with a diameter of a few centimeters, illuminated from within by all the light it contains. To describe the experience, "Borges" struggles against the limits of language. Every object, seen from every possible perspective, is infinitely complex. He sees oceans, night and day at once, innumerable eyes, all the mirrors on the planet (none of them reflecting his image), snow, metal veins in the earth, deserts, a cancer growing in a chest, teeming crowds, horses, obscene letters that Beatriz had written to Carlos Argentino Daneri, the circulation of his own blood, the Aleph from every perspective, the Earth within that Aleph, the Aleph within that Earth, his own face, your face, the universe. The experience is shocking and debilitating. "Borges," faced with Daneri, avoids confirming that he saw anything and, out of a desire for a kind of revenge, recommends that Daneri rest for a while in the countryside after thanking him, benevolently, for his hospitality.

The Aleph is widely considered Borges's most influential literary invention. Writers and scholars have often emblematically associated it with Borges and, more specifically, with his seemingly limitless capacity for imagination and invention.[6] It has been described as epiphanic, pointing to the unrepresentable vastness of the universe as encountered by the mind of a genius. These interpretations are, in part, encouraged by the narrator's reflections on the difficulty of using language (or any human system of representation) to communicate experiences or concepts of totality or infinity. For example, in a "postscript" that accompanies the story, "Borges" writes that in the Kabbalah, the word "Aleph" refers to "En Soph," "la ilimitada y pura divinidad" (pure and limitless divinity [1:931]); it is also said to represent the form of "un hombre que señala el cielo y la tierra, para indicar que el mundo inferior es el espejo y es el mapa del superior" (a man who gestures to the sky and the earth to indicate that the world below is the mirror and the map of the world above [1:931]).[7] The word "Aleph" also has a mathematical context that "Borges" details for the reader: "para la *Mengenlehre*, es el símbolo de los números transfinitos, en los que el todo no es mayor que alguna de las partes" (in the *Mengenlehre* [mathematical set theory], it is the symbol of transfinite numbers, in which the total is not greater than one of its parts [1:931]).[8] These theological, cartographic, and mathematical attempts to represent infinite or total concepts are joined by the projects of mystics, including the Persian poet Farid ud-Din Attar's 1177 *Mantiq ut-Tait* (*The Conference of the Birds*), Alain de Lille's paradoxical description of an infinite sphere, and a four-faced angel from the book of Ezekiel (1:929).[9] Given this set of references, it is reasonable to read the story as a literary attempt to evoke grand abstractions such as "reality," "the universe," or "divinity," while simultaneously acknowledging that each is a partial, incomplete human invention.[10]

Yet there is a less-often discussed aspect of the story that complicates the impulse to see in Carlos Daneri's Aleph an epiphanic emblem of Borges's mind or literary work. After mentioning infinite set theory and the Kabbalah, "Borges" writes that the object that he encountered in the basement of Daneri is not, in his opinion, a "true" Aleph. Specifically, he states that "por increíble que parezca, yo creo que hay (o que hubo) otro Aleph, yo creo que el Aleph de la calle Garay era un falso Aleph" (as incredible as it might seem, I believe that there is [or that there was] another Aleph; I believe that the Aleph on Garay street was a false Aleph [1:932]).

This pronouncement is not easy to decipher. What could it possibly mean to be a "false" Aleph? The narrator does not contradict his previous description of how the Aleph provided him with a simultaneous, total vision of the universe. It is, nevertheless, marked as "false" in a casual manner that belies the ambiguity of the statement.

In the next paragraph, the reader is promised that proof of the Aleph's falseness is forthcoming.[11] Despite this promise, the odd label of "false" remains puzzlingly unexplained. Instead, we are presented with a description of a manuscript written by Richard Francis Burton during his 1867 stay in Brazil as British consul. This manuscript (an invention of Borges) describes a set of fictional objects that are similar to the Aleph found in Daneri's house. These objects are: the mirrors of Iskandar Zu al-Karnayn, Tarik Benzeyad and Lucian of Samasota; the seven-ringed cup of Kai Khosrow; the "lanza especular" (mirrored lance [1:932]) of Jupiter; and Merlin's crystal ball.[12] "Burton" dismisses these fictional examples for being "meros instrumentos de óptica" (mere optical instruments [1:932]).

This statement (by "Burton") is, ostensibly, the reason why the Aleph is to be considered false: namely, because it—like these fictional examples—is a *mere* optical instrument. This is particularly confusing since the Aleph, itself, is initially described in wholly visual terms. For it to be dismissed, afterwards, for being visual is plainly contradictory. Not only does "Borges" never fulfill his promise to explain why the Aleph of Daneri is false, we are never even shown what this "falseness" might mean.

The story continues, however, with a description of *another* object from "Burton's" manuscript that is, crucially, *not* visual:

> Los fieles que concurren a la mezquita de Amr, en El Cairo, saben muy bien que el universo está en el interior de una de las columnas de piedra que rodean el patio central. . . . Nadie, claro está, puede verlo, pero quienes acercan el oído a la superficie, declaran percibir, al poco tiempo, su atareado rumor. . . . La mezquita data del siglo VII; las columnas proceden de otros templos de religiones anteislámicas, pues como ha escrito Abenjaldún: "En las repúblicas fundadas por nómadas, es indispensable el concurso de forasteros para todo lo que sea albañilería." (1:932)

> The faithful that gather at the Amr mosque, in Cairo, know very well that the universe is located within the interior of one of the stone columns that encircle the central patio. . . . No one, it is clear, can see it, but those who bring their ears close to its surface attest to perceiving, after a few moments, its muted rumbling. . . . The mosque was built in

the seventh century; the columns are from other temples belonging to pre-Islamic religions, for, as Abenjaldún has written, "In the republics founded by nomads, the participation of outsiders is indispensable for everything related to construction."

The implication is, in my view, that the *unseen* object encased in a pillar of the Amr Mosque is the "true" Aleph while the other examples (including the Aleph of Carlos Argentino Daneri) are "false" Alephs. The fact that this Aleph in Cairo is not visual—it cannot be seen—places it in clear opposition to the "mere optical instruments" mentioned up until this point.

We must still, however, consider why "visuality" or "nonvisuality" would be associated with "falseness" and "truth" in the context of Borges's story.[13] In order to do so, it is important to refer back to the story mentioned at the beginning of this chapter, "Un pincel nuestro: Tafas." The similarity between the pair of Alephs (one visually blocked by the surface of the mosque's pillar and another delivering incredible visual details) to the pair of canvases created by Tafas (one blocked by black shoe polish and another delivering astounding realism) is not difficult to perceive. Both involve an emphasized visual field and its later obfuscation. What is less obvious is the shared allegorical context of these oppositions. Borges and Bioy black out Tafas's canvas while highlighting the written label in order to transform a seen painting into an interpreted text: the black canvas conceptually joins the black text on the wall of the museum in stimulating the imagination of the viewer. Both the canvas and its label require effort and interpretation; neither presents passive viewers with visual delights. These viewers must stop, read, and imagine if they are to enjoy the "content" of the art and the writing.

Tafas's canvas, in this sense, draws dramatic attention to our capacity for active visual imagination as readers. The story reminds us that to read is to conjure a "visual" world using the power of our own minds and not, crucially, waiting passively to be provided with entertaining stimuli. When this idea is applied to "El Aleph," other parts of the story become suddenly far more important. Its two main characters are, after all, writers. One of them, Carlos Argentino

Daneri, relies on a device (the Aleph) that visually delivers the world to him. He is very much like the "modern man" that he evokes in his first appearance in the story, yet instead of being connected to telephones, telegraphs, newspapers, bulletins, radios, magic lanterns, and movie projectors, Daneri has, in the Aleph, a way to access perfect visual knowledge of the universe.

The *effortlessness* of the experience, however, means that Daneri does not encounter or surmount any difficulties while seeing "the world."[14] Everything is delivered to him as a perfectly satisfied passive consumer and his poetry, as a result, is unconcerned with the challenges of imagination and interpretation. When he reads his verses, Daneri cannot stop himself from celebrating them in front of "Borges" in a way that shows that he is oblivious to the fact his poetry is failing to have any of its intended effects. "Borges" offers backhanded praise to Daneri while communicating his disdain to the reader (a disdain that may have echoed frustrations that Borges felt with regard to James Joyce and Ramón Gómez de la Serna, whom he "marked" with the sign of the "Alef" in an essay that predates the story).[15] Daneri's lack of mastery suggests that the Aleph—for all of its wondrous sights—has the effect of atrophying the mind. Skill and artistry are born of a struggle to understand and work with the limits of language, interpretation, and knowledge, not of an easy, boundless access to the world-as-spectacle.

If the story is understood in this light, it becomes difficult to associate the Aleph in Daneri's basement with the limitless potential of the mind or with Borges's own writerly prowess. Instead, this Aleph becomes far more specific, suggesting a particular kind of passive encounter with the world that overwhelms us with its totalizing visual allure.[16] According to Borges, the effects of the Aleph—especially with regard to literary creativity—are almost all profoundly negative.[17] After the experience of looking into the Aleph, "Borges" finds himself in a stupor, dulled and depressed by the fact that he can no longer hope to see a new face on the street. Thankfully, he writes, forgetfulness eventually begins to do its work.

What "Borges" and Daneri experience when they look into the Aleph can, in this sense, be understood as precisely the *opposite* of the difficult, creative experience of reading literature. Faced with black text set against the white of the page, one must actively create an internal world; it is not possible to experience anything without the effort of interpretation. As one expends this effort and, over time, becomes more skillful at reading, the experience changes, becoming richer and more dynamic. Returning to the problem of "truth" and "falseness" within the story, we can offer the interpretation that *within the context of fiction*, the visual Aleph of Daneri is *false* in the sense that it presents a passive mode of engagement thoroughly incompatible with the very nature of reading. It provides an optical—and not an imaginative—experience in a literary context requiring interpretive effort and creativity.

The *unseen* Aleph in Cairo, however, can be understood as "true" within this context of fiction due to the way in which it successfully allegorizes the experience of the actual reader of the story—its truth is the truth it tells about itself and its medium. Just like the black canvas of Tafas and the black text that accompanies it, the perfect darkness within the stone of the pillar gives us no direct visual information. We must, instead, *listen*.[18] Only when the ear touches the surface of the stone can anyone get an indirect sense of the "universe" through its distant rumbling: it is a universe that must be actively imagined into existence. For those of us who are blind, "reading" through listening is, of course, a daily practice. The fact that Borges knew that he would soon be unable to see makes this turn toward the truth of the obscured Aleph all the more important.

It would have been possible to include these allegories about the nature of literary interpretation without any kind of theological component. Borges, however, associates *both* the black canvas of Tafas and the obscured Aleph of Amr with Islam. While the Islamic context of Tafas's black canvases is made clear in "Un pincel nuestro: Tafas," in the case of "El Aleph" the influence of Islam is stronger than might initially be apparent. If one seeks out the original manuscript of the story it is possible to see that instead of referring to the "point within which all points reside" as an "Aleph," Borges uses, in the very first version of the story, a completely different term. The manuscript shows the following set of alterations: "[. . .] en un ángulo del sótano había un ~~mihrab~~ Aleph. [Carlos Daneri] aclaró ~~que un mihrab~~ que un <u>Aleph</u> es uno de los puntos del espacio ~~en el cual están contenidos~~ q. contiene todos los puntos" (in a corner of the basement there was ~~a mihrab~~ an <u>Aleph</u>. [Carlos Daneri] explained ~~that a mihrab~~ that an <u>Aleph</u> is one of the points in space ~~in which are contained~~ that contains all points).[19] The word "mihrab" can clearly be seen struck out and replaced by "Aleph." A mihrab is, traditionally, the empty, concave space situated within the wall of a mosque; it points (from the perspective of the worshippers inside) to "qibla": the direction of Mecca.

The similarities between the visible Aleph described by Daneri and the mihrab are numerous. Both are "empty" spaces found within buildings that invite prolonged contemplation. They are meant to be visually addressed. One points to a universe without a fixed center (viewed from infinite perspectives), while the other points to the center of the Islamic universe (from the privileged perspective of a mosque's interior). Yet there are also clear differences. A mihrab simultaneously points one's gaze toward Mecca and, also, blocks that gaze. Instead of instantly delivering a rapturous vision, it forms part of a set of devotional practices designed to invite contemplation and imagination in the absence of icons.[20] It seems, in this sense, to have more in common with the second, visually blocked Aleph buried within one of the columns of the Amr Mosque than with the lens that instantly delivers a visual totality to the eyes of Carlos Argentino Daneri.

A closer look at the history of the Amr Mosque confirms that Borges was, in fact, associating the idea of a mihrab with the unseen, "true" Aleph found within its pillar. According to the historian Eustace Corbett, the original architectural construction of the Amr Mosque was relatively simple.[21] The feature that it is most famous for is, however, its initial lack of a concave mihrab.[22] Instead of the hollow niche, another structure (also referred to as a mihrab) marked by *four columns* originally served to indicate the direction of Mecca.[23] In 710–11, however, Kurra ibn Sharik removed this unknown marker in the process of an architectural expansion. A new southern wall was erected with a concave mihrab. The old mihrab, however, was not forgotten; to commemorate its importance the four columns that enclosed it were kept and their capitals were gilded.[24] The space occupied by the Amr Mosque's original (and, today, invisible) mihrab was, in this sense, quite literally enclosed within the four pillars occupying a central location in the patio.

Borges, we must conclude, decided to make the unseeable Aleph in his story reside within one of the pillars of the Amr Mosque due to the specific history of the Mosque's transformation. We can thus say that the true Aleph is, in an absolutely literal (and figurative) sense, an unseen mihrab.

The specific manner in which Borges came to be interested in the history of the Amr Mosque is an open question. It is likely that two sources were especially important. The first is the 11th edition of the *Encyclopedia Britannica*, which he owned and frequently used.[25] This encyclopedia's general entry on "Mosque" features only one illustration on its initial page: the architectural plan (see fig. 1) of "Mosque of 'Amr, Old Cairo" (18:899). The encyclopedia explains that the Amr Mosque was rebuilt, while also—echoing Borges's story—asserting that "the columns and capitals were all taken from ancient buildings, Egyptian, Roman, and Byzantine, and they carry arches of different forms, semicircular, pointed and horseshoe" (18:899). The entry also states that in a typical mosque "the principal feature [. . .] is the niche (mihrab), which is sunk in a wall built at right angles to a line drawn from Mecca, and indicates the direction towards which the Moslem should turn when engaged in prayer" (18:899). There is no mention, however, of the shifting, transformed mihrab within the Amr Mosque.

The second text that may have led Borges to the Amr Mosque is Edward William Lane's *An Account of the Manners and Customs of the Modern Egyptians*. While the index of the two-volume work does not mention architecture, Section II of "Appendix F: Editor's Notes" does provide a summary of "Arabian Architecture." In this summary, the transformations of the Amr Mosque are emphasized (333–34) and, most importantly, an abstract of "El-Makreezee's" account is added in a separate section titled "History of the Mosque of 'Amr" in order to provide even more detail.[26] This account states the following:

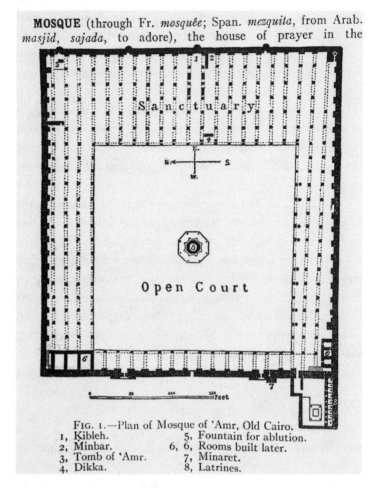

MOSQUE (through Fr. *mosquée*; Span. *mezquita*, from Arab. *masjid*, *sajada*, to adore), the house of prayer in the

FIG. I.—Plan of Mosque of 'Amr, Old Cairo.
1, Ḳibleh.
2, Minbar.
3, Tomb of 'Amr.
4, Dikka.
5, Fountain for ablution.
6, 6, Rooms built later.
7, Minaret.
8, Latrines.

FIGURE 1 Illustration of the "Plan of Mosque of 'Amr, Old Cairo" on the first page of the general entry for "Mosque" in the 1911 *Encyclopedia Britannica*.

In the beginning of the year 92, by the order of El-Weleed, El-Kurrah Ibn-Shureyk, the governor of Egypt, pulled it down, and began to build it in Shaabán of that year, completing it in Ramadán, 93. The enlargement of Kurrah was on the southern and eastern sides, and he took part of the house of 'Amr and of his son, and enclosed it in the mosque, with the road which was between them and the mosque.—Kurrah made the recessed niche which is called the mihráb of 'Amr, because it is in the direction of the niche of the old mosque which 'Amr built. The kibleh of the old mosque was at the gilt pillars in the row of táboots [wooden chests] at this day: these are four pillars, two facing two, and Kurrah gilt their capitals: there were no gilt pillars in the mosque except them. (349)

This detailed description of the original mihrab being replaced by four specially gilded pillars would have been accessible to Borges. It appears to be the most likely source for his invention of the "true Aleph" and therefore, of course, of the central Aleph in the story.

Borges mentions this particular book by Lane in the essay "Las mil y una noches" (3:259), and Adolfo Bioy Casares, additionally, recalls Borges referring to an anecdote from the book in conversation in 1963 (*Borges*, 896). Norman Thomas di Giovanni has written that it was "one of Borges's favourite books" (*Lesson of the Master*, 202) and the obvious source material for Borges's story "El espejo de tinta" (despite the fact that the narrator asserts that it is a literal translation of Richard Burton's *The Lake Regions of Equatorial Africa*).[27] "El espejo de tinta," is, in fact, a crucial text for this investigation. It provides an important link between "El Aleph" and "Un pincel nuestro: Tafas" that points to Islam as a common framework. While Borges's "El espejo de tinta" reproduces many aspects of Lane's "historical" account of his experiences in Egypt, it also deviates in ways that speak to the unique goals of his literary project.

Both texts—Lane's nonfictional account and Borges's fictional story—describe an act of magic in which a circular pool of ink is dripped into an individual's hand; in both texts this person is then asked to look within the pool. In Borges's "El espejo de tinta," however, this person is "Yakub el Doliente," a fictional ruler of Sudan who is holding the magician Abderráhmen El Masmudí hostage.[28] This magician asks Yakub if he can see his own face in the pool of ink; when he says yes, the ruler is then instructed not to look away. What follows in Borges's story is a series of visions that are not present in the account of Lane. Yakub asks first to see a perfect wild horse, then a pack of these horses. The next day, the visions that he asks for begin to become more complex. He commands his captive magician to show him cities, treasures, instruments of war, medicine, and music. He asks to see beautiful women, planets, stars, and even "la sombra proyectada por el toro que sostiene la tierra y por el pez que está debajo del toro" (The shadow cast by the bull that carries the earth and the fish that is below the bull [1:629]). For our purposes, however, the most important sights that he asks to see are "los colores que emplean los infieles para pintar sus cuadros aborrecibles" (the colors that the unbelievers use to create their abhorrent paintings [1:629]). Lane makes no mention of any Islamic proscriptions of visual representation in his anecdote; for Borges, however, they are clearly important.[29]

In Borges's story, the circular pool of ink in the palm of Yakub's hand seems to allow him to magically circumvent the proscriptions that make Western paintings impossible for him to view. He beholds these paintings without (technically) ever seeing them. The story soon reveals that this is, nevertheless, a transgression. Yakub—in his pool-of-ink visions—sees an individual that reappears in diverse cities and countries, each time wearing a cloth that (appropriately, given these very proscriptions) covers his face; he is referred to as "El Enmascarado" (The Masked Man). After asking to see many scenes of cruelty, Yakub demands to see a just killing. The circle of ink shows him the executioner of his own castle; the condemned man is, to his great surprise, the masked individual that he had seen in his other visions. Yakub commands that this man be unmasked: he is revealed to be Yakub himself, who watches himself be decapitated within the ink pooled in his own hand before falling to the floor, dead.

With regard to "El Aleph," this story of a magical, circular pool of ink is important in several ways. The first, and most general, is that it further establishes the relationship between the Aleph and the proscription of visual representation that Borges associates with Islam. In both stories, a "magical" circular aperture allows a viewer to behold great distant sights; in both stories, this aperture is presented (at the end) as more of a curse than a blessing. While I have argued that "El Aleph," by virtue of its evocation of a hidden mihrab and its relationship with "Un pincel nuestro: Tafas," makes *indirect* use of the perceived proscriptions against representing living beings in Islam, the extremely similar visual device in "El espejo de tinta" *explicitly* presents its visuality as antagonistic to these "Islamic" prohibitions.[30]

The second way in which it is useful to consider "El espejo de tinta" is within the context of allegory. Peering into *ink* and "seeing" distant sights brings the act of reading easily to mind. The important (allegorical) distinction that Borges makes in his story, however, is that the "reader"—Yakub—is not using his imaginative faculties. He desires to see something, demands it of his magician, and it appears. As in the case of Daneri's Aleph, no *effort* is expended in the satiation of curiosity. Instead of referring directly to the reading experience, the magical circle of ink comments on a set of desires that are, in fact, wholly incompatible with the context of literature.[31] Instant sensory gratification is not what fiction can offer.

This, I believe, is precisely what Borges finds most compelling about the version of "Islam" that he constructs within his fiction. In each of these stories "Islam" is a system of belief concerned principally with questions of representation, interpretation, and imagination. These departures from a historical understanding of Islam align with the literary concerns of Borges as an author. Tafas's religion, for example, is presented only in terms of the limitations that it imposes on him as an artist (limitations that transfer the burden of representation and interpretation from the painted canvas to the written word). In "El Aleph," the devoted "Muslims" at the Amr Mosque do not face a mihrab as a way to contemplate the Prophet Muhammad praying toward Mecca; instead, they encounter the immensity of the physical universe through the power of their imaginations. In "El espejo de tinta," Borges's Muslim protagonist uses the mirror of ink to pursue his desires for an illicit Western form of artistic representation. Borges's reimagined "Islam" thus ceases to function as a "historical" religion in any meaningful way so as to take on the characteristics of an allegorical mode of literary exploration related to the author's own ideas about visuality, iconicity, and interpretation.[32]

Accordingly, when the characters and narrators within Borges's stories show "devotion" within Borges's "Islam" we find them *favorably* associated with an imaginative, active form of literary interpretation that is unburdened by everyday desires for direct sensory stimulation.

While these sensory desires might be perfectly at home in the everyday world, in the context of literary reality they are—for Borges—out of place. Conversely, a *lack* of devotion to "Islam" is associated with desires that are framed as incompatible with the author's ideal literary experience. Daneri's Aleph, Tafas's as-yet unwashed canvas, and Yakub's mirror of ink can each be seen as visually lush (non-"Islamic") distractions from the author's meditations on the nature of reading, writing, and literary existence. All of these passive entertainments are challenged by "Islamic" ideas that are, in fact, representations of the author's own literary principles.

Many of these literary ideas—especially those dealing with the tension between visuality and textuality in literature—were developed in conversations between Borges and Macedonio Fernández. Borges and Macedonio began their friendship in 1921, when Borges returned to Buenos Aires from Europe with his family. Macedonio, twenty-five years older than Borges, was a friend and classmate of his father who, in his writing and in his conversations, was interested in fashioning a philosophy that radically reimagined the limits of identity while using a peculiar variety of metaphysical humor. Álvaro Abós writes that Borges sought out a relationship with Macedonio partially as a way to begin to enter into the intellectual circles of Buenos Aires after seven years in Europe.[33] Reflecting back on that time, Borges suggested that Macedonio represented the possibility of reimagining everything anew, outside of the scholarly structures that other mentors, such as Rafael Cansinos Assens, had introduced him to.[34] Borges acknowledged Macedonio's influence on his earliest works of fiction explicitly, writing:

> Yo por aquellos años lo imité hasta la transcipción, hasta el apasionado y devoto plagio. Yo sentía: Macedonio *es* la metafísica, *es* la literatura. Quienes lo precedieron pueden resplandecer en la historia, pero eran borradores de Macedonio, versiones imperfectas y previas.[35]

> I, in those years, imitated him to the point of transcription, to the point of impassioned, devoted plagiarism. I felt: Macedonio *is* metaphysics, *is* literature. Those who came before him may shine in history, but they were just drafts of Macedonio, imperfect, earlier versions.

Their relationship is often recalled in the context of café conversations (at La Perla, in the Once) in which philosophy, fiction, and a playful sense of humor combined in unexpected ways.[36]

One of Macedonio's fundamental ideas about literature was that by virtue of being composed strictly of language, it represented a unique opportunity to consider (and experience) existence in a context free from the everyday limits of corporeality and social norms. The mind, in the moment of reading fiction, is tasked with creating a universe riddled with inconsistencies, contradictions, and surprises: a new world only tangentially related to our own, guided by lines of language printed on paper. Becoming adept at this was, in Macedonio's view, freeing, as it could loosen the reader from the grasp of pervasive cultural conventions and everyday assumptions about reality: immersed in reading, our experience of being is different than it might be at the supermarket, at the bank, in an office. Yet some kinds of literature were more freeing than others. He doubted that fiction based on the direct representation of everyday fears, desires, pleasures, and difficulties could have the liberating effects that he was interested in. Instead, such works of realism could in fact reinforce social norms while delivering experiences that could not help but pale in comparison with the real thing. "El horror del Arte" Macedonio writes, "es el relato y la descripción, la copia como fin en sí" (The horror of Art is storytelling and description, imitation as an end in itself).[37] Excessively "sensory" literature was regarded as "culinary."

In one of his early essays on the literary principles of his contemporaries, Borges expresses a similar wariness with regard to the allure of sensory content in fiction and poetry. The fact that he does so by employing a series of theologically inflected metaphors makes the essay—"Después de las imágenes" (1925)—of particular interest here. Borges begins by evoking a conservative mindset (influenced by positivism and the book of Genesis) that understands the order of language as fixed to the order of conventionally understood reality. Borges then points to a few of the ways in which young poets like himself have tried to *unsettle* the notion that language and reality are bound together in an immutable relationship. He refers to their metaphors as "conjuros" (spells), the tricks of a few literary magicians heretically challenging an entire religious and philosophical tradition.

Yet this early essay is not an ode to the power of the metaphor. Borges states that while metaphorical "witchcraft" might be interesting, there is a more radical, powerful approach to consider. Instead of presenting the passive reader with a parade of unusual composite *images*—birds that drink of mirrors, thunderstorms that swirl in bonfires—that challenge initial expectations and assumptions, he writes that it might be possible to create an entire *literary reality* into which the reader could enter so as to engage with the specific peculiarities of fictional experience and artifice. This "literary reality" would not necessarily be beholden to the laws of physics or even to the norms of sense perception. He asserts that "hay alguien superior al travieso y al hechicero. Hablo del semidiós, del ángel, por cuyas obras cambia el mundo. Añadir provincias al Ser, alucinar ciudades y espacios de la conjunta realidad, es aventura heroica" (there is someone superior to the trickster and the conjuror. I speak of the demigod, the angel, through whose work the world is changed. To add provinces to Being, hallucinate cities and spaces of a conjoined reality, is a heroic adventure [1:76]).

Borges goes on to explain that he is interested in *investigating* and *exploring* the radically different nature of such literary spaces, but not necessarily from the distanced perspective of literary studies. He hopes to make sense of them from within, as a character or a narrator.

> Ya no basta decir, a fuer de todos los poetas, que los espejos se asemejan a un agua. Tampoco basta dar por absoluta esa hipótesis y suponer, como cualquier Huidobro, que de los espejos sopla frescura o que los pájaros sedientos los beben y queda hueco el marco. Hemos de rebasar tales juegos. [. . .] [H]ay que mostrar un individuo que se introduce en el cristal y que persiste en su ilusorio país (donde hay figuraciones y colores, pero regidos de inmovible silencio) y que siente el bochorno de no ser más que un simulacro que obliteran las noches y que las vislumbres permiten. (1:76)

It is not enough to say, as do so many poets, that the mirrors are like water. Neither is it enough to take the hypothesis to its absolute extreme and suppose, like any Huidobro, that through mirrors blow fresh breezes or that thirsty birds drink of them until each frame is empty. We should reject such games. . . . [I]t is necessary to show an individual who enters into the glass and who persists within its illusory country (where there are figures and colors, but caught in an immovable silence) and who feels the shame of being nothing more than a simulacrum obliterated by night, permitted to exist only by glinting lights.

The central idea that Borges offers here is that the exploration of literary space could be done from within literature *instead of* from a position of formal criticism: through characters and narrators that (directly or indirectly) consider the literary artifice that surrounds them and, at the same time, constitutes their very existence.

How would such characters carry out this exploration of their artificial surroundings? The structure of Borges's essay suggests that these characters and narrators should have their own forms of philosophy and theology to contrast with the positivism and the biblical context that he mentions early on. Borges thus points to the possibility of an as-yet-unarticulated literary philosophy or, on the other hand, the possibility of a *literary theology*, at a very early age.[38]

The question for Borges becomes how to begin to imagine a system of philosophical or theological belief that could correspond to these literary dimensions.[39] With regard to philosophy, the often contradictory system of thought proposed by Macedonio Fernández combines the idealism of George Berkeley with instability, humor, and even mysticism in a way that made it especially vital for Borges's literary project.[40] When it comes to creating a *theological* system of belief appropriate for considering the nature of a fictional universe from within, Borges, I argue, turned principally to Islam.[41]

Three interconnected aspects of Islam made it especially useful for Borges as the basis for his "literary theology."[42] The first, which we have already encountered, is its association with aniconism. The second aspect of Islam is its history of iconoclasm: works of art that violated the prohibitions of visual representation would sometimes be altered or destroyed in very specific ways.[43] The third aspect of Islam that Borges is drawn to is the special status (and the divine origin) given to language.[44]

Borges highlighted these three aspects of Islam within an unpublished, undated draft of an essay titled "Místicos del Islam" currently housed at the Harry Ransom Center at the University of Texas, Austin. In the draft, Borges describes the religion as "una guerra contra los ídolos, un odio encarnizado de las imágenes, que llevó a sus prosélitos a proscribir todo arte representativo y a descubrir/idear el arte austero y abstracto de los arabescos" (a war against idols, a fierce hatred of images, that led its devotees to prohibit all representative art and to discover/invent the austere and abstract art of arabesques). The essay states that while the Qur'an is said to have been revealed gradually to the Prophet over the course of years, the original text, "la Madre del Libro" (The Mother of the Book), is held to exist in heaven as an eternal *attribute* of God (and not, for example, as one of his creations). Borges seems to enjoy the contradictions that this implies, writing that the Qur'an "es así anterior al idioma árabe y a los seres que nombra" (in this way, precedes both the Arabic language and the beings that it names [1]). The way in which a book is considered to be part of the divine (and not simply the vehicle through which God speaks or is recorded by inspired scribes) is underlined here with a sense of wonder.[45]

While the concept of a divine language—and, especially, a divine book existing outside of history—would, most likely, not be especially compelling to Borges in the context of the everyday, it applies very nicely to a context in which everyone and everything is, in fact, composed of imagination based upon fixed language. If you and your universe are mental projections based on lines of text (as is the case for fictional characters), then it makes sense that language would be considered sacred, that the book containing these lines would be positioned outside of (imagined) reality as an essential part of a divine creator.

When Borges decided to use theology within his stories to explore contradictions of literary existence, these three characteristics associated with Islam took on radically new functions, pointing to the irreconcilable relationship between everyday reality and the nature of fiction. In "La busca de Averroes" (1949), for example, all three of these elements come together to create a singular crisis of contradiction. The "Averroes" mentioned in the title of the story is a fictional character based on a historical figure, a Muslim scholar (1126–198) who wrote commentaries on Aristotle's philosophical works. Borges uses this text to *explicitly* bring "Islam" in conversation with his own writing practice, demonstrating how his literary ideas can be expressed through theologically inflected narrative.

The story's extraordinarily lengthy initial sentence describes the centuries-long transformation of the proper name "Abulgualid Muhámmad Ibn-Ahmad ibn-Muhámmad ibn-Rushd" into "Averroes" before informing the reader that the man to whom these names belong is, at the moment, sitting at his desk writing the eleventh chapter of the *Tahafut-ul-Tahafut*.[46] The second sentence of Borges's story continues to develop the "spatial" surroundings of his character, describing Averroes's gestures, the manner in which he writes, and the way he perceives the open interior of the house in which he is sitting. This description becomes emphatic and expansive, including the doves outside his house and the hidden sounds of a fountain. The reader is informed that further beyond are gardens and that beyond them is the Guadalquivir River and Córdoba and, in fact, all of Spain "en la que hay pocas cosas, pero donde cada una parece estar de un modo sustantivo y eterno" (in which there are few things, but where each seems to exist in an eternal and substantive state [1:885]).[47] These two elements—a transformed, textual identity in flux and a more "stable" visual and spatial setting—are, as we will soon see, placed in profound tension within the story.

The story soon describes a central conflict: in addition to the *Tahafut-ul-Tahafut*, Averroes is writing a commentary to Aristotle's *Poetics* but cannot understand the terms "tragedy" and "comedy." The narrator of the story explains that "nadie, en el ámbito del Islam, barruntaba lo que querían decir" (no one, in the sphere of Islam, could guess what they referred to [1:886]).[48] Islam, in other words, is presented as the principal context for Averroes's difficulty; it is implied that theatrical representations are antithetical to its tenets.[49]

Which tenets might these be? Once again, the issue seems to be that the perceived proscription of visual representation makes the theater *unimaginable* as a high art form. (Averroes is shown ignoring a group of children playing a game in which they pretend to be a tower, congregation, and the muezzin calling everyone to prayer; this activity does not, to him, register as anything approaching a form of art, much less as something relevant to Aristotle's text.)

Averroes leaves his work to attend a gathering in the house of "el alcoranista Farach." In attendance is a traveler named Abulcásim Al Asharí, who had just returned from Morocco and who had travelled as far as China. The conversation at the house of Farach soon turns to the nature of language; the suspiciously regarded traveler is challenged to confirm or deny the existence of a rosebush—described by Ibn Qutaybah—whose undying roses have petals that contain characters that spell out "No hay otro Dios que el Dios, Muhámmad es el Apóstol de Dios" (There is no God but God, Muhammad is the Apostle of God [1:887]).[50] The traveler demurs by saying that all things green and withered are registered "en Su Libro" (in His Book [1:887]). Averroes, however, offers a more direct challenge, stating that he would be far less surprised if Ibn Qutaybah (or a copyist) had erred than if such a plant were to exist. He goes further, suggesting that "los frutos [. . .] pertenecen al mundo natural, pero la escritura es un arte" (fruits [. . .] belong to the natural world, but writing is an art [1:887]).

The potential *divinity* of language is, in this way, positioned as a key aspect of the story. Averroes has to contend with the statement that "el original del Qurán—*la madre del Libro*—es anterior a la Creación y se guarda en el cielo" (the original Qur'an—the mother of the Book—predates Creation and is safeguarded in the heavens [1:887]). Another guest mentions "Cháhiz de Basra," who stated that the Qur'an "es una sustancia que puede tomar la forma de un hombre o la de un animal" (is a substance that can take the form of a man or an animal [1:887]).[51] While Farach, as the resident expert, explains that the orthodox position is that everyday language and writing are, indeed, tools of mankind, the connection between language and divinity is highlighted by the conversation. Language is presented as a tool available for use by man whose origins are, nevertheless, divine.

Soon the tension between visual representation and linguistic representation is brought into high relief. Abulcásim Al Asharí, after sidestepping the question of the text-petaled rosebush, relates the story of a strange house that he came across while traveling in China. This was a painted structure in which masked individuals "[p]adecían prisiones, y nadie veía la cárcel; cabalgaban, pero no se percibía el caballo; combatían, pero las espadas eran de caña; morían y después estaban de pie" (suffered imprisonment, and no one could see their prison; they rode horses, but no one could discern the horse; they fought, but the swords were made of bamboo; they died and then got to their feet [1:888]). The traveler explains that these actions combined to tell a story for a seated public but everyone, including Averroes, seems confused as to what this means. The theater, even when described, remains out of view. Farach replies that if these strange people were indeed speaking then the rest of the performance was clearly unnecessary; it would have been enough for just one person to speak in order to tell the story, given the extraordinary power of language.

The final conversation in the story concerns the nature of poetry. Abdamálik offers the opinion that poetry ages and that old metaphors should be renovated with new inventions. Averroes disagrees, suggesting instead that poetry is made new not through the invention of metaphors but instead through new contexts of interpretation. He gives the example of a line of verse by Abd al-Rahman directed, originally, to an African palm "en los jardines de Ruzafa" (in the gardens of Ruzafa [1:890]) that, for Averroes, eased his feelings of separation from Córdoba while he was in Marrakesh.[52] The meanings of words, according to Averroes, are not fixed in one form. By placing an emphasis on the felicitous progression of distinct interpretive situations, the character appears to locate the value of poetic language in the chance encounters between readers, texts, and contexts.

After returning to the home that was so clearly described in the first paragraph of the story, Averroes cautiously writes that Aristotle "denomina tragedia a los panegíricos y comedias a las sátiras y anatemas" (calls panegyrics tragedies and refers to satires and anathemas as comedies [1:891]), noting that the Qur'an contains admirable examples of both. He then has the following encounter with a mirror:

Sintió sueño, sintió un poco de frío. Desceñido el turbante, se miró en un espejo de metal. No sé lo que vieron sus ojos, porque ningún historiador ha descrito las formas de su cara. Sé que desapareció bruscamente, como si lo fulminara un fuego sin luz, y que con él desaparecieron la casa y el invisible surtidor y los libros y los manuscritos y las palomas y las muchas esclavas de pelo negro y la trémula esclava de pelo rojo y Farach y Albucásim y los rosales y tal vez el Guadalquivir. (1:891)

He felt tired, felt a little cold. With his turban unraveled, he looked at himself in the metal mirror. I do not know what his eyes saw, because no historian has described the contours of his face. I know that he suddenly disappeared, as if fulminated by a fire without light, and that with him disappeared the house and the unseen fountain and the books and the manuscripts and the doves and the many slaves with black hair and the tremulous red-haired slave and Farach and Albucásim and the rosebushes and, perhaps, the Guadalquivir River.

Here the dissolution of the principal literary space of the story begins with the dissolution of a face: "Averroes," looking at himself in the mirror, finds a troubling aporia. There is nothing there, we read, because the "author" of the story ("Borges") had read no historical accounts of his features. This crisis of representation does not, however, remain contained within the borders of the protagonist's visage. Instead, the entire visual register of the story collapses, erasing Averroes's body, his house, and all his surroundings, including the Guadalquivir River described so placidly in the opening paragraph of the story.[53]

While the narrator explains that Averroes is impossible to describe due to a lack of sources, the same explanation does not hold, clearly, for the Guadalquivir River, for the doves, for the rosebushes. One does not need a history text to describe a dove within a short story. A shift in representation has occurred but it is *different* than the one explicitly pointed to by the narrator. It is important to note that, after showing Averroes's pronounced inability to conceptualize visual representation, Borges shows that he, too, has suddenly become just as incapable. I find that this is not because of any religious restrictions or cultural blind spots, but rather because of a very specific aspect of textual representation that Borges wishes, at this juncture, to highlight. It is, in fact, the *very same* aspect that was emphasized in the first sentences of the story: the idea that instead of delivering sensory information directly (as a *theater* might) literature can only communicate indirectly, through words whose meanings change depending on the contexts that different readers bring to them. (This was also the concept delivered rather conveniently by "Averroes" himself in his anecdote.) The reassuringly stable presence of the initial landscape, river, home, and protagonist was always, from the very beginning, laced with the instability of language and imagination: the landscape was a mere noun (*sustantivo*), not an actual substantive (*sustantivo*) place.

This challenge to the visual register of literary representation is once again articulated through the utilization of an "Islamic" context in which the *word* is placed in far higher esteem than visual artistic traditions such as, here, the theater. The black canvas of Tafas and the unseen Aleph within a pillar of the Amr Mosque are now joined by a fulminated theatrical fiction, a context of nonrepresentation that explicitly poses questions about our relationship to the familiar illusions of realism.

Borges's inability to represent the scene has typically been understood as an acknowledgement of the *difference* between his cultural background and that of the historical figure of Averroes. His narrator helpfully suggests that the story be read in this way, as a doubled failure that includes both the difficulties of Averroes to understand the concept of drama without being able to imagine a theatre and, of course, the failure of Borges (or is it "Borges"?) to imagine Averroes with only a few books at his disposal.[54] While Borges is pointing, clearly, to many of the limits of the books written by Orientalists such as Renan and Lane (and to his own lack of knowledge), his story, I argue, is principally designed to unsettle the theatrical literary norms that he and Macedonio mistrusted. The disintegration of the visual and spatial register of the story, in other words, performs an *affinity* between Borges and a *fictional* representative of an imaginary version of "Islam" concerned more with artificial representation than with

divinity, politics, or society. Borges does not contrast Averroes's failure to understand the visuality of the theater with his own personal,
"Western" *faith* in that visuality. Instead, Borges essentially agrees with
his literary character: emphatic "visual" displays (in the context of
fiction) can distract the reader from the ways in which textual meanings develop and change over time and across contexts. He concludes
his story with a performed rejection of theatrical literature, not with
an affirmation of the vitality of Western theater.

The story seems to present the realization that the "literary milieu"
of Averroes is unstable as a surprise for Borges; as a sudden epiphany
that interferes with his supposed "efforts" to create a traditional, realistic narration. Yet this is a pose; we have been set up (from the first
paragraph of the story) when the easily understood spatial description
of Averroes's immediate surroundings was paired with a far more
disorienting series of proper names and a description of their transformation in time. An abstract textual development based on a series
of cultural changes (the transformation of "Abulgualid Muhámmad
Ibn-Ahmad ibn-Muhámmad ibn-Rushd" to "Benraist" to "Avenryz"
to "Aben-Rassad" to "Filius Rosadis" and then, finally, to "Averroes")
was contrasted, implicitly, with the visual and spatial development of
a "scene" presented as the easily imagined backdrop—as the theatrical
stage—upon which the story was to develop.[55] Borges, by dissolving
the visual and spatial "stage," reaffirms that language is, by its very
nature, meaningless without contextual change, and that the stability
that it can suggest is, often, an illusion and a trap. Averroes's own
name becomes a textual microcosm of the literary ideal he expresses
within the story: it is altered through time just like the shifting poem
that he describes to his friends.

While the relationship between aniconism—seen in the characters' inability to conceptualize the theater—and the divine origins of
language is clearly a driving force in the story, the role of iconoclasm
is perhaps more difficult to perceive. It is important to know that
iconoclastic encounters with art objects in Islamic contexts were often
not characterized by wanton violence.[56] Instead, specific gestures
were employed in order to render the offending object "powerless"
while also managing to preserve its essential form. In "Between Cult

FIGURE 2
Detail from a painting by Mir
Musavvir, ca. 1530. British
Museum, acc. no. 1930,1112,0.2.

and Culture," Finbarr Flood, for example, mentions the example of
a luster tile in the early fourteenth century in which the diminutive
depictions of birds had their heads chipped off, leaving only the
"empty" spaces of the clay beneath (647). A useful example of this
strategic erasure is a painting by Mir Musavvir (active as a painter
1525–50, according to the British Museum) that has been altered in
a similar fashion (see fig. 2).

While the obliteration of Averroes's universe may have been set
up in the initial paragraph of the story, it begins, importantly, with
his face—with his face and also with his own gaze. Looking into the
mirror causes Averroes to encounter an absence that soon takes the
Guadalquivir River along with it. The context of Islamic aniconism
maintained throughout the story is thus mobilized as, effectively, an
iconoclastic erasure.

This is especially true since "La busca de Averroes" is not the
only story that combines references to Islamic prohibitions on representation and pronounced erasures of faces. A principal example
is found, in fact, within the conclusion of "El Aleph." The narrator
of the story asks himself whether he might have seen the "true"
Aleph within the Amr Mosque while peering through the Aleph of
Daneri. He is uncertain but affirms, regardless, that "[n]uestra mente

es porosa para el olvido; yo mismo estoy falseando y perdiendo, bajo la trágica erosión de los años, los rasgos de Beatriz" ([o]ur minds are porous for forgetfulness; I myself am falsifying and losing, with the tragic erosion of years, the features of Beatriz [1:932]). The erasure of Beatriz's face is the final gesture in the story.

The significance of this erasure is augmented by the fact that, in the beginning of the story, her home is described as filled with representations of her physical form:

> Beatriz Viterbo, de perfil, en colores; Beatriz, con antifaz, en los carnavales de 1921; la primera comunión de Beatriz; Beatriz, el día de su boda con Roberto Alessandri; Beatriz, poco después del divorcio, en un almuerzo del Club Hípico; Beatriz en Quilmes, con Delia San Marco Porcel y Carlos Argentino; Beatriz, con el pekinés que le regaló Villegas Haedo; Beatriz, de frente y de tres cuartos, sonriendo, la mano en el mentón. . . . (1:921–22)

> Beatriz Viterbo, in profile, in color; Beatriz, with a mask, in the 1921 carnival; the first communion of Beatriz; Beatriz, the day of her wedding to Roberto Alessandri; Beatriz, right after the divorce, at a lunch in the Club Hípico; Beatriz in Quilmes, with Delia San Marco Porcel and Carlos Argentino; Beatriz, with the Pekinese that Villegas Haedo gave her; Beatriz, facing forward and at an angle, smiling, her hand on her chin . . . .

For a story that relies, as I have argued, on the perceived Islamic prohibition of visually representing living beings, this is a crucial, emphatic parade of portraiture. The peculiar "love" that "Borges" feels toward Beatriz is, perhaps, best seen as a superficial infatuation with this very mode of visual representation.

By the end of the story, however, the narrator's infatuation with the spectacle of artificial visual representation has been disrupted. This is both because the narrator has seen "obscene" letters exchanged between Carlos Argentino Daneri and Beatriz and, more importantly, because the overdose of visuality has made infinitely perfect vision less appealing. The false Aleph of Daneri has redirected us to something more "true" within this literary context: the promise of indirect, imaginative interpretation offered by the Aleph at the Amr Mosque. "Borges" is in this way set free from a desire for sight-as-spectacle that is, at least in Macedonio's estimation, profoundly anti-literary. Beatriz's face fades from view.

Neither is this the sole example of such an iconoclastic gesture.[57] "El espejo de tinta" began, as we noted earlier, with a magician asking Yakub el Doliente to look into a pool of ink and see his own face. It ended, however, with this same governor seeing a *masked* individual in the visions contained within the ink. When he asked that this individual be magically unmasked within his vision, it was revealed that the man represented was, in fact, himself. This revelation of a face was followed by a decapitation: the head of the represented human figure was chopped off by the executioner. Yakub, watching this painterly vision of his own death, then died as well. This set of gestures connecting the occultation, revelation, and decapitation of the represented face is paired, in the story, with an explicit mention of Islamic aniconism and, as such, may have been informed by Borges's knowledge of iconoclastic practices within Islam.

This is due to the fact that while abrasion or erasure were sometimes used to deal with works of art that inappropriately represented human or animal figures, another act of iconoclasm was that of gestural decapitation. A detail from an illustration of the *Maqamat* of Al-Hariri (1054–1122) shows this form of alteration: lines drawn across the necks of the depicted individuals have symbolically decapitated them, rendering them inoffensive to the proscriptions of representation familiar to Borges (see fig. 3). The fact that Yakub el Doliente is punished for "seeing" prohibited paintings with his own virtual (and actual) decapitation points strongly to this iconoclastic tradition.

In "El tintorero enmascarado Hákim de Merv" (1935) we encounter the face, again, as a troubled site of representation within an Islamic context. The protagonist in this story is a prophet who states that his powers originate, in fact, from an act of divine decapitation: his head was cut off by the Angel Gabriel and brought before God. God, in turn, "le dio misión de profetizar y le inculcó palabras tan antiguas que su repetición quemaba las bocas y le infundió un glorioso

FIGURE 3 Illustration by Irakischer Maler, ca. 1225–35. The Institute of Oriental Manuscripts (IOM) of the Russian Academy of Sciences in St. Petersburg. Photo: Yorck Project (2002).

resplandor que los ojos mortales no toleraban" (gave him a prophetic mission and taught him words so ancient that their repetition burned mouths and infused him with a glorious resplendence that mortal eyes could not bear [1:611]).[58] When he was younger, interestingly, the prophet had worked as a dyer; this job provoked a series of internal questions as to the propriety of dyeing wool:

> Así que pequé en los años de juventud y trastorné los verdaderos colores de las criaturas. El Ángel me decía que los carneros no eran del color de los tigres, el Satán me decía que el Poderoso quería que lo fueran y se valía de mi astucia y mi púrpura. Ahora yo sé que el Ángel y el Satán erraban la verdad y que todo color es aborrecible. (1:610)

And so I sinned in the years of my youth and altered the true colors of living beings. The Angel told me that rams were not the color of tigers; Satan told me that the All Powerful wanted them to be and used my cunning and my purple dyes. Now I know that the Angel and Satan were in error and that all color is abominable.

Hákim's internal debate about the propriety of *visually* altering the appearance of even the *remains* of a living being through man-made artifice eventually leads (after his revelation) to the conclusion that any representation—any color—is "aborrecible." This leap is important. We are no longer considering "Islamic" prohibitions of visuality in terms of represented artistic practices (painting, the theater, etc.). Hákim connects a rejection of artful alteration of the natural order of things (is it proper to alter the color of animal pelts?) to the rejection of all color in his (fictional) world. This rejection of color soon extends to a total rejection of visuality. The focus, in other words, shifts from the nature of art in the fictional context of the story to *the very fabric* of the fiction itself, just as in "La busca de Averroes" the disintegration of the visual originates with an iconoclastically altered face (Hákim's divine decapitation) but leads to the radical questioning of the entire artificial reality.[59]

While I have pointed to the ways in which other stories can be read *allegorically* as referring to the nature of literary interpretation (through Tafas's two canvases, the "true" and "false" Alephs, and the mirror of ink), this is the first moment in which a fictional character (who is not "Borges") relates to all of his artificial surroundings as *explicitly* composed of pure artifice. This shift in narrative strategy is also accompanied by a shift in the represented "theology" of the character. While the context of the story is "Islamic," the protagonist is a heretic. This heretical position, however, represents an *amplification* of "Islam's" prohibition of visual representation: where previously only man-made visual representations of life were to be mistrusted by the literary characters, we now find that the whole visible world of the character is to be internally disdained and abhorred as—crucially—a work of artifice.

In "Después de las imágenes" Borges called for the creation of literary works of art that could allow internal characters and narrators to consider their artifice from within. Here, Hákim undergoes a radical shift of perspective: he comes to believe that he and his surroundings are all composed of artifice and, as such, should be detested as others detest the paintings of living beings that are (rightly) prohibited. Hákim, from our perspective as readers, is correct: both he and his world are composed of man-made artifice.[60]

In Borges's story, Hákim de Merv asserts that at the beginning of time, the image of God, an unalterable and faceless being, projected nine shades that, in turn, provided and ruled over the first heavens. From this demiurgical circle emerged a second group that created their own lower, symmetrical heaven. This process continued until the 999th version, which was governed by a shadow god whose fraction of divinity "tiende a cero" (approaches zero [1:612]):

> La tierra que habitamos es un error, una incompetente parodia. Los espejos y la paternidad son abominables, porque la multiplican y afirman. El asco es la virtud fundamental. Dos disciplinas (cuya elección dejaba libre el profeta) pueden conducirnos a ella: la abstinencia y el desenfreno, el ejercicio de la carne o su castidad. (1:612–13)

> The earth that we live on is an error, an incompetent parody. Mirrors and fatherhood are abominable because they multiply and affirm it. Disgust is the primary virtue. Two disciplines (whose election the prophet left open to choice) can lead us there: abstinence or complete indulgence, the use of flesh or its chastity.

If one exists within a context that is composed of simulacra—a copy of a copy—and desires nothing more than truth, then it is clear that "disgust" could be considered a fundamental virtue. One's enlightened perspective would consist of total rejection. Mirrors would only repeat the essential falseness of the world with yet another copy: a glimpse of that wholly redundant 1000th universe symmetrical to one's own.[61]

The fact that the Prophet describes himself as divinely decapitated may, furthermore, speak to the larger Islamic context of the story: this is, after all, the gesture reserved for simulacra depicting living beings (as was seen in fig. 3). Given the ubiquitous context of artifice that Hákim believes in, he is, like the characters of the illustrated *Maqamat*, just as much of an artificial representation as any drawn figure. What neutralizes this falsity, we have seen, is a line drawn through the neck, a virtual decapitation that, in the case of Hákim de Merv, arrived from a divine hand.

"Heaven," in this story, is fittingly described as the knowledge that one is fictional: it is a peaceful understanding of the falsity of the world, its distance from reality. "Hell," on the other hand, is a belief in the reality of a body that, nevertheless, suffers pain and desires pleasure within these repeated copies of worlds. Again, the fact that Hákim de Merv is, in fact, *fictional* makes his "theological" belief system profoundly relevant to our experience as readers. We, in this story, encounter a protagonist who intuits his status as a fictional character in theological terms and reacts with complete disgust toward everything that would suggest otherwise.[62] Protected and empowered by his own decapitation, he has the ability to make others blind by simply looking in their eyes. We might ask if this blindness is a curse or, in the context of being surrounded by so much repulsive falsity, an act of mercy that might lead others to a kind of *literary enlightenment*. We might also ask if it is relevant to interpret it in terms of Borges's own understanding that he would likely one day be blind.

"El tintorero enmascarado Hákim de Merv" (1935) is often seen, fittingly, as a precursor to "Tlön, Uqbar, Orbis Tertius" (1940). In this later story, Borges expands on the ideas that we have already traced to create what is perhaps his most elaborate allegorical exploration of fictionality. It begins with "Borges" and "Adolfo Bioy Casares" conversing about the possibility of a work of literature that would communicate to a select few—by means of certain contradictions, omissions, or peculiarities—an appalling or banal reality. As an apparent aside, "Bioy" anecdotally mentions something that he had once read in an encyclopedia: that, for certain heresiarchs of a country called "Uqbar," copulation and mirrors were considered abominable because of the way that they increased the number of men. This observation sends them in search of information about the country, which does not appear in any of the references at their disposal. Soon they determine that the country and the quote that pertains to it (which was remembered incorrectly by Bioy, who replaced "fatherhood" with "copulation") are both pure inventions. Uqbar, they learn, is fictional.

The parallels with "El tintorero enmascarado Hákim de Merv" are difficult to miss. In both cases we hear the belief that mirrors are abominable due to the manner in which they visually reproduce people who are, for the most part, unaware of the fact that they are derivative copies of copies. Copulation (or, more accurately, "fatherhood") is, in this view, simply another means of "artificial reproduction." When we read these ideas while paying attention to the fact that they are being articulated by artificial characters it is possible to perceive an important allegorical resonance.[63] Mirrors and reproduction—in the context of *literature*—add falsity to falsity, fiction to fiction: for someone (especially a literary character) desiring freedom from so much simulacra, they might easily be abhorrent.

This unusual discovery of an invented country piques the curiosity of "Borges." Soon he discovers a volume of an encyclopedia that details certain aspects of the literature of "Uqbar." It mentions that these literary works take place in one of two possible regions. One of them is called "Tlön." In a later discovery, he comes across a very different encyclopedia in which Tlön is represented as, it seems, a whole planet that operates according to unfamiliar rules.

Within Tlön, "el mundo [. . .] no es un concurso de objetos en el espacio; es una serie heterogénea de actos independientes. Es sucesivo, temporal, no espacial" (the world [. . .] is not a set of objects in space; it is a heterogeneous series of independent acts. It is successive, temporal, non-spatial [1:727]). Instead of an everyday spatial context in which discrete objects are in proximity to one another, the narrator describes a version of reality in which a series of independent, heterogeneous acts combine with one another, in time, without ever materializing in a physical form.

While this is, at first, not an easy context to visualize, it is worth considering the degree to which the above description corresponds with the line of text that you are currently reading: these words are, in fact, independent and heterogeneous acts experienced successively, in time, without ever materializing in physical form.[64] Literary reality can easily be understood in this way: as nonspatial, successive, and temporal, as originating from a series of independent acts of textual expression (words).

Language within Tlön, given this absence of concrete objects, is peculiar: there is a corresponding absence of nouns. Instead of a fixed noun such as "moon" one might find a verb "que sería en español *lunecer* o *lunar*" (that in English would be *moonify* or *to moon* [1:727]). Verbs and adjectives take on central roles, creating a method of description that resides within the impossible dimensionality of an immaterial, imaginary world.[65] In this world (of fiction, if my interpretation holds), there is no *there* there: people, places, and things are but fleeting impressions gathered from interpreted gestures.

Causality is also an everyday principle that disappears within fiction; a set of actions in a short story are, of course, nothing more than the associated ideas of an author.[66] Similarly, in Tlön, "[l]a percepción de una humareda en el horizonte y después del campo encendido y después del cigarro a medio apagar que produjo la quemazón es considerada un ejemplo de asociación de ideas" (the perception of smoke on the horizon and then of the countryside on fire and then of the still-burning cigar that originated the first flame are, together, considered to be an example of mental association [1:728]).

It should come, then, as no surprise to learn that certain Tlönian schools of thought hold that most minimal details of life and the greatest episodes of history are all "la escritura que produce un dios subalterno para entenderse con un demonio" (the writing that a subaltern god produces to communicate with a demon [1:729]). To live in Tlön is, in other words, to struggle existentially and, in certain cases, theologically, with the fact of one's profound artificiality.[67] If the author is a subaltern god then we, as readers, are their demons.

In Tlön, the spectacle of Daneri's Aleph is replaced by the wonders of a *thing-less universe*: perfect, simultaneous vision is rendered useless in a context in which there is no "thing" to observe.

Within the story, "Borges" relates his encounter with the volume of the *Encyclopedia of Tlön* in this way: "[e]n una noche del Islam que se llama la Noche de las Noches se abren de par en par las secretas puertas del cielo y es más dulce el agua en los cántaros; si esas puertas se abrieran, no sentiría lo que es esa tarde sentí" (on a night in Islam called the Night of Nights the secret doors of the sky open wide and the water sweetens in its pitchers; if those doors were to open I wouldn't feel what I felt that afternoon [1:726]). The volume that causes this ecstasy is, tellingly, composed of 1001 pages: while Borges draws from his understanding of Gnosticism, "Islam" is inscribed upon this literary allegory in a manner that is difficult to ignore.

The account of the wonders of Tlön does not end ecstatically, however, as a great triumph of creativity. Instead, we are presented with a note of caution, even fear, with regard to this fantastical order. This fear stems from an unsettling incursion of fictionality into the space (and the morality) of the everyday. We read, in a "1947" postscript, that a letter discovered in 1941 revealed the full project of Tlön.[68] It describes how a secret society dedicated to the perpetual elaboration of Uqbar was founded in the seventeenth century. The disciples of this society continued the work until, in 1824, one of them spoke with an ascetic millionaire named Ezra Buckley. Buckley, a nihilist and a defender of slavery from Mississippi, derisively suggests that in America the invention of a country would be absurd and that, instead, it would be more appropriate to invent a full planet. There is only one condition: the encyclopedia that he proposes—The Encyclopedia of Tlön—must not, he states, include "el impostor Jesucristo" (the impostor Jesus Christ [1:733]). While Buckley insists that this encyclopedia should be hidden from the world, in 1944 it is discovered (possibly with the help, "Borges" notes, of Buckley's disciples). People everywhere soon become obsessed with its perfectly ordered version of reality and in time begin neglecting the far more challenging disorder of the real world.

As "Borges" witnesses the world abandon its everyday concerns, immersed in Tlön, he compares the situation to the rise of Marxism, Nazism, and anti-Semitism, closing the story with the report that he is secluded in a hotel in Adrogué writing "una traducción quevediana [. . .] del *Urn Burial* de Browne" (a Quevedian translation [. . .] of Browne's *Urn Burial* [1:736]). The disconcerting turn in the story—in which the fantastical world of Tlön becomes a terrifying delusion associated with violence and genocide—can be approached from many different perspectives. One of the most direct (and surprising) ways in which this shift is prefigured, however, is through a text that Borges references early on in his story: Thomas De Quincey's *Historico-Critical Inquiry into the Origin of the Rosicrucians and Free-Masons.*

"Borges" describes how the initial encyclopedia entry on "Uqbar" found by "Bioy" included, in its bibliography, a text by Johann Valentinus Andreä titled *Lesbare and lesenswerthe Bemerkungen über das Land Ukkbar in Klein-Asien* (1641).[69] "Borges" elaborates on the importance of this find:

> El hecho es significativo; un par de años después, di con ese nombre en las inesperadas páginas de De Quincey (*Writings*, decimotercer volumen) y supe que era el de un teólogo alemán que a principios del siglo XVII describió la imaginaria comunidad de la Rosa-Cruz—que otros luego fundaron, a imitación de lo prefigurado por él. (1:725)

> The fact is significant; a few years later I came across that name in the unexpected pages of De Quincey (*Writings*, 13th volume) and I found out that it belonged to a German theologian who in the early seventeenth century described the imaginary community of the Rosy Cross—which others later founded, imitating what he had prefigured.

Turning to the actual volume of De Quincey mentioned by Borges reveals a historical account that closely parallels the events in the story.

De Quincey describes how Andreä, a German theologian, sought to create a brotherhood of men that would attract followers by *evoking the mysteries of the Orient.* To do so, the theologian invented a fictional tale centered on a protagonist named "Christian Rosycross." His writings—which presented themselves as factual—described how Christian Rosycross had lived hundreds of years before and, after discovering the secrets of the Orient, returned to the West to create a benevolent secret society. De Quincey reveals, quite dramatically, that he is able to prove that Rosycross is, in fact, no more than a mythical, reconfigured version of his "biographer" Andreä: "That Andreä was that author I shall now prove by one final argument:

it is a presumptive argument, but in my opinion conclusive: The armorial bearings of Andreä's family were a St. Andrew's Cross and four Roses. By the order of the Rosy-cross he means therefore an order *founded by himself*."[70] De Quincey goes on to write that soon after the publication of Andreä's texts, many people began to seek out membership in the order of the Rosy-cross. Things, however, did not go as Andreä planned. Some of the individuals seeking entrance into the mysterious guild became frustrated (as they received no replies to their public petitions) and eventually decided to simply declare themselves Rosicrucians. Instead of laboring to help others under a renovated Christianity, as Andreä seems to have hoped, De Quincey writes that they often focused their efforts on using the allure of Oriental alchemy to take their followers' money. Andreä, regretting his actions, turned against the Rosicrucian order.[71]

The same progression occurs within Borges's story. Following the initial inventors of Uqbar, who base their fictional order on a reconfigured "Islam," generations of initiates labor to create a more and more intricate world. This is a world that, for all of its complexity, is far more comprehensible than anything not deliberately created by mankind. Just like the alchemically revealed universe promised by the Rosicrucians, Tlön—for all its mysteries—is attractive for the way in which it is, in a word, *legible*. Therein, according to Borges, also lies the danger:

> Hace diez años bastaba cualquier simetría con apariencia de orden—el materialismo dialéctico, el antisemitismo, el nazismo—para embelesar a los hombres. ¿Cómo no someterse a Tlön, a la minuciosa y vasta evidencia de un planeta ordenado? Inútil responder que la realidad también está ordenada. Quizá lo esté, pero de acuerdo a leyes divinas—traduzco: a leyes inhumanas—que no acabamos nunca de percibir. Tlön será un laberinto, pero es un laberinto urdido por hombres, un laberinto destinado a que lo descifren los hombres. (1:735)

> Ten years ago, any kind of symmetry with an appearance of order was sufficient—dialectical materialism, anti-Semitism, Nazism—to bewitch mankind. How then to avoid submitting to Tlön, to the minute and

vast evidence of an ordered planet? It is useless to respond that reality is also ordered. Perhaps it is, but according to divine laws—I will translate: to inhuman laws—that we will never cease to discover. Tlön might be a labyrinth, but it is a labyrinth plotted by men, a labyrinth destined for men to decipher.

As readers, we are left to ask whether the "ordered planet" that we are being warned against is not, in fact, literature itself.

If, as I have argued, Tlön represents the most coherent allegorical performance of Borges's experience of literary reality (a reality in which causality, physicality, and permanence are notably absent), then this warning about its allure is crucial for our understanding of his literary work in general. Specifically, the warning issued by Borges seems to be that in seeking out intricate and pleasurable games of interpretation and authorship, it is very possible to lose sight of the experiences, questions, and responsibilities that *resist* literary representation.[72] Understanding literature on its own terms is to not lose sight of how partial it is, of how much of life is not represented in the imaginary worlds that we create from lines of text. To follow Borges's analogy, one can become lost in the labyrinth of human artifice not because it is difficult but, instead, because it is *simple*, because it—literature—is a human invention with human solutions.

It is worth remembering the distinction between standard theology and the "literary theology" that Borges has put to use in the preceding stories. Where theological ideas often grapple with the questions that *supersede* the human capacity to create and understand, the kind of literary theology that Borges constructs focuses, instead, precisely on the manner in which human beings are *capable* of communicating and interpreting meaning. The end of Borges's story suggests that there is an important limit to the literary exploration that he initiates, a boundary that circumscribes his literary theology. Despite the richness and urgency of the questions that he explores within his work, the everyday world is a far more difficult context of interpretation, one where political and social questions of meaning, responsibility, fear, and desire do not necessarily have answers lying in wait to be discovered.

Borges's literary theology is, in this sense, generally unconcerned with guiding moral behavior. It, instead, allegorically questions the traditional laws that guide the imagination of a reader (or an author) in momentary isolation, playing with the possibilities of an active, creative relationship with visuality and textuality. In opening toward the internal "experience" of literary characters grappling with literature, it also allows the reader to sense their own experience of being-while-immersed-in-literature with a renewed sense of clarity. While there are aspects of Borges's work that are indeed quite political and can have the effect of unsettling orthodoxies and sources of imagined purity and superiority (as well as others that reinforce existing power structures), this story points to the way in which immersion in fiction (and in the pleasures and possibilities that it offers) can, when overly emphasized, distract us from other aspects of life that are far more consequential.[73] "Tlön, Uqbar, Orbis Tertius" was first published in May 1940, which, as Edna Aizenberg points out, is "the month when Hitler overran Holland, Belgium, and Luxembourg."[74]

Echoing the beginning of the story, one might say that our discovery that the individuals in Tlön are *emphatically fictional characters* is banal: of course we are reading a fictional story, of course these individuals and spaces are composed of human artifice. The second context, carefully considered, is appalling: we are shown that the attraction that one feels (that I feel and that you feel) to the order of fiction can, if uncritically followed in the context of the everyday, lead to violence, suffering, and death. It is banal to state that literature is imaginary. It is appalling to see how fictions are used to injure, kill, and oppress (or to distract from violence and oppression).

The fact that Borges ends his story writing a Quevedian translation of Sir Thomas Browne's "Urn Burial" marks, finally, the importance of mortality and the contemplation of death in his consideration of the allure of literary artifice.[75] It is framed, in the story, as a turning *away* from Tlön and, given the nature of the translated text, can be read as an admission that it is both futile and vain to hope to live beyond one's years within memories, monuments, and texts. In this gesture, we might sense an idea: that not all forms of literature are equally dangerous in terms of their capacity to foment or distract from violence and injustice, that a glance toward death, toward one's own mortality, can be a stark reminder of more important things.

This "urn burial" in the story is complex. Within the word "urn" is the word "Ur": the name of the city that, as Alan White has written, one *actually finds* when seeking out the nonexistent "Uqbar" in the 1911 *Encyclopedia Britannica*.[76] I mention the buried "Ur" within the word "urn" because this encyclopedia entry describes that the city of Ur is, in turn, a famous burial ground. In this way, the "Urn Burial" reconfigures the burial grounds of Ur, which are only accessible for readers who seek out "Uqbar" between "Ural-Altaic languages" and "Upsala," as the story gently suggests. (There is more: within the context of Tlön the fantastical objects that come into existence solely due to the *hopes* of someone who seeks them out are called, in fact, "ur." The hopeful reader who seeks out "Uqbar" is, in this way, greeted with a wink. They have found one such fantastical object carrying, strangely, the name of its category.)[77]

Within this tangle of references lies the dichotomy between the imaginary and the tangible, between the objects made "real" in Tlön by the hopes of their seekers and the physical geographic expanse of a historical burial ground. Borges chillingly associates those who are so enthralled with fiction that they chase his riddles into encyclopedias with others who have become lost within other imaginary, artificial orders: white supremacy, Nazism, anti-Semitism, extreme nationalism, etc. This is not a relationship that is resolved within the story: fiction and violence remain entangled to the point where it is difficult to maintain the separation between the reality of the literary and the reality of the everyday, between Orbis Tertius and our own third planet from the sun. We are asked, quite simply, to be careful.

Given the ways in which the invention of Tlön combines theology and literary ideas, it is worth returning to the condition that Ezra Buckley, the nihilist, ascetic millionaire in the story, sets for the project of Tlön: that it not include any mention of the "impostor" Jesus Christ. This can, in fact, be seen as yet abother oblique reference to Islam given that Borges writes the following in his "Místicos del Islam":

Una religión que proclama un Dios personal, un Dios único, una religión cuyos artículos fundamentales enseñan un Juicio Final, en el término de la historia, y después un infierno eterno o un cielo eterno, con demonios o ángeles, no difiere excesivamente de la cristiana—salvo en que falta el Cristo. (1)

A religion that proclaims a personal God, a single God, a religion whose fundamental articles teach of a Final Judgment, at the end of history, and afterwards an eternal hell or an eternal heaven, with demons and angels, does not differ excessively from that of Christianity—save for the absence of Christ.

The above fragment from Borges's manuscript draft suggests that he imagines Islam as very nearly a copy of Christianity, with the notable absence of Jesus Christ as a divine being and, of course, a fierce rejection of iconicity and Western visuality.

It is nearly inevitable that the representation of Christ would enter into Borges's exploration of his (literary) culture's reliance on iconicity: there is no more central an example of a revered, visualized image to point to.[78] The oppositional relationship between Islam's aniconism and Christianity's iconicity is, additionally, at the very center of a riddle within Borges's "El Zahir" (1949). Solving this riddle brings us face to face with iconicity in a way that will ultimately help to recontextualize Borges's unique use of his 'literary theology.'

"El Zahir" begins, enigmatically, with the following statement: "En Buenos Aires el Zahir es una moneda común, de veinte centavos; marcas de navajas o de cortaplumas rayan las letras N T y el número 2; 1929 es la fecha grabada en el anverso" (In Buenos Aires the Zahir is a common coin, of 20 cents; razor or penknife marks trace out the letters N T and the number 2; 1929 is the date printed on the other side [1:892]).[79]

Though the narrator ("Borges") does not immediately explain precisely what a "Zahir" is, he does mention that at the end of the eighteenth century a tiger was a "Zahir" in Gujarat. At other times and places, it took the form of a blind man in a mosque, an astrolabe, a compass, a vein within a marble pillar, and the bottom of a well.

"Borges" announces that he came across the Zahir months before and that he, as he writes, is struggling to hold on to his identity: "[a]ún, siquiera parcialmente, soy Borges" (still, if only partially, I am Borges [1:892]).[80]

What follows this peculiar introduction is a description of two very different contexts of visuality that should, by now, seem familiar. The first is related to a Western tradition of visual allure—the narrator ("Borges") is in love with a model who is obsessed with the perpetually changing rules of fashion that connect Buenos Aires with Europe and Hollywood. The second context is explicitly Islamic and relates to the Zahir, a word used to describe certain cursed objects that, when *seen*, lead to debilitating obsessions. The text states that "[l]a creencia en el Zahir es islámica y data, al parecer, del siglo XVIII. [. . .] Zahir, en árabe, quiere decir notorio, visible; en tal sentido es uno de los noventa y nueve nombres de Dios" (The belief in the Zahir is Islamic and dates, seemingly, to the eighteenth century. . . . Zahir, in Arabic, means known, visible; in this sense, it is one of the ninety-nine names of God [1:896]). Those who visually behold the Zahir are rendered incapable of thinking of anything but the Zahir.

Both of these contexts are, additionally, presented in theological terms. Borges associates the routines of the fashion model with the practices of a religious devotee. The rigor with which she follows the ever-shifting edicts of fashion is compared with following the *Mishnah* and the *Book of Rites*. "Teodelina se mostraba en lugares ortodoxos, a la hora ortodoxa, con atributos ortodoxos, con desgano ortodoxo, pero el desgano, los atributos, la hora y los lugares caducaban casi inmediatamente" (Teodelina would present herself in orthodox places, at an orthodox hour, with orthodox attributes, with an orthodox indifference, but this indifference, hour, and set of places would expire almost immediately [1:892]). Even her name—Teodelina Villar—suggests a theological identity tied to fashion: "Teo-de-lina" can be read as "the god of cloth" or (in other words) fashion-as-religion. (This interpretation is strengthened by Borges's own note within his manuscript draft "Místicos del Islam," which explains that the etymology of "Sufi" is "vestido de lana" [dressed in wool]; "Teo-de-lina" and "vestido de lana" form a punning pair that

I believe would have appealed to Borges, given the references in the story to Islamic mysticism.)[81]

Teodelina Villar is, in other words, an extreme case of a living being whose reproduced image is propagated (and perhaps even worshipped, in a secular sense) within society. Her decline begins as World War II makes her devotional practice more difficult; the Buenos Aires–Paris connection is severed. After appearing in less prestigious advertisements, Teodelina decides to retire and, shortly afterward, passes away.

It is after her funeral that "Borges" acquires the coin that is the Zahir. After he sees it, he cannot help but think of coins. As he ponders Charon's obol, the obol of Belisarius, the thirty coins of Judas, Ahab's gold doubloon, and the florin of Leopold Bloom he finds that he has wandered, without realizing it, in a circle. Even his footsteps trace the contour of the imagined coin. The obsession, over the next several pages, changes shape. Unable to see outside of the abstraction of money, "Borges" finds that he is trapped by an object that he finally identifies, with the help of a (fictional) book, as a "Zahir."[82]

The relationship between the coin that cannot be unseen and Teodelina Villar is not difficult to discern. The power of both the fashion icon and the cursed coin lie in their visual allure. In the context of Borges's "Islam," however, the Zahir is framed as a curse and in the Western context of fashion, the reproduced image of Teodelina is celebrated for its attractiveness.

The riddle that initiates the story, however, complicates this apparent tension. The puzzle is, in many ways, a visual one: as previously mentioned, it involves the letters N and T as well as the number 2 carved in the coin at the center of the story.[83] Given the larger theological themes that Borges appropriated in the stories mentioned within this chapter, it occurred to me that the $N\,T$ likely stood for "Nuevo Testamento." The number 2 could, of course, refer to either a chapter or a verse but this was not enough information to clearly identify a specific textual reference. The coin, however, being worth twenty centavos, would already have the number 20 on its face and could have led its previous (obsessed) owner to the twentieth chapter found in the Bible far more easily than it could have led to every twentieth verse. Placed together, it seemed possible that chapter 20, verse 2 of the first book of the New Testament could be relevant to the story. In fact, Matthew 20:2 contains *the exact moment* in which Jesus describes the divine reward offered to his followers by comparing it to a single coin.

It is, however, a strange coin. Jesus is here responding to a question from Peter, who points out that he and the other disciples have "forsaken all" and need to know "what shall we have, therefore?" The response takes the form of a story: it begins with a landowner who goes out in the morning to hire laborers for his vineyard. Verse 20:2 (the verse that solves Borges's riddle) states: "And when he had agreed with the laborers for a *denarius* a day, he sent them into his vineyard" (emphasis mine). Later on, the man goes out again and, seeing idle workers, hires them to work for the rest of the day. They agree to receive "what is right." In the evening, he finds more men idle and hires them as well. Finally, when it is time to be paid, every man receives one coin, the aforementioned denarius, despite having labored for different periods of time. After the first workers complain, the man says: "Take what is thine, and go thy way; I will give unto this last even as to thee." The story concludes with the statement "So the last shall be first, and the first last; for many are called, but few chosen" (King James Version [Schofield]).

The coin that Borges references in his biblical riddle is peculiar in a number of ways. The first is that it refers to the infinite, divine reward that awaits the faithful. Its value, in this sense, is indeterminate and unquantifiable. The second peculiarity of the coin is that, in having infinite value, it is not exchanged for labor as normal coins might be exchanged. Mathematically, infinity divided by ten is equal to infinity divided by two. Theologically, the parable suggests that the reward of divinity is the same for all of the devotees of Jesus, regardless of what they had to give up or how long they have held their faith.

Within the context of this chapter it is important to note the ease with which, in this Christian parable, a *denarius*—a coin that features the representation of a person's face (Caesar's, most likely either Augustus's or Tiberius's) on one of its sides—is used to illustrate allegorically the divine reward of God. (See fig. 4 for an example.)

FIGURE 4 Denarius of Augustus, Lugdunum, ca. 8–7 B.C.E. Harvard Art Museums / Arthur M. Sackler Museum, purchase through the generosity of Celia and Walter Gilbert Claude-Claire Grenier and the Marian H. Phinney Fund, 2005.115.91. Photo: Imaging Department © President and Fellows of Harvard College.

As we have seen, Borges's "Islam" was focused on the prohibition of visual portraiture. That a coin with a representation of Caesar's face on it could be used, by Jesus himself, to represent the divine reward of God stands in stark contrast to the ideas that Borges associated with his literary theology.

Toward the end of "El Zahir" the narrator comes to terms with the fact that he will soon become insane, anaesthetized by a single, simple repeated thought. The story, regardless, ends with a note of optimism: "Para perderse en Dios, los sufíes repiten su propio nombre o los noventa y nueve nombres divinos hasta que éstos ya nada quieren decir. Yo anhelo recorrer esa senda. Quizá yo acabe por gastar el Zahir a fuerza de pensarlo y de repensarlo; quizá detrás de la moneda esté Dios" (To lose themselves in God, the Sufis repeat their own names or the ninety-nine divine names until these no longer mean anything. I hope to follow this path. Perhaps I will end up consuming the Zahir through its repeated evocation; perhaps behind the coin is God [1:898]).[84]

The resolution of the story thus draws from a Sufi tradition of *textual* repetition to propose that the repetition of an imagined *image* might, also, lead to a similar encounter with the sublime. It is an interesting shift in strategy; the curse of the ubiquitous icon is here reframed as, possibly, a path of liberation. While this could easily be interpreted as a particularly tragic aspect of the narrator's delusion, we must also contend with the fact that Borges did hide a riddle within his story that mentions a coin behind which the infinite gifts of heaven do in fact (allegorically) reside. In the last line of the story, this coin, adorned with the visual representation of a human being, bridges the Bible with Islamic mysticism.

What does this bridge between iconicity and aniconism tell us? One possibility is that Borges was never interested in simply deposing a visual literary regime with the radical elevation of textuality. The idea, instead, was to unsettle his readers' relationships with literary norms, complicating approaches to reading that focused on theatrical representation and elaborate imagery without paying sufficient attention to the medium of the written word and the peculiarity of the act of reading. None of the texts presented in this chapter eschew visuality; on the contrary, stories such as "El Aleph" are successful largely because of their intense visual impact. Yet they all introduce an oppositional perspective that questions the habits of writers and readers, destabilizing some of their familiar practices and expectations. Borges, in other words, develops his literary theology around a reimagination of Islam in order to recontextualize the icon—complicating it, not destroying it. He subverts an iconicity that he also carefully cultivates, making use of impactful visual displays while revealing that they are composed of nothing more than black text set against white paper.[85]

Instead of arguing for a new kind of literature that elides the image, Borges points to a form of interpretation and writing focused on the contradictory truth that all of the rich "sensory" experiences that one has as a reader are conditioned by an active engagement with words and, thus, are also brimming with instability and possibilities for reinvention. Overvaluing the visual register of literature can lead to a general forgetfulness regarding the conditioned, artificial, and even uniquely literary nature of these experiences. Overvaluing the textual can cause an interpretation to lose its grasp of the senses, the body, and everyday experience. Together, these ideas create a restless, shifting strategy designed to perpetually upset our desires as readers and, more optimistically, point to new forms of reading, writing, and engagement with the stories that we tell and believe.

While one way of understanding this project is through an analysis of Borges's literary ideas and the way in which he sought to push against the expectations of his readers, there is another, more personal dimension to the strategies that this chapter has described. It is based upon the idea that Borges's strategies of visual representation are difficult to appreciate fully without reflecting on the fact that he, from a very early age, expected that he would one day be blind. There is, in other words, a corporeal and embodied dimension to these ideas that might otherwise be framed purely in terms of their abstract, conceptual, and literary functions.

The possible relationship between Borges's blindness and his interest in "Islam" is supported by an obscured allusion in "El espejo de tinta." I previously mentioned that the story is presented by its narrator as a translation of R. F. Burton's *The Lake Regions of Equatorial Africa*. While there is no book by that title, Burton did write *The Lake Regions of Central Africa*. Regardless, Norman Thomas Di Giovanni writes that this actual book is a red herring: it is Lane's *An Account of the Manners and Customs of the Modern Egyptians* that provides the material for Borges's "El espejo de tinta" (which, as we saw, is not a translation at all). While Di Giovanni is clearly correct in pointing to Lane's book as the inspiration for the story, it is possible that he is mistaken in asserting that *The Lake Regions of Central Africa* is a book that Borges never read and, moreover, a book that has nothing to do with the story.

This is due to the fact that within Burton's *The Lake Regions of Central Africa* there is a mention of a circular pool of ink. It is a pool of ink that serves a purpose perfectly opposed to that of Lane's: this pool of ink delivers no transcendent visions, only blindness.

We halted three days on the western extremity of the Usagozi district, detained by another unpleasant phenomenon. My companion, whose blood had been impoverished, and whose system had been reduced by many fevers, now began to suffer from an inflammation of a low type, affecting the whole of the interior tunic of the eyes, particularly the iris, the choroid coat, and the retina; he describes it as "an almost total blindness, rendering every object enclouded as by a misty veil." The Goanese Valentine became similarly afflicted, almost on the same day; he complained of a "drop serene" in the shape of an inky blot— probably some of the black pigment of the iris deposited on the front of the lens—which completely excluded the light of day; yet the pupils contracted with regularity when covered with the hand, and as regularly dilated when it was removed. (1:406)

In this brief passage, Burton combines the primary gestures that were referenced in Borges's story: a pool of ink, an eye, and a hand. Instead of magically transporting his readers to visual wonders, this ink is described as both a blockage and as a veil.

While its connection to "El espejo de tinta" is speculative, it does fit the pattern of paired visual apertures and occlusions that I have pointed to in Borges's other stories. If we allow ourselves to consider it as part of the textual puzzle, Burton's passage would provide a link between Islam's perceived visual proscriptions and the author's own conflicted personal relationship with sight, reading, and mental visualization. If we remain skeptical, it nevertheless is difficult to imagine that Borges would have written about the allure of perfect sight without contemplating his own experiences with blindness.

In his essay "La ceguera," Borges writes that "quien es poeta lo es siempre, y se ve asaltado por la poesía continuamente. De igual modo que un pintor, supongo, siente que los colores y las formas están asediándolo. [. . .] Para la tarea del artista, la ceguera no es del todo una desdicha: puede ser un instrumento" (He who is a poet is a poet always, and is assaulted by poetry constantly. In the same way that a painter, I suppose, feels that colors and forms are besieging him. [. . .] For the work of the artist, blindness is not completely a curse: it can also be an instrument [3:310–11]). Blindness can be used as a tool in myriad ways, of course. One of these is as a critique of a culture obsessed with sight, seeing, and visuality that, as a result, is less interested in the ways in which the mind creates complex "visualized" worlds without direct ocular information. Insight does not require sight, nor does imagination.[86]

This idea is most clearly articulated in "El hacedor" (1960). Here blindness is positioned, in fact, as a kind of "starting point" for a turn inwards, away from the apparent immediacy of the senses and toward the careful examination of the cultural discourses that make life meaningful. The text describes a man who, first, lives in the sensory present: he lives for sensation, for the intuitive urgency that calls him to action. Soon, however, the universe begins to retreat as blindness blurs his surroundings. With this blindness comes a journey into memory. The memory that is most compelling to him is from his childhood: he remembers fleeing from his father's house, dagger in hand, imagining himself as Ajax or Perseus in order to steel himself for the violent encounter that would soon follow. This is a moment in which his sensory experiences are revealed to have *always* been embedded within long-standing narratives of myth. It suggests the possibility that his previous experiences of the "immediate present" were, in fact, *only compelling* due to a set of stories that, at the time, remained both unperceived and unmentioned. Turning the reader's attention to the power of narrative is thus reframed as the revelation of the cultural foundations of the senses.

The story, in other words, describes how one blindness (the inability to see the cultural discourses that construct "immediate" experiences) is replaced by another (the inability to directly participate in visual sensory experiences). The first (cultural) blindness is positioned within the story as far more tragic than the second (visual) blindness. Developing the second sight of imagination through language is made all the more urgent when it is revealed that the protagonist is, in fact, Homer: the writer that sits at the center of Borges's cultural tradition.

Borges's "Islam" can be understood, in this sense, as a mode of literary inquiry designed to return us, as readers, to this invented (mythical) origin in which Homer's language, imagination and sensory privation work productively against one another. Perhaps Borges began to sense the need for such a return "home" to the beginnings of his writerly tradition as his sight began to leave him, as he foresaw his own future need to rely more on memory and invention. A personal odyssey, then.[87]

It should at least register within our understanding that Borges, knowing that he would likely one day be blind, is most well known for inventing a magical object that grants everyone perfect sight. The fact that this astounding orb is positioned as a dangerous trap, a stultifying spectacle that atrophies the mind and its abilities to imagine and create, indicates to me that Borges was pushing back against his culture's emphasis on visuality in a way that was, ultimately, extraordinarily personal. The Aleph buried within the stone column at the Amr Mosque in Cairo is encountered through touch and through listening—the two ways in which those of us who are blind are able to read. It can be understood, in this way, as the place at which *anyone* can momentarily enter into a state of sightless contemplation of the universe. As such, I believe that it deserves to be understood as a monument to both blindness and the creative capacities of the mind.[88]

Borges, toward the end of his life, often expressed a desire to be the invisible man.[89] Often this desire was understood as an expression of social anxiety, an aversion to fame and publicity. It occurs to me, however, that it may somehow be related to his experiences as a blind person. Unable to see, the wish to be unseen strikes me as a just balancing of the scales. The statement may also be relevant to the ideas that this first chapter has explored: literature, for Borges, was a medium that offered a rich universe that could only be perceived indirectly, through the imagination instead of through the senses. One might even say that there is a kind of invisibility that goes hand in hand with reading: the characters do not see us, nor do the narrators, authors, and other readers. Perhaps for those of us who are blind, these aspects of the literary experience are also received, at times, as especially welcome. Reading, we perceive without seeing and also without *being seen*; we are tasked with exploring a world that is not built solely for those with functioning eyes.

It seems reasonable that if one wanted to highlight the essential *invisibility* of experience rendered in textual form, the use of aniconic, even *iconoclastic*, literary acts would be especially useful tools. To impress upon fully sighted readers that an obsession with visuality can be a distraction from the creative acts of reading and writing and imagining, one would have to be willing to encase even the wonders of the Aleph in stone as black as text.

Sex, Borrowed Bodies, and the Idea of Literary Progeny

Si el mundo externo fuera algo más que una magia, sería indestructible. El mundo es irreal. Las cosas vacías engendran cosas vacías; el culto de un Buddah ilusorio confiere un mérito ilusorio; el asesinato de un fantasma proyecta dolores imaginarios en infiernos mágicos.

If the external world were something other than an act of magic, it would be indestructible. The world is unreal. Empty things engender empty things; the worship of an illusory Buddha confers an illusory benefit; the murder of a ghost projects imaginary pain within magical hellscapes.

—**L. de la Vallée Poussin**, *Boudhism* (from Borges and Bioy Casares, *Libro del cielo y del infierno*, 37)

In conversation with Antonio Carrizo, Borges wonders out loud whether or not he has a personal life. Not, however, because he has become so famous that journalists are documenting his every step, or because scholars have written books about him using every scrap of information at their disposal. Instead, Borges contemplates the idea that he, as a writer, has inevitably decided to allow his personal life to be made public. This shift from private to public occurs, in his view, at a level that is imperceptible even to him, defying every effort to manage the boundary between the experiences that are strictly his and those that he offers, codified and altered by literary language, to his readers.

> Yo no sé si tengo vida personal. Sí, yo creo que sí. Pero esa vida personal sirve para mi literatura. Si no qué importancia tiene. [. . .] [P]ara un escritor, todo lo que le ocurre puede ser un estímulo literario. Aunque no lo sepa, aunque en ese momento lo ignore.[1]

> I don't know if I have a personal life. Yes, I think that I do. But that personal life exists in the service of my literature. If not, then what importance does it have. [. . .] For a writer, everything that occurs can be a literary stimulus. Even if they do not know it, even if in that moment they are unaware of it.

There is one story, however, that Borges consistently holds up as the exception to this rule—a story that he states, over and over again, did not come from him, that is not his, that is fundamentally disconnected from his personal life. In this chapter I aim to show that, in fact, this story—"Emma Zunz" (1948)—lies at the very center of one of Borges's most personal and challenging literary projects. This project was the literary representation and transformation of the author's difficult relationship with sex and sexuality, a relationship that began with a traumatic experience when he was a young man. It expanded, over the course of years and stories, to encompass ideas about gender, procreation, intimacy, power, and family—ideas that found themselves articulated (and partially hidden) within some of his most well-known and celebrated texts.

"Emma Zunz" was first published in 1948 in the magazine *SUR* and then, soon after, within the collection *El Aleph* (1949). Bella Brodzki suggests that it is Borges's least characteristic work.[2] Borges was happy to agree with this opinion, commenting to his friend Adolfo Bioy Casares in 1953 that if all his writing were to be destroyed with the sole exception of "Emma Zunz," then nothing of his, truly, would be left.[3]

In the epilogue to *El Aleph*, as well as in numerous interviews, Borges distances himself from "Emma Zunz," maintaining that he was only a scribe who wrote down the ideas of his friend Cecilia Ingenieros. In *Borges, el Memorioso*, Borges suggests that in writing it he had, in truth, *returned* the story to Cecilia Ingenieros. He continues, explaining that he (in 1979) no longer likes "Emma Zunz" for the way in which it is built around the idea of revenge, which he now considers cruel and ridiculous. "Además," he says, "la única venganza, como ya he dicho tantas veces, es el olvido" (Moreover, the only true revenge is, as I have stated countless times, forgetting [234]). While it is clear that Cecilia Ingenieros played a role in the idea for the story, I will demonstrate that Borges's attempts to distance himself from the story are strategic and, in fact, purposefully misleading. In order to do so it is important, first, to pay close attention to the plot of Borges's story.

"Emma Zunz" opens with the news of a death. Emma, upon returning home from work, finds a letter that describes the "accidental" poisoning of "el señor Maier." Her reaction to this letter is both physical and emotional: she feels cold and ill, her knees become weak. Fear, guilt, and a sense of unreality sweep over her body; the narrator states that she feels as though the death of her father were the only event ever to occur in the universe and that it would continue to occur ad infinitum. Emma weeps for Manuel Maier, a man whose name was once Emanuel Zunz.

This corporeal reaction is paired with a series of vivid memories, the strongest of which is her father's declaration, six years ago, that "el ladrón era Loewenthal" (the thief was Loewenthal [1:865]). She told no one of this accusation. While her father was vilified for being a thief, his partner Loewenthal, in turn, eventually became one of the owners of their factory, the very factory in which Emma Zunz is now working. The implication is that her father's fate, his suicide, hinged upon this central injustice.[4]

After a sleepless night, Emma constructs an unusual and elaborate plan. She purposefully goes through the motions of her day as though she had not received the news of her father's suicide. She gossips with friends, discusses movies, and listens while other girls discuss boyfriends. (No one expects her to share anything, the narrator explains, as she, despite almost turning nineteen, suffers from an almost pathological fear of men.) The next day she finds a ship in the newspaper that would soon be leaving the docks. She calls her boss, Loewenthal, and arranges for them to meet, explaining that she has information about a strike. Finally, she destroys the letter communicating the death of her father.

In the afternoon, Emma Zunz goes to the docks. She enters a few bars until she finds men from a ship, the *Nordstjärnan*, that is about to leave. One of these men is too young for her plan; she fears that he might inspire some degree of tenderness in her. Instead she chooses a short, older man who then leads her through a door, a hall, up some stairs, to a landing, another hall, and then a room. What follows this oddly prolonged journey through the building is an experience that is described as being beyond both time and space: the sensory descriptions end, and we are left with sex communicated as complete horror, subjection, and torture.

The traumatic nature of this act has, importantly, very little to do with questions of consent, with the physical repulsiveness of the man Emma found or, in fact, with any particularly violent aspect of the sexual act. Instead, the experience is traumatic for the manner in which it conjures—in Emma's mind—the sexual relationship of her parents. In this imaginary transposition, she is her mother passively enduring sex with her own father.

> ¿En aquel tiempo fuera del tiempo, en aquel desorden perplejo de sensaciones inconexas y atroces, pensó Emma Zunz *una sola vez* en el muerto que motivaba el sacrificio? Yo tengo para mí que pensó una vez y que en ese momento peligró su desesperado propósito. Pensó (no pudo no pensar) que su padre le había hecho a su madre la cosa horrible que a ella ahora le hacían. Lo pensó con débil asombro y se refugió, en seguida, en el vértigo. El hombre, sueco o finlandés, no hablaba español; fue una herramienta para Emma como ésta lo fue para él. (1:867)

> In that time out of time, within that perplexing disorder of disconnected, atrocious sensations, did Emma Zunz think *even once* of the dead man motivating the sacrifice? I myself believe that she thought, once, and that

in this moment she put her entire desperate goal at risk. She thought (she was unable not to think) that her father had done to her mother the horrible thing that was now being done to her. She thought this with weak surprise and sought refuge, immediately, in vertigo. The man, Swiss or Finnish, did not speak Spanish; he was a tool for Emma, just as she was a tool for him.

The narrator refuses to directly represent the trauma for the reader, drawing back into a distanced position that evokes confusion and a kind of dissociative sensory revulsion. Yet this narrator also intervenes, in an unusual way, by stating "Yo tengo para mí que pensó una vez" (I myself believe that she thought, once). The question of her internal state of mind at this crucial moment in the story is linked, loosely, to the speculations of a narrator who, elsewhere, paradoxically knows (omnisciently) her internal state of mind. One way of approaching this inconsistency is to sense that the narrator either rhetorically (or actually) creates some distance out of respect for the "privacy" of Emma Zunz; this is consistent with the manner in which direct descriptions of the sexual encounter are also avoided. Afterwards, Emma Zunz destroys the money that had been left for her (she had posed as a prostitute) and makes her way to the factory.

In the factory, she is received by Loewenthal, the alleged thief whose crime she believes had been pinned on her father, leading eventually to his suicide. She asks for a glass of water and his momentary absence allows her to grab the revolver that she knew was in his desk. She shoots him, twice, when he returns and then shoots a third time to quiet his curses in Spanish and Yiddish. Emma then arranges the scene to make it look like an attempted rape before calling the police and reporting it as such. The narrator explains that despite the unlikeliness of the story, everyone believes her due to the fact that her tone of voice, her shame, and her hatred were all completely authentic. The specific wording of this explanation is important:

La historia era increíble, en efecto, pero se impuso a todos, porque sustancialmente era cierta. Verdadero era el tono de Emma Zunz, verdadero el pudor, verdadero el odio. Verdadero también era el ultraje que había padecido; sólo eran falsas las circunstancias, la hora y uno o dos nombres propios. (1:869)

> The story was, in short, unbelievable, but it imposed itself on everyone as it was, in essence, true. True was the tone of Emma Zunz, true was her shame, true was her hatred. True, also, was the affront that she had suffered; the only falsehoods were the circumstances, the hour, and one or two proper nouns.

The profound truth of the trauma, in other words, shone through the fictional story that she created. Because of this truth, her story is given social currency and power. She becomes, through her fiction, an adult who avenges her father and, also, surpasses his passive victimhood. It is a transformative moment.

And yet the story strains against this final idea: it is not particularly easy for us, as readers, to accept the notion that someone would purposefully undergo a sexual trauma in order to create a slightly more believable alibi for a murder. In terms of a realistic representation it does not strike me as very successful.[5] It is improbable enough, in fact, to seem a bit false, a bit wooden.

Here, I would like to argue, is where things get especially interesting.

Instead of approaching this lack of believability as a *weakness* in the narration, I would like to suggest that it is one of its *principal features*: the story is designed, in my opinion, to be implausible, to ring false.

It would do us good to recall that the conclusion of the story deals with *precisely* the nature of the problem that we face as its doubting readers: it states that a series of *implausible narrated events* can, nevertheless, be accepted as true under the right conditions. What are these conditions? The story, we are informed, must communicate the emotional truth of an obscured, parallel experience that makes the cumbersome nature of the invented fiction less than important. If, in other words, we are dissatisfied with the "realism" or psychological acuity of "Emma Zunz," the narrator indirectly suggests a course of action: that we consider the possibility that it might communicate, in fact, a set of powerful lived experiences that are purposefully obscured by the less-than-believable plot. Instead of accepting the story at face value (as the police do), we are thus compelled to ask: which lived experiences of its author—of Borges—could serve as the parallel to the story, buttressing its implausibility with hidden emotional depth?

The answer, I believe, is one that Borges may not have intended for us to discover. Estela Canto's biography of Borges, *Borges a contraluz*, provides enough information, however, for the discovery to take place. Canto's book was published first in 1989, in Spain, and then published again in Argentina in 1999. It combines photocopies of letters sent to her by Borges with a description of her impressions of him, his life, their relationship, and a selection of his stories. She met Borges in 1944 and, over time, developed a friendship with him that became more intimate.

Canto characterizes their relationship as imbalanced. For her, Borges was an interesting person whose company she enjoyed and valued; she did not mind that their relationship crossed into physical intimacy but also did not feel particularly attracted to him. Borges, on the other hand, is presented as deeply in love. Canto, for example, describes the experience of having Borges propose marriage to her—on a park bench during one of their walks—in great detail.

Instead of explaining that she did not want to marry him, Canto writes that she—on this park bench—replied disingenuously so as to avoid a direct rejection. She told Borges they could get married, but only if they had sex first. This statement was based, she writes, in the knowledge that sex was terrifying for Borges, that it was physically impossible for him. While their relationship did not progress any further, Canto states that Borges nevertheless repeated his desire to marry her, adding that he wanted them to have children together. A year later, as their relationship waned, Borges—still hopeful, it seems, that they might be able to be together—asked her to accompany him to a meeting with a psychoanalyst named Dr. Cohen-Miller. She agreed.

In this session, Canto writes that she heard Borges's situation described in more detail. Dr. Cohen-Miller, believing, it seems, that Canto wanted to have a full, intimate relationship with Borges, recommended that they marry in order to alleviate his sense of shame with regard to sexual intimacy. He explained that one experience in particular had led to Borges's inability to have sex. In Geneva, when Borges was eighteen or nineteen, his father—after verifying that his son was a virgin—attempted to accelerate his sexual development in order to deliver him into "adulthood." He gave his son a specific address, a time to arrive, and the news that a woman—a prostitute— would be there, waiting for him.

As the younger Borges made his way to this encounter, it occurred to him that if his father had arranged for a woman for him to have sex with, then he surely must have known her very well. It did not seem logical that he would arrange for him to be intimate with someone of whom he had no intimate knowledge. Borges became certain, in other words, that his father had previously had sex with the woman that he was going to meet. She was, in his mind, his father's woman. As his "father's woman" was closely associated, in Borges's mind, with his own mother, this created a deep sense of dread and unease. Borges was unable to have sex with the prostitute at the time and place that his father had chosen for him.

His parents, to make matters worse, learned of this "failure" and saw the problem as a physical one. They gave him a series of treatments: tonics and pills for a "weak liver" that likely intensified and sustained his sense of shame, inadequacy, and difference.[6] As one might expect, Estela Canto, despite the advice and pleas of Dr. Cohen-Miller, was unwilling to marry Borges and their relationship diminished over the years. Canto writes that the analyst had asked her to marry him for the good of literature, a plea that she found laughable, nonsensical, and insulting. The session with Dr. Cohen-Miller took place in 1946, according to Canto's recollection. "Emma Zunz" would be published only two years later, in 1948.

To place my cards on the table: I believe that events experienced by Borges in Geneva are being directly expressed within the plot of "Emma Zunz." To prove this assertion, it is best to begin with the clearest correspondences between the story of Borges and the trauma that Estela Canto described in her book.

Borges, eighteen years old and a virgin, has a sexual encounter with a stranger that involves an exchange of money. It is, for him, horrific. Emma Zunz, also eighteen and a virgin, has a sexual encounter with a stranger that involves an exchange of money. It is, for her, horrific.

The reason for Emma's encounter with the stranger is not sexual desire. Instead, it occurs due to a sense of obligation to her father. Borges is also not motivated by sexual desire. Instead, he meets the woman out of a sense of obligation to his father, whose command he is directly obeying.

The specific experience of the sexual encounter is, for Borges, very difficult both because of his inexperience and, also, because the connection between the prostitute and her father brings the sexual relationship between his parents to mind. Emma Zunz also has a traumatic sexual encounter because of her inexperience with sex and, far more importantly, because she acts as a prostitute in the service of her father. This role leads her to mentally visualize herself as her mother enduring sex with her father. The moment of imagining herself in the role of her mother (not the sex act itself) is, according to the narrator, what makes the encounter horrific.

The story of Emma Zunz turns, however, on the protagonist's mastery of language. Her ability to weave a plot—despite the physical, emotional, and sexual trauma that she has undergone—allows her to finally resolve her relationship with her (absent) father as an adult firmly in control of her actions.[7]

Borges's story also turns on his use of language. He is able to weave a plot (about a female protagonist undergoing a parallel situation) that involves the transformation of a difficult physical, emotional, and sexual trauma that he experienced. Borges's father, at the time of the story's writing, is also absent. He had died ten years before, in 1938. And as it is through storytelling (and not sexual or physical prowess) that Borges finds the kind of success that might have aided in showing his family that he was indeed a full adult, the resolution of the story is fitting. While his father wanted to be a successful author it is Borges who earns his adulthood through the mastery of fictive language.

The text specifies that Emma received the letter announcing her father's death on the 14th of January; Borges's father dies on the 14th of February. Emma Zunz is given a name that is inscribed within her father's name (Emmanuel Zunz). Jorge Luis Borges's father is named Jorge Guillermo Borges.[8]

The role of "revenge" in "Emma Zunz" (which Borges mentions frequently when he discusses the story) has a clear parallel in Borges's experience if we agree that it would not be unusual to resent being forced to perform sexually for one's family and then, subsequently, finding oneself being shamed for being unable to do so. In this reading, the idea of revenge would be directed against Borges's father. If this idea is imported into "Emma Zunz," the oppositional figures of "Loewenthal" and "Emmanuel Zunz" collapse into one paternal figure of authority: one male, older protagonist who is both obeyed and murdered. This collapsing of "enemies" is rather frequent in Borges's work (see "Los teólogos" and "La muerte y la brújula," for prominent examples). The result: Borges, in the story, through the figure of "Emma Zunz," both follows his father's command (going to a traumatic sexual encounter out of duty) and, also, rebels against his father, murdering him (as Loewenthal) at the end of the story in order to surpass him in terms of storytelling dexterity. Everything is covered up twice, with the alibi of Emma Zunz and the literary artifice of "Emma Zunz." This interpretation is, of course, almost emblematically Freudian. The fact that Borges was, at the time, visiting a psychoanalyst may be a particularly relevant part of the text's genesis.

Some of these parallels are circumstantial and speculative. Together, however, I believe that they offer a compelling proof: that Borges reencountered his own personal trauma through the literary figure of Emma Zunz.

It is also worth noting the fact that Emma Zunz found a sexual partner who was not from Buenos Aires; she sought out someone from Europe, "[un] sueco o finlandés" (1:897), in order to properly prepare the horror that would buttress her alibi. Borges, in this sense, can be seen as drawing an arrow pointing northward, to Europe, back (indirectly), to the Geneva of his past.

This idea is supported by a bit of wordplay. The name of the ship that Emma Zunz finds is the *Nordstjärnan*. There was, in actuality,

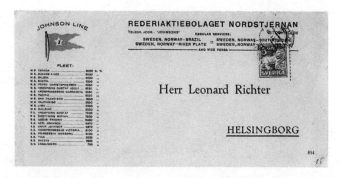

FIGURE 5 Johnson Line brochure, 1921, close to the time in which Borges's story is set. Note that the *Prinsessan Ingeborg* is part of the "Nordstjernan" line (in the upper right corner). Photo from the collection of Björn Larsson, www.timetableimages.com.

a ship by this name. As far as I have been able to tell, however, the *Nordstjärnan* would have never reached Buenos Aires. There was also, though, a shipping company called *Nordstjärnan* that connected directly to Buenos Aires via what was termed the "Johnson Line" (see fig. 5). One particular ship would have docked at both Malmö and Buenos Aires, as the story specifies: it was the MS *Prinsessan Ingeborg* (see fig. 6). Ignoring the actual name of the ship (*Prinsessan Ingeborg*) to rechristen it *Nordstjärnan* is, in my view, a potentially significant gesture given the manner in which it can, quite literally, direct our attention *northward*, like the star for which it is named. Perhaps we are being asked to direct our attention toward Europe, toward Geneva, the place that provides the setting for the "true" story at the center of the fictional one. (That the story appeared first in the magazine *SUR* creates an interesting opposition of geographical gestures.)

In summation, if we do look beyond the specific circumstances of the place, time, and identity of "Emma Zunz" (as the story strongly suggests in its final lines), then we can see a plot emerge that applies to *both* Borges and to Emma Zunz. Consider the following story while thinking, simultaneously, of the author and his character. An eighteen-year-old has a horrific sexual encounter with a stranger from Europe who speaks a different language; it involves prostitution. The reason for the encounter is not, however, sexual desire. Instead, it is

FIGURE 6 Postcard with an image of the ship that may have been utilized in the creation of "Emma Zunz." Sjöhistoriska museet, Stockholm, F024865AB.

an experience designed to allow this person to connect to and honor a father for whom they are named (yet toward whom they also feel a certain degree of anger). The sexual experience is traumatic both because of the inexperience of the individual and, also, because it strongly brings the sexual relationship between this person's parents to mind. Surviving the trauma provides the emotional urgency behind a fictional story that, despite its falsity, resonates with truth and redeems a failing of a paternal figure. It also, however, involves an indirect repudiation of this paternal figure. Becoming a successful, convincing storyteller channels the intensity of the experience while also maintaining enough control to alter names, places, and times in ways that grant its author a sense of personal safety and adult mastery.

Returning to the title of the story, we might notice now that the four-letter near-palindromes "Emma" and "Zunz" look—almost—like textual fragments ("em" and "zu") being held up to a mirror. Each word, in this sense, might suggest a close but ultimately imperfect reflective symmetry. The story works, similarly, as warped mirror. It represents both an intimate, autobiographical self-portrait and, also, an encounter with a new, transformed entity: Emma Zunz.[9] Borges constructs both a disguised portrait of himself (as Emma Zunz) and creates a fictional woman (Emma Zunz) with whom he shares a version of his initial sexual encounter. The peculiarity of literary interpretation creates a situation in which both Emma Zunz and Borges experience their traumas completely alone and, also, together.

One of the main questions that Brodzki asks in her essay is: "How do the meanings generated by this text pivot on the fact that the subject is a woman?"[10] Meaning, as Brodzki points out, can shift depending on how masculinity and femininity are positioned within our interpretations, especially in a story that pivots around representations of sex and trauma. Here I am proposing that the meanings generated by the text rely on the fact that the subject is, simultaneously, a woman and a man: Borges and an imaginary, female partner who experiences a parallel set of traumas.

The fact that Borges chose a woman instead of a man when imagining his story's protagonist has made it, clearly, more difficult for his readers (including Estela Canto) to identify the parallels described here. While we might sense that a strongly binary approach to gender may have played a role in preventing the female protagonist from being identified with Borges, it is also true that he made every effort to distance himself from the story and the story of its creation.

Borges, I believe, was hoping for these difficulties to occur: obscuring the content of his story was likely just as important as expressing it publicly. The story works, in a nearly therapeutic sense, insofar as it both expresses and conceals the traumatic event at its core. (If it had revealed too much, Borges would have had to negotiate questions about his own sexual challenges in the open; if it had not revealed enough, then it would not have truly brought the events tied to his private difficulties into the public sphere, failing to truly respond to the conclusion of the story.) This interpretation reframes Borges's repeated disavowals of the story, turning them into acts of preservation and perhaps even fear with regard to his own sense of pride and public identity.

At times, Borges made statements that could have served to guide us toward the way he joined his own experiences with those of Emma Zunz. For example, in conversation with Néstor Montenegro, Borges responded to the observation that very few of his characters are women by stating that "no tengo ningún personaje, ni femenino ni masculino. Hay autores que crean personajes: Dickens, Balzac, Zola, Jules Romains. Yo nunca dejé de ser Borges, ligeramente disfrazado, en diversas épocas o países" (I don't have any characters, masculine or feminine. There are authors that create characters: Dickens, Balzac, Zola, Jules Romains. I never ceased being Borges, slightly disguised, in different times and countries).[11] With a few alterations of time, space, and the requisite proper nouns, Borges invents and transforms. Here, at least, he points to his possible connection to his most well-known female character.[12]

Bella Brodzki closes her essay on "Emma Zunz" with a question: "Could this story *be* if Emma were a man?"[13] The answer seems to be an emphatic *yes*, one that does not, however, require that Emma Zunz ever cease to "be" a woman. The gender binary, on the other hand, must be released. Seeing the protagonist as a doubled character in this way, however, leads to peculiar effects. The character is, in this sense, at once a mirror and a window, a reflection of the author and an *aperture* through which he is able to glimpse a "female" doppelgänger who shares the complex shame of his sexual trauma together with the same desire for revenge that he disavows, later, as an older man.

If the question of Emma Zunz's identity is in flux here it is also relevant to ask what happens to Borges's identity in the process.[14] What does it mean for him to encounter himself as a fictional female protagonist and also to find in this (artificial) woman an ideal part-ner-in-crime (and partner-in-intimate-trauma)? What happens to his sense of self as this relationship is created and entered? One way of framing "Emma Zunz" is as a story that requires Borges, himself, to undergo a transformation—to become, in a sense, a kind of lit-erary character—in order to consider Emma Zunz within a context of partnership (or, in a more direct sense, to allow his experiences to be restaged through hers). The manner in which traditional gender roles fall apart within these doubled transformations can be seen as contradictory and yet also as potentially freeing. It can be fruitful to imagine the paradoxical refashioning of identity here as pushing against the traditional binary understanding of maleness and femaleness just as it pushes against the limits between the literary and the everyday. In the context of a ritual designed to perpetuate a narrow understanding of adult masculinity (the ritual that bound Borges together with his father and the prostitute), it strikes me as particularly (and appropriately) disruptive.

"Emma Zunz" is, for all these reasons, an attempt to hold a diverse set of mental operations together within the same text. It is a cathartic expression, masked pseudonymously, that allows the author to publicly represent and conceal a secret, destructive shame. It is also a meditation on the importance of technical mastery, designed to communicate adulthood and skill both *to and against* a father figure who is obeyed and rebelled against. And finally, it is the creation of an imaginary woman with whom Borges shares one of his most intimate challenges. Unlike Estela Canto in the office of Dr. Cohen-Miller, Emma Zunz "knows" something close to what Borges went through, having gone through a parallel experience herself. With Emma Zunz, Borges creates a unique possibility of literary intimacy that is not easy to articulate. Their implied relationship of partnership and solidarity straddles the real and the fictional, just as the final line of the story suggests.

It may be useful, as well, to repeat that this interpretation does not imply that there is no connection between "Emma Zunz" and Cecilia Ingenieros. (There clearly *is* a link between the two, demonstrated by Borges's frequent public statements and, more privately, by the fact that he sent her an early typed manuscript of the story for her opinion.)[15] It simply attempts to show that Borges presents that connection as part of a strategy of misdirection that conceals a more complex, personal register. One way of considering this connection, in fact, is to note the relationship between Cecilia Ingenieros and *her* father, the positivist writer José Ingenieros.[16] His *La simulación de la lucha por la vida* (1903), in particular, may have been a strong influence on the story. It borrows Darwinian ideas to theorize about how individuals who perpetrate crimes can, strategically, decide to feign psychological states of mind to avoid punishment. In a "contextualizing" section of the book, Ingenieros writes that deception is often used by women and prostitutes for their own personal, and especially monetary, gain.

> De la tendencia general al fraude, y por consiguiente a la simulación, sólo diremos que estando la mujer excluida por la naturaleza del uso de algunos medios violentos de lucha, encuéntrase obligada a perfeccionarse en los medios fraudulentos.[17]

> Of the general tendency toward fraud, and thus also fakery, we will say only that as women are by nature excluded from the use of certain violent forms of combat, they find themselves obligated to perfect their abilities through fraudulent means.

While Borges may have used José Ingenieros's text to create some of the "visible" setting of the story, it is especially tempting to speculate that Cecilia Ingenieros had a strong role in these aspects of the plot. One can imagine her crafting a female protagonist that is just as capable as a man when it comes to intricate plots of deception, revenge, and psychological fakery that, furthermore, transcend the categories of prostitution and gold-digging that her own father emphasizes, later in his text, with sexually explicit descriptions. (We can, in this sense, recall Emma tearing up the money after she poses as a prostitute in a very different light.) If this suspicion is true, Borges and Cecilia may have both been trying to push back against the gendered ideas of their fathers while, to a degree, following in their respective footsteps.[18]

A significant part of the importance of "Emma Zunz" is that it is not an isolated text. It forms part of a constellation of writings by Borges that bring sexuality and procreation into a literary dimension that radically alters their significance. The next story in the series is crucial for the way in which it takes the same basic elements as "Emma Zunz" and reconfigures them within a violent triangle that accentuates Borges's own sense of being cast out from his family's sense of normality and adulthood. "La intrusa" (1966) is, in this sense, far less triumphant than "Emma Zunz." It is more about pain than it is about mastery. Given that the story was published eighteen years after "Emma Zunz," I believe that it is worth approaching it not as a second restaging of the events that occurred in Geneva but rather as a kind of corrective that explores a dimension of Borges's experiences left out of the first story.

"La intrusa" is remarkable, first of all, for the way in which it presents itself as a series of events that occurred in historical reality. The entire first paragraph functions as a distancing mechanism that traces the story's origin to another writer, Santiago Dabove, who heard it second- or thirdhand from someone at the funeral of Cristián, one of the story's main characters. The narrator, "Borges," states that he will try to be faithful to the story as he understands it but anticipates that a degree of fictionalization is inevitable. The reader is thus primed to interpret the story as a set of events that may not have a direct connection to the interior creative or psychological life of the author. Similar techniques (the use of framing devices such as "I was told that" or "I found out that") continue this separation throughout the story. It is as though Borges found a way to transform the disavowals that he used *after* publishing "Emma Zunz" into a narrative framework; the effect is largely the same.

It is in the second paragraph where the plot begins in earnest. We read that two brothers, Cristián and Eduardo Nilson, live together in Turdera, near Buenos Aires in an austere rural setting. The only book in the house is an old Bible, the back of which is used to record their family history. They are described as tall and red-haired. Short, terse sentences detail their life, their possessions, and their habits.

Cristián, one day, brings a woman, Juliana Burgos, to their home. Her presence is noted by the neighbors. The narrator suggests that while she is treated as a servant, as a subjugated, lesser being by Cristián, he also expresses fondness toward her. Eduardo, Cristián's brother, begins to react negatively to their relationship. He leaves the house to take care of some business and returns with a woman as well but, in a few days, casts her out of the house. Eduardo, infatuated with Juliana, becomes more difficult, drinks more, and isolates himself.

One night, Cristián offers Juliana, sexually, to his brother in a tone described as both cordial and authoritative. He states: "Yo me voy a una farra en lo de Farías. Ahí la tenés a la Juliana; si la querés, usála" (I'm leaving for a party at Farías's. Juliana is over there; if you want, use her [2:432]). The younger brother is not sure how to react; he is stunned. Cristián leaves, saying goodbye to his brother while ignoring Juliana, who was "una cosa" (a thing [2:432]).

At this point the description of that night cuts off. We are only told that the brothers "share" her for several weeks but that the arrangement is not sustainable. They refuse to pronounce her name and find themselves in bitter arguments. "En el duro suburbio," the text states, "un hombre no decía, ni se decía, que una mujer pudiera importarle, más allá del deseo y la posesión" (In the rough outskirts a man would not say, even to himself, that a woman could matter to him beyond desire and possession [2:433]).

The narrator states that while Juliana serves both brothers with animalistic submission, she cannot help but show preference for Eduardo; despite having participated in the arrangement, he had not come up with it. The conflict between the brothers persists until they decide to sell Juliana to a brothel far away from their house. They tell her to pack her things and to get ready for the long journey. After they leave her there, they try to return to the life that they had experienced before Juliana was introduced in their relationship. Yet they both, secretly, travel to the brothel. When they realize that they have not resolved the situation, they buy Juliana back. The anger and violence that could have turned one brother against another is channeled, we are told, in other directions, against strangers, their dogs, and Juliana herself.

Months later, Cristián takes his brother out on a trip to sell some hides. After night falls, Cristián pauses and tells his brother to get to work, explaining that he has killed Juliana and that this is where they are going to bury her so that there would no longer be any animosity between them. They embrace at the story's close, united, now, by the bond represented by Juliana: "la mujer tristemente sacrificada y la obligación de olvidarla" (the woman sadly sacrificed and the obligation to forget her [2:434])

The story, then, is a horrific description of abuse, prostitution, debasement, and murder. The focus on the relationship between the two brothers, their conflicts and their states of mind, combines the representation of violence with the narrative erasure of Juliana; she is literally given no voice at all throughout the story. This is overlaid on a racial dimension that differentiates between the two brothers (who are white, with ancestors from Denmark or Ireland, and look different enough from other men in the Costa Brava that the narrator suggests that they have to be especially united) and Juliana, who is described as having dark skin. That she is treated like an animal, a slave, and an object is made explicit by the text. Jorgelina Corbatta describes a common reaction to this story as one of profound unease, a sense of repulsion in the face of "la crueldad del tratamiento de la Juliana por los hermanos Nilsen, expresado en un lenguaje que pareciera complacerse hasta la vanagloria en el primitivismo y la bestialidad de lo narrado" (the cruelty of the Juliana's treatment by the Nilsen brothers, expressed in a language that seems to take pleasure—to an almost prideful degree—in the animalistic, bestial nature of the narrated events).[19]

The relationship between this story, however, and Borges's sexually traumatic experience in Geneva can complicate our interpretation. Both of these stories (one personal, one literary) deal with the question of family identity and the "disruption" caused by the "sharing" of a woman, a prostitute, between an older and a younger man in a family. One might suggest that Borges and his father could be identified with the two brothers: the story, after all, details how an older man in a family (Borges's father/Cristián) has a sexual relationship with a woman (the prostitute in Geneva/Juliana Burgos) before suggesting that the younger man (Borges/Eduardo) follow him sexually. The tension in the story reaches its heights in the aftermath of a conflict within the space of an actual brothel.[20] With regard to "La intrusa's" connection to "Emma Zunz," we should note that both stories begin with the framing device of the death of the "father figures" of Cristián and Emanuel Zunz and explore the consequences of their decisions for their families.

There is, additionally, a quiet intertextual reference that joins "Emma Zunz" with "La intrusa." In 1954, a movie based on "Emma Zunz" opened in Buenos Aires. The name of the director of *Días de odio*, who sometimes went by "Babsy" or "Leo Towers," was Leopoldo

Torre Nilsson. Borges, by borrowing the Swedish last name of the director, pairs Cristián and Eduardo with "Emma Zunz" and, perhaps, with the sailor from the *Nordstjärnan*, who may also have been from Sweden.[21]

Yet there is a problem with this simple overlaying of the two stories. In "La intrusa," Cristián "gives" his younger brother the option of having a sexual relationship with Juliana: Eduardo is allowed the freedom to agree or disagree to participate in this arrangement. His younger brother, additionally, is described as a sexual being with a certain degree of desire. The story hinges on their shared complicity within an arrangement that is profoundly inhumane. For this reason, we should strongly consider a second possibility: that Borges is, in fact, represented by *Juliana*, who has no choice and no agency as she/he is sent back and forth between the house and the brothel. (This was the journey that Borges described as constituting the important lead-up to his original encounter with the prostitute.)

Caught, with no voice and no desire, between two sexual beings who are uncomfortably linked by family bonds, Juliana Burgos and Jorge Luis Borges are *commanded* to perform sexually irrespective of their desires or preferences. The similarity between their names (Jorge Luis Borges clearly echoes Juliana Burgos in terms of both sound and etymology) encourages this interpretation.[22] It singles Borges out as the weakest, most powerless individual in the triangle, according to Borges—the individual who ultimately feels rejected by the family for failing to sexually prove his adulthood. The specific terms of this rejection are worth contemplating given the parameters of the story. We should recall that the only book within the brothers' house is the family Bible that serves as a record of their successive generations: procreation is thus subtly underscored as an act of familial survival valued as a sacred, if unstated, ritual. The sense that the story marks a rupture, somehow, in the genealogy, is lightly suggested by the fact that, after describing this Bible, the narrator asserts that it, and the family tree within it, are now lost: the book is described as "la azarosa crónica de los Nilsen, perdida como todo se perderá" (the tumultuous chronicle of the Nilsens, lost as all things will be lost [2:432]).

Borges, of course, is likely quite aware—as an adult—that it will be difficult for him to participate in the creation of successive generations as a father. He interrupts the genealogical tree precisely because he was traumatized by being commanded to perform sexually in a way that entered into conflict with his understanding of family boundaries. As a young man, the conflict with his father (and his mother, indirectly) was based upon the notion that he was, in this situation, being valued only in sexual terms. "Juliana Burgos" thus enacts these different aspects of Borges's own experiences in a way that allows her to stand in for his own powerlessness, his own voicelessness, and the sexual demands that his family placed on him. The unease and repulsion that the story traditionally elicits, reoriented toward the sexual objectification of its male author (as opposed to its female protagonist), can be remarkably disorienting. While this approach to reading "La intrusa" seems counterintuitive due, once again, to the switching of genders that it requires, it allows the story to represent what is perhaps the most difficult aspect of Borges's traumatic experience: the fact that his father *coerced him* to sexually perform with someone who was, in his mind, intimately connected to his father (and associated with his mother). From Borges's perspective, he was treading where he did not belong: he was, in this sense, the intruder.

This approach to "La intrusa" is strengthened if we consider how "Emma Zunz," eighteen years earlier, restages Borges's experience in terms of a successful, nearly triumphant act of writerly mastery. Emma Zunz emerges victorious at the close of the story; she is in control of the narrative and successfully executes her plan. In the later story, however, the tone is darker, the message more attuned to that which cannot be resolved through fiction and renown. It works, in this view, as a corrective: a restaging of "Emma Zunz" in which the outcome emphasizes the devastation and the silence that reigns in the wake of what occurred. The emphasis on procreation, and on family, suggests that Borges is considering the larger consequences of his inability to have children. Instead of focusing on his capacity of entering adulthood as a writer independent from his father, the story gestures toward other questions of belonging and familial continuity.

It is perhaps not surprising that Borges, in interviews, wrote that he did not end the story himself and that it was his mother who provided the conclusion in the dictation process.[23] Beyond providing a disavowal similar to the one involving Cecilia Ingenieros, the statement uncannily suggests that his family helped bring the story into being.

If "La intrusa" and "Emma Zunz" are understood to be different restagings of a conflict and a humiliation that, for Borges, was both foundational and sexually traumatic, there is another story that more *directly* represents the author's attempt to engage with the idea of sex. It has, generally speaking, been dismissed as a somewhat simple riddle-story (whose answer, clearly, is "sex"). I would like to suggest, however, that Borges inserted an enigma at the center of this story that is not so easily solved, one that will point us in a new direction within this chapter. The story is titled "La secta del Fénix," and was first published within *SUR* in 1952.

The story's narrator begins by describing a secret society whose members form part of every society and culture. It is a group of people that shares only one thing in common: the practice of a rite—carried out privately—that allows for the possibility of exceeding the limits of one's own mortality.

While the story begins with a series of scholarly references (to Heliopolis, Amenophis IV, Herodotus, Tacitus, Rabanus Maurus, and Titus Flavius Josephus),[24] the first time that the narrator describes an actual personal experience it is—fittingly—set in Geneva, Switzerland. This is, of course, the city in which Borges had his traumatic encounter, at eighteen or nineteen, with the prostitute hired for him by his father. Here, instead, we simply read that "en Ginebra he tratado con artesanos que no me comprendieron cuando inquirí si eran hombres del Fénix, pero que admitieron, acto continuo, ser hombres del Secreto" (in Geneva I came across artisans that did not understand when I inquired if they were men of the Phoenix, but that admitted, immediately after, to being men of the Secret [1:821]).

As the story progresses, the narrator adds more details about the nature of the sect and the secret upon which it is based. We read that beyond the Secret there was once, also, a legend and perhaps even a myth related to the origin of the universe. What remains, however, is only an obscured act—a punishment, pact, or privilege—that points to the divine promise of eternity offered to those who, generation after generation, execute a particular rite. This rite is the only religious act of the devotees of the sect, though it is never taught by mothers or priests. Initiation, we read, is performed by only the lowest members of society. There are no temples for the ritual, which can occur in many hidden-away places. For many of the members of the sect, the rite is now so natural as to be considered a simple instinct.

There are a few moments in the story that echo Borges's own personal struggles with sex. His narrator writes that while "[e]l acto en sí es trivial, momentáneo y no require descripción" ([t]he act in itself is trivial, momentary, and does not require description [1:822]) there are those who are unable to perform it: "[u]na suerte de horror sagrado impide a algunos fieles la ejecución del simplísimo rito; los otros los desprecian, pero ellos se desprecian aun más" ([a] kind of sacred horror prevents some of the faithful from executing the very simple rite; the others despise them, but they despise themselves even more [1:823]).

The story ends with a paragraph that echoes the "horror" experienced by Emma Zunz (and by Borges himself). The narrator states that the members of the sect "[n]o se avenían a admitir que sus padres se hubieran rebajado a tales manejos" (they could not bring themselves to admit that their parents had lowered themselves to such practices [1:823]). Once again, the act of copulation is complicated by the mental imagination of sex between one's parents. The conflict between sexual desire and maternal and paternal relationships is brought to the foreground in a way that only makes sense if we understand the trauma that followed Borges for his entire life.

In this story, we see that Borges—as a fifty-three-year-old man— inscribes the idea of (heterosexual, procreative) sex as a secret into his fiction in a rather sophomoric way that is difficult to understand without knowledge of his own struggles with sexual intimacy. In this specific case, sex is presented to the reader as a practice that in and of itself is trivial but, nevertheless, acquires meaning due to the way in which it accomplishes two central goals: as a rite it, first, creates a powerful group identity and, second, promises a kind of eternal life that can be experienced by successive generations.

Each of these outcomes is highlighted, respectively, by "Emma Zunz" and "La intrusa." The first story explores the question of how to negotiate belonging and agency within adulthood, balancing a troubled relationship with sex carried out as a duty to one's family against a capacity to order reality through complex fiction. The second frames the author's conflicts within a more isolating, final context echoed by the interrupted, lost family tree traced in the Bible of the Nilsen brothers.

It is important to draw attention to the fact that these two possible outcomes are the only sources of importance and legitimacy given to sex within the story. As a way, for example, for two people to be together in a physical, intimate, and mutually pleasurable encounter, sex is completely ignored. Within the logic of the story, sex is not presented as a form of physical communication between two people. Instead, it is a clandestine, animalistic ritual that human beings find themselves instinctively falling into, benefitting along the way from social acceptance and procreation. This story, about heterosexual sex, manages to avoid the mention of a single woman.

What is also absent is the word "sex." And while almost every aspect of the story points to it as the "solution" to the riddle, there is one sentence that complicates matters for us as readers. After the narrator states that the act in question is not worth describing, we are given a peculiar description of the specific materials used within the rite: "[l]os materiales son el corcho, la cera o la goma arábiga. (En la liturgia se habla de légamo; éste suele usarse también)" ([t]he materials are cork, wax or gum arabic. [In the liturgy clay is also mentioned; this tends to be used as well] [1:822]). No other explanation of these materials is given. They do not correspond to the act of sex yet fail to point in any particularly clear direction. While they make our interpretation more complex they cannot logically displace the common understanding that the rite in question is, in fact, procreative copulation.[25] Neither, however, are they red herrings, as we will see later in this chapter.

In order to understand the placement of clay, gum arabic, cork, and wax within "La secta del Fénix" it is important to understand that the very idea of procreation, of creating life, functions in Borges's stories within both an everyday and a literary context. The story that most strikingly demonstrates these intertwined discourses is "Las ruinas circulares" (1940), which—like "La secta del Fénix"—involves a rite and a notable absence of women. This text provides, in other words, a crucial bridge between the explicit ideas posited in "La secta del Fénix" and the obscured rationale behind the materials of its peculiar rite.

This story describes a man who emerges mysteriously from a river with the project of dreaming another person into existence. He finds the circular ruins of an old temple, sits there, and begins to dream. At first, he dreams that he is instructing timid, dreamt students in a way that might prepare them for existence in reality. This project soon fails, however, and he begins again, this time composing a man, part by part, as he dreams. He begins by dreaming a beating heart, which takes several weeks. The dreamer then continues on to the other vital organs. Almost a year is required to mentally conjure the skeleton, the skin, the hair. The man he creates will not, however, wake up until the god of the temple—who takes many different forms but whose earthly name is Fire—instructs him in the required rites. The man is told by the god that he must, when the time comes, send his creation further down the river, to a similar temple, so that he might worship him there. This god explains that only the dreamer and fire itself will be able to tell that he is not a normal man.

The dreamer then instructs his creation (in his dreams) how to worship the god of fire. When he brings his creation into the world, right before sending him down the river, the dreamer makes his son forget everything about his unusual origins. This way, he would not be humiliated by the knowledge that he was a mere work of artifice, a false man.

The story ends with the dreamer, alone, watching the horizon light up with a forest fire that is descending on his temple. He resigns himself to his death only to find that, when the fire approaches him, it does not burn his skin. "[C]omprendió que él también era una apariencia, que otro estaba soñándolo" ([H]e realized that he, too, was an artificial being, that someone else was dreaming him [1:749]).

There are, clearly, many ways of approaching this story. In the context of this chapter, however, it is worth viewing it as an example of sexless procreation, as the solitary, meditative creation of another being. A man creates another man, and no woman is involved; there is no physical encounter. Creation is reconfigured as a mental operation.[26]

Yet there is a way in which this simple observation is complicated when we see that the "mental operation" being referred to relates directly to the experience of conjuring a literary character. The relationship between a (male) author and his (male) character has been described in terms of a sexless, cognitive act of creation before—in a text, additionally, that was very important to Borges: Miguel de Cervantes's 1605 prologue to *Don Quijote*. In fact, Borges references this prologue slyly with the borrowed phrase "el hijo que he engendrado" (the son I have engendered [1:748]), which echoes the first few sentences of Cervantes's prologue, together with a playful reference to the multiple "narradores" (narrators, 1:748) within *Don Quijote*. In the prologue, Cervantes writes:

> Quisiera que este libro, como hijo del entendimiento, fuera el más hermoso, el más gallardo y más discreto que pudiera imaginarse. Pero no he podido contravenir al orden de naturaleza, que en ella cada cosa engendra su semejante. Y, así, ¿qué podría engendrar el estéril y mal cultivado ingenio mío, sino la historia de un hijo seco, avellanado, antojadizo y lleno de pensamientos varios? (1:Prólogo, 7)

> I would like that this book, as a child of my intellect, be the most beautiful, the wisest, the most daring imaginable. But I have not been able to defy the order of nature, which dictates that everything engenders its own likeness. And, as such, what could the sterile and poorly cultivated mind that I possess engender but the story of a dry, withered, capricious son filled with all manner of thoughts?

Borges, in his story, writes, "[e]n general, sus días eran felices; al cerrar los ojos pensaba: *Ahora estaré con mi hijo*. O, más raramente: *El hijo que he engendrado me espera y no existirá si no voy*" ([i]n general, his days were happy ones; upon closing his eyes he would think: *Now I will be with my son.* Or, more infrequently: *The son that I have engendered waits for me and will not exist if I do not go* [1:748]).

In his prologue, Cervantes playfully confuses authorship with fatherhood, and the book's protagonist with the book itself. Both are his "sons" and the reader cannot keep track of which is which—the text and the human being that we are imagining combine into a text-body that resists easy interpretation (and foreshadows the unique condition of Don Quijote). The confusion builds until it implicates even Cervantes as "Cervantes," an artificial version of the author who is more of a literary character than a flesh-and-blood author evoked in a stable historical context. The world of the everyday and the world of the fictional in this foundational text are in chaotic flux.

The closest the prologue gets to providing guidance—some kind of framework through which Cervantes's novel might be read—is when another character jokingly suggests that the ideal prologue would include a list of all of the books ever published, organized according to their authors' names beginning with A and ending with Z. In other words: to enter into the book and begin to understand the confusion that emerges as the everyday world combines with fiction one should consider its literary antecedents. According to the aforementioned rule of nature, like engenders like. Therefore, literature begets literature and authors are simply the conduits for this process—stepfathers adjacent to the vastness of any literary genealogy.

Borges's story involves precisely the same turn: he points to the way in which the literary character is "authored" by other characters, existing only as one knot within a vast tapestry of interconnections. He, too, repudiates the notion of a concrete, authorial (and authoritative) origin for a work of art, replacing it, instead, with an *alternative genealogy* made of literary links that creatively control authors through the inevitable influence of their patterns. We are asked to imagine a series of circular ruins, each sending dreamt dreamers into the next. If each dreamt individual represents a literary creation, then these connections (linking the circular ruins of temple A to B to C . . . to Z) approach Cervantes's list of all the books ever written, organized from A to Z.

I would like to suggest that Borges is indeed writing about writing, about the process of creating a literary character. Yet the way in which he does this is, nevertheless, informed by his complicated relationship with the idea of sex and procreation.

It is important to recall that Borges, in "Las ruinas circulares," creates a story about a form of reproduction that is immune to fire, that relies on a rite worshipping fire, and promises a generational circularity that—protected from fire—bends toward eternity. This can be stated more plainly: Borges, in "Las ruinas circulares" (1940), creates "La secta del Fénix" (1952). Both stories link fire, eternity, and reproduction under the sign of the mythical phoenix, a being for whom *fire* is transformative instead of lethal. In the earlier story, however, we find a version of reproduction that directs our attention toward *literature* more than to corporeal, procreative sex. Crisscrossing between the two stories is the idea of *writing* as an alternate form of biological procreation.[27]

The tension between the act of writing and the act of copulation is highlighted, additionally, by the strange set of materials utilized in the rite at the center of "La secta del Fénix."

Wax. Clay. Gum arabic. Cork. These are the materials used within an act that the story's clues tell us *should* be sexual procreative copulation. Since the "solution" to the riddle is telegraphed to such a high degree within the story, these materials tend to be disregarded as peculiar red herrings, as ways of distracting the reader while adding some mystery to the narration.[28] I have consistently found that Borges, however, is far more interested in the inscription of different interconnected ideas within his stories than, say, the evocation of ambiguity and open-endedness.[29] While the obscured dimensions of his stories successfully function as strange, colorful complications for many readers, disrupting the coherence of their interpretations in a way that is evocative, they also tend to contain coherent internal discourses. The fact that this story (about copulation) so closely parallels "Las ruinas circulares" suggested that the solution, in this case, would likely have something to do with the act of writing or printing. After searching through diverse texts, I was able to come upon the answer.

The initial discovery that helped lead me to the solution was that burnt cork was once used to create an ink referred to as "el humo de imprenta" (printing smoke) by, among others, Tulio Febres Cordero in his 1888 book *El Lápiz* (which draws from the newspaper by the same name that he founded).[30] Burnt cork is more infamously associated in the United States with blackface vaudeville routines, but it seems to also have been an inexpensive way of generating a black tint for presses. I also found that gum arabic was associated with the creation of inks. Yet the use of wax and clay remained elusive.

Finally, I turned to Borges's favorite resource, the 11th edition of the *Encyclopedia Britannica*. After reading the entries under "encaustic painting," "printing," "ink," and innumerable other headings I decided to look up the word "pencil." At the very end of the entry on the composition and history of pencils is an offset paragraph in which the writer describes a way to create a variety of nonstandard pencils: "Black pencils of an inferior quality are made from the dust of graphite melted up with sulphur and run into moulds. Such, with a little tallow added to give them softness, are the pencils commonly used by carpenters. Coloured pencils consist of a mixture of clay, with appropriate mineral colouring matter, wax, and tallow, treated by the Conte method, as in making lead pencils. In indelible and copying pencils the colouring matter is an aniline preparation mixed with clay and gum."[31] In this concluding section we have, in short, a set of materials that mentions clay, gum arabic, wax, and coloring matter together, in concert. Together, they are used to create the inside of pencils: the core column of pencil "lead." Since the burnt cork was used to create "colouring matter" this is a completely viable explanation of Borges's peculiar list. In other words: a writing implement lies at the very center of Borges's story about sex.

The very beginning of this encyclopedia entry mentions, additionally, that the word "pencil" has an etymological origin in Latin that translates to "little tail." This is, more or less, the same etymological origin as the word "penis." The connection, I believe, would not have been lost on Borges. These two stories quite literally transpose pencils and penises, literary creation and copulation. The "wax, cork, clay, and gum arabic" at the center of the story form part of the joke, describing the male author's writerly sex organ (or, more specifically, its contents) within a story about copulation. For Borges, it bears repeating that these were likely not easy stories to write. They traffic in shame as well as pride and prowess.

"El jardín de senderos que se bifurcan" (1941) is a story that is not usually associated with sex. It is known, instead, as a somewhat philosophical text that introduces a meditation on time—and the possibility of alternate realities and parallel timelines—within a spy story set in World War I. Nevertheless, I believe that it is Borges's most developed attempt to reconcile the tension that he saw between his abilities as a writer and his difficulties with physical intimacy. If "La intrusa" offers a traumatic interruption, a devastating end to both a family line and a sense of familial belonging, then "El jardín de senderos que se bifurcan" explores the possibilities of literary inter-connectedness opened up by "Las ruinas circulares."

The story begins with a paragraph (written in a disinterested, dry tone) that describes how new information has shed light on the reasons for the two-day postponement of a British offensive planned for the 24th of July in 1916. This information, we read, is contained in a declaration that was dictated, reread, and signed by a spy for the Germans named Yu Tsun. The rest of the story is this declaration, which is missing its initial pages.

Yu Tsun begins by recalling the moment in which he called his compatriot Viktor Runeberg, and Captain Richard Madden answered the telephone instead. Hearing his voice, Yu Tsun describes how he knew immediately that Viktor had been arrested or killed and that Madden would soon be in pursuit of him. From the perspective of Yu Tsun, Madden is particularly relentless because he is Irish—the successful capture of two German spies (him and his friend Viktor) would help him to be seen as less untrustworthy by his British comrades.

The narration then veers into a more introspective tone. Yu Tsun looks out the window and contemplates the peculiar nature of time, how everything occurs precisely in the present and has always done so, for millennia, and will continue to do so, far in the future. He considers it strange that everything always seems to happen only to him, from his perspective, in the present, and that this is the way it is for everyone.

Yu Tsun, returning to the problem at hand, considers his options. Not only must he escape, he also has to find a way to communicate what he refers to as the 'Secret': the geographical position of British artillery above the Ancre River in France. Yu Tsun decides to create a plan to send this position to the Germans before his capture or demise. He knows that they will be examining newspapers for clues; this is the only medium he has to reach them in time. After going through the items in his pockets, he arrives at an idea and consults the phone directory to find the person who might allow him to transmit the Secret. It turns out that he lives about a half an hour away by train.

A break in the narration allows him to reflect on why he carried out his plan, and why he became a spy. The wording of these thoughts is important: "Lo hice, porque yo sentía que el jefe tenía en poco a los de mi raza—a los innumerables antepasados que confluyen en mí. Yo quería probarle que un amarillo podía salvar a sus ejércitos (I did it, because I sensed that the boss looked down at the members of my race—at the innumerable ancestors that converged within me. I wanted to prove to him that a yellow man could save his armies [1:770]). The argument provides a parallel to Yu Tsun's understanding of Richard Madden's specific motivations as an Irishman and, beyond this, subtly points to a far more complex idea that we will return to shortly.

After Yu Tsun gets on the train he sees Richard Madden on the platform; he is in pursuit, exactly as was feared. At his destination, Ashgrove, a child asks him if he is on his way to Stephen Albert's house. Yu Tsun replies affirmatively, and another child suggests that if he takes every possible left turn then he will arrive safely. Yu Tsun recognizes this peculiar instruction since he is the great-grandson of Ts'ui Pên, a governor of Yunnan who famously renounced his position in order to write "una novela [. . .] más populosa que el *Hung Lu Meng* y para edificar un laberinto en el que se perdieran todos los hombres" (a novel [. . .] more populous than the *Hung Lu Meng* and construct a labyrinth in which all men might lose themselves [1:771]). He knows that the directions given to him by the child were also used to arrive at the central patio of certain labyrinths. Yu Tsun drifts off into another introspective set of associations, writing: "[p] ensé en un laberinto de laberintos, en un sinuoso laberinto creciente que abarcara el pasado y el porvenir y que implicara de algún modo los astros" (I thought of a labyrinth of labyrinths, a sinuous, growing labyrinth that would include the past and the future and somehow involve the cosmos [1:771]).

He continues forward, noticing music that he only later registers as Chinese. A house comes into view; the man inside mistakes Yu Tsun for a Chinese consul and asks if he has come to see the garden of bifurcating paths. Yu Tsun instantly recognizes this garden as the creation of Ts'ui Pên; he (truthfully) tells this man, Stephen Albert, that he is Pên's ancestor and is welcomed in.

They walk through a library and Tsun notices manuscripts of a never-published encyclopedia and a gramophone with a record spinning alongside a bronze phoenix. Soon they sit under a circular clock placed high on the wall; Yu Tsun wonders how long it will take Madden to reach him. Albert explains his fascination with Yu Tsun's ancestor Ts'ui Pên as a man who abandoned his studies, his political power, his relationships and his social life all to create two works of art: a book and a labyrinth. Yet only chaotic manuscripts were found after his death, which were published by a monk against the wishes of his family.

The legend, Albert notes, suggests that the true labyrinth of Pên was infinite. A letter by Ts'ui Pên that he had discovered added to the mystery. It read: "Dejo a los varios porvenires (no a todos) mi jardín de senderos que se bifurcan" (I leave to various futures [though not to all of them] my garden of bifurcating paths [1:773]). Albert explains that in time he came to believe that the labyrinth and the book were, in fact, the same object. He thus had to consider the ways in which a book could be infinite. He thought of the structure of *One Thousand and One Nights* and "una obra platónica, hereditaria, transmitida de padre a hijo, en la que cada nuevo individuo agregara un capítulo o corrigiera con piadoso cuidado la página de los mayores" (a platonic, hereditary work, transmitted from father to son, in which each new individual adds a chapter or corrects, with pious care, a page of the elders [1:774]). None of these possibilities seemed satisfactory.

Albert decides, ultimately, that the fragmentary nature of the novel left behind by Pên is the (visible) result of his characters experiencing every possible path forward through time, each branch bifurcating at different key moments. Albert believes that Ts'ui Pên conceived of an infinite series of timelines, in a vertiginous network of "divergent, convergent, and parallel" possibilities. The book he left behind is the incomplete but faithful expression of his understanding of time itself.[32] As Yu Tsun listens to Albert, he visualizes all of the invisible, possible versions of himself in the garden. Suddenly he sees Richard Madden advancing through this garden off in the distance. He asks Albert to see the letter again and then shoots him in the back with his revolver. Despite being arrested and condemned to die, the daily newspaper communicates that an unknown man, Yu Tsun, shot the famous sinologist Stephen Albert. This was enough for his German boss to understand the name of the city in which the British artillery was located: Albert.

Most approaches to this story have centered on its explicit content: the idea, helpfully provided by Albert, of an "infinite" text that branches off at various points, creating alternate timelines and multiple fictive worlds. Often, this branching text (following the logic of the story) is related to a nonfictional conceptualization of time and space that allows for all possible universes to exist parallel to one another.[33] The interpretation that I offer here takes a very different route: I argue that there is a way of solving the riddle of Ts'ui Pên's dual masterpieces that is at odds with Albert's interpretation. This solution has very little to do with hypertexts, multiverses, or alternative conceptualizations of time—it refers, instead, to the more *everyday* challenge of considering one's own life in relation with the past and the future (a challenge that is directly represented in the story). It has the benefit, additionally, of being more logically coherent than the solution that Albert delivers to us.

To proceed, however, we have to notice a peculiar signpost that Borges inserts within the story: it is the record of the phonograph spinning alongside a bronze statue of a phoenix. This statue, I argue, directs the reader toward both "La secta del Fénix" and "Las ruinas circulares," the stories in which a similar deity of fire is linked with cyclical, infinite existence by means of an ambiguous combination of writing and copulation. The cyclical concept of time that appears in both stories (and in the title of one) is suggested by the spinning, circular record of the phonograph that accompanies the statue. There are other echoes as well: after mentioning the spinning record of the phonograph, the story describes a "circular" clock hanging high on the wall. (Referring to a clock as "circular" is either redundant or extraneous unless we allow the adjective to emphasize the idea of circular/cyclical time, in opposition to a more linear temporal model.) Together, these objects reintroduce the central question posed by the story in a new context: how might Ts'ui Pên have attempted to extend his life beyond its mortal limit (as in the case of the cyclical existence of the phoenix) through his creative work in a way that can be considered infinite? What is the book that he is referring to? What, truly, is the labyrinth?

Albert, as was previously noted, believes that the book and the labyrinth of Ts'ui Pên are essentially the same object: the incomplete novel that was published by the monks that shows characters appearing and reappearing on different timelines. Yet this explanation does not take into account the requirement that Ts'ui Pên articulated: that the garden be, in fact, *infinite*. While the book is fragmentary and involves multiple timelines, it is impossible to categorize it as "infinite" in a way that *differentiates* it from any other text.[34] According to the story, the first work of art, the labyrinth, was referred to as the "garden of bifurcating paths." The second work of art, the book, was supposed to be the novel that Ts'ui Pên fashioned in solitude. I believe that maintaining this distinction is important; collapsing them into one object (as Albert does) derails the interpretation.

The solution to this puzzle is based on the relationship between the two stories that it references—"La secta del Fénix" and "Las ruinas circulares"—and the way in which they positioned the acts of *sex* and *writing* as modes of forming relationships with the past and future. This was done through a special emphasis on the creation of future generations of descendants (in "La secta del Fénix") and readers (in "Las ruinas circulares") and also through past generations of ancestors ("La secta del Fénix") and literary influences ("Las ruinas circulares").

Accordingly, I would like to argue that the garden of bifurcating paths fashioned by Ts'ui Pên is neither a garden nor a novel. It is, instead, a genealogical tree—his genealogical tree.

The garden of bifurcating paths is the conceptualization of Ts'ui Pên's family—his entire family, including every member of the past and future generations that he was never able to know personally. To imagine one's family from the limits of the present moment—in its conceptual totality—is to mentally construct a complex temporal figure that includes individuals in the past, present, and future. This work of the imagination stands up to the legend: in considering the future branchings of his genealogical tree, of course Ts'ui Pên had to conceive it as an infinite structure, one with unlimited potential forms. Even the past includes, after enough generations, mysterious and unknowable branches of relation. Extending this figure to its logical limit would, moreover, involve tracing one's family to the very first human beings and therefore, perhaps, out toward all people that have ever lived and will ever live. Recall that this is a labyrinth in which "all men might lose themselves."

There are multiple ways of considering the form of this genealogical tree. One strategy is to imagine it as though it is a branching, linear map being viewed from afar. Another far more compelling approach is to consider the branching structure from within; if you (like Yu Tsun) are a member of this family, you would quite literally be travelling within one of its branches. This shift in perspective converts a simple genealogical chart into a labyrinth that one walks from birth until death. One can see that every bifurcation in such a labyrinth is the result of procreation. In this way, sex and the garden edenically combine within *El jardín de senderos que se bifurcan*, as well as in Ts'ui Pên's genealogical masterwork.

This interpretation has a number of serious consequences for the story. It allows us to recontextualize some of its more peculiar elements in a way that provides a more coherent explanation. Yu Tsun's reasons for working as a spy for the Germans are not, for example, particularly convincing when we consider them in isolation. We read that he is motivated to kill and die for his racist, odious German boss in order to prove to him that he and his ancestors are people that are worthy of respect, trust, and confidence. He acts, in other words, motivated by an attempt to defend a particular conceptualization of his family. (Madden, in Yu Tsun's view, is doing the same. They both want the victors to carry forward a positive account of their individual contributions and, by extension, the value of their "people"). Yu Tsun's act of murder is in this way intended to *preserve the integrity* of his own garden of bifurcating paths, the version of his great-grandfather's masterwork that he intuitively carries with him.

There is, nevertheless, a peculiar tension between the decision to murder a man—and communicate a Secret (written with a capital *S* in the story) that will lead to the deaths of many more—in order to protect the way that one's family (and ancestors) are conceptualized and known. Given how each "bifurcation" in the garden is a birth (the result of procreative sex), it can be disorienting to see how the attempt to preserve it relies so heavily on death (the result of intentional killing). We should recall that Yu Tsun's project is to communicate a Secret that is the location of the artillery in the town of Albert. This capitalized Secret strongly recalls the "Secret" of "La secta del Fénix," a group that was alternately referred to as "La secta del Secreto." While the most obvious answer to this riddle in this story was, as we know, "sex," its *obscured* answer was "writing." And write is precisely what Yu Tsun does when he kills Albert: the murder forces a newspaper to print a message detectable by Yu Tsun's racist German boss. One cannot help but consider that there was another option: if he had, instead of engineering a solitary, murderous act of writing to protect his ancestors from insult, taken the route suggested by the garden, he could have formed a family instead of joining the war. He could have had a son or a daughter instead of killing a man. Yet the story seems to require the tension between births and deaths, between procreation and murder.

To clarify: Yu Tsun, through his act of murder, converts the person "Stephen Albert" into a sign to be written and read: "Albert." He indirectly authors a story (in a newspaper) so that a very particular reader (his boss) can interpret it and use it to kill even more people. Having turned away from the possibilities of fatherhood suggested by his great-grandfather, he engages in an act of writing (with the newspaper acting as his instrument) that yields, conversely, only death. At the center of both of their stories is family: Yu Tsun chooses to kill, absurdly, for the Secret when he just as easily could have sought to love.

If we are prepared to separate the book from the garden (the two works of art authored by Ts'ui Pên) then the book exists as the garden's obverse. While the garden, the branching genealogy of his family, advances forward in time with every act of procreative sex (and extends backwards in time as far as the mind can follow), the book, in contrast, is a catalog of death. From the excerpts presented to us by Stephen Albert, we can see that the text is exclusively preoccupied with *death*, *killing*, and *dying*. It is a solitary meditation on isolation, authorship, and the various ways in which we meet the end of our existence.

Consider the content of the book, as it is presented to us in the story.

Leyó con lenta precisión dos redacciones de un mismo capítulo épico. En la primera, un ejército marcha hacia una batalla a través de una montaña desierta; el horror de las piedras y de la sombra le hace menospreciar la vida y logra con facilidad la victoria; en la segunda, el mismo ejército atraviesa un palacio en el que hay una fiesta; la resplandeciente batalla les parece una continuación de la fiesta y logran la victoria. Yo oía con decente veneración esas viejas ficciones, acaso menos admirables que el hecho de que las hubiera ideado mi sangre y de que un hombre de un imperio remoto me las restituyera, en el curso de una desesperada aventura, en una isla occidental. Recuerdo las palabras finales, repetidas en cada redacción como un mandamiento secreto: 'Así combatieron los héroes, tranquilo el admirable corazón, violenta la espada, resignados a matar y morir.' (1:774–75)

He read with slow precision two versions of the same epic chapter. In the first an army marches to battle across a deserted mountain; the horror of the rocks and the shadows make them scorn life and they achieve victory easily; in the second version, the same army goes through a palace in which a celebration is being held; the shining battle seems to them to be a continuation of the party and they achieve victory. I listened with respectful veneration to these old fictions, which were perhaps less admirable than the fact that they had been created by my bloodline, and that a man from a distant empire was giving them back to me in the course of a desperate adventure on a western island. I remember the final words, repeated in every version like a secret command: 'Thus fought the heroes, their admirable hearts at ease, their swords violent, resigned to kill and die'.

Every time that the book is referenced it refers to a conflict between men, usually involving killing.[35] Each encounter may very well result in a new bifurcation of causes and effects, but it also (importantly) *cuts short* the branch of the genealogical tree of an individual's family. Even the novel is an unfinished work, cut short by death: Ts'ui Pên is killed by a stranger before he can write a conclusion. (Perhaps this is the only conclusion that is possible within its internal logic: to kill, and only to kill, is to actively conclude.) The book (of death) and the garden (of life) are, in this way, set in direct opposition to one another.

Together, *these* distinct works of art can be seen as representing the totality of the temporal, social universe as conceived by Ts'ui Pên. Dying/killing and engaging in procreative sex are the two acts that balance out a worldview based on a cyclical, *familial* story of human existence. Yu Tsun, in turn, participates in the tradition of his ancestor's written text without fully realizing it, laboring to kill and write a message at the very same time, motivated by an obscured desire to protect his family.[36] He, as a descendant of Ts'ui Pên, walks—without knowing it—within the garden of the forking paths, heading toward the very end of one of its branches. Yu Tsun was, in truth, walking through his ancestor's garden from the very beginning.

With this duality in mind, notice, now, the name of Yu Tsun's ancestor. He is a *Pen* whose name is handed down through the generations only through the act of procreative sex. (Ts'ui Pên can even be misheard as "Soy Pen" [I am Pen].) Borges's previous riddle—which relied rather heavily on the 1911 *Encyclopedia Britannica*—now has another possible link. From "penis" to "pencil" to "Pen," his game links procreation with writing once again. With his writing implement,

Pên creates a book (of death and dying). With his other implement, he creates a family (through a potentially infinite series of births).

This doubled work of art is alluded to in an essay of Borges titled "La muralla y los libros" (1950). The essay also describes a man from China known for two remarkable feats that, while different from one another, reflect and support each other in terms of their internal logic. These two projects can, together, be considered as the echo of Ts'ui Pên's genealogical labyrinth and book of literary death.

Shih Huang Ti, Borges writes, is known for creating both the "casi infinito" (nearly infinite, 2:13) Great Wall of China and, also, ordering the burning of all of the books of the past. The essay is framed as an exploration of the possible connection between these two projects. Setting aside the most intuitive reasons (the defense of the Emperor's territory and the destruction of texts used by the opposition to praise previous rulers), Borges emphasizes that the scale at which the projects functioned gives them a nearly metaphorical quality. He writes that they amount to efforts to destroy the past and fix in place the limits of a world.

The Emperor's works, seen through this lens, become world-making acts that reshape space and time. Borges writes that "Shih Huang Ti, según los historiadores, prohibió que se mencionara la muerte y buscó el elixir de la inmortalidad y se recluyó un en palacio figurativo, que constaba de tantas habitaciones como hay días en el año" (Shih Huang Ti, according to historians, prohibited the very mention of death and sought out the elixir of immortality, seeking refuge in a figurative palace that contained as many rooms as the year has days [2:14]). Borges interprets these actions as indications that the wall and the burning of the past were magical acts designed to elude death. He wonders whether Shih Huang Ti named himself Huang Ti as a way of refashioning himself after the legendary emperor who created written language and the compass (tools, after all, for navigating space and time). After a series of conjectures about the wall and the fire, Borges takes a step back to offer the idea that the doubled project of Shih Huang Ti does not require any further speculation, that its form and its scale are enough for us to feel their impact, as one might feel the power of music.

It was music, also, that Yu Tsun felt as he approached the house of Stephen Albert:

> La tarde era íntima, infinita. El camino bajaba y se bifurcaba, entre las ya confusas praderas. Una música aguda y como silábica se aproximaba y se alejaba en el vaivén del viento, empañada de hojas y de distancia [. . .] Comprendí, de pronto, dos cosas, la primera trivial, la segunda casi increíble: la música venía del pabellón, la música era china. Por eso, yo la había aceptado con plenitud, sin prestarle atención. No recuerdo si había una campana o un timbre o si llamé golpeando las manos. El chisporroteo de la música prosiguió. (1:771–72)

> The afternoon was intimate, infinite. The path descended and bifurcated within the already confusing meadows. A sharp and almost syllabic music came forward and receded with the rhythm of the wind, muffled by leaves and distances [. . .] I understood, suddenly, two things, the first trivial and the second almost incredible: the music came from the pavilion, the music was Chinese. For that reason, I had accepted it fully, without even paying attention. I don't remember if there was a bell or a buzzer or if I clapped my hands. The crackling sparks of music continued.

While there are parts of this story that suggest a discrete puzzle for us to consider (and potentially solve) as readers, here we encounter the tensions of the story in another form. When Yu Tsun, after stepping off the train, hears music in the air and senses its naturalness, effortlessly accepting it as he travels his path, we can sense the physical and emotional pull of his own ancestral and familial traditions. We are asked to feel—not think about—the way he finds himself intuitively a part of his family and his culture, even while working for a government that rejects him in its racism. Beyond the answer to the riddle (what are Ts'ui Pên's works of art?), beyond the interpretation that we can offer to respond to the gaps and contradictions present in the story, this experience of sensing (and not being able to fully understand) the pull of one's cultural roots contains the essential force of the story.

In both texts, Borges draws from an idea: that it is not "baladí pretender que la más tradicional de las razas renuncie a la memoria de su pasado, mítico o verdadero" (inconsequential to claim that the most traditional of races could renounce the memory of its past, whether it be mythical or true [2:13]). In choosing a Chinese cultural context, Borges is foregrounding the 'traditional' idea of using family identity as a lens through which the world can be understood and ordered. Borges traces the way both protagonists attempt to take control of forces that are greater than their individual talents for creation and destruction.

Yet while Borges utilizes a Chinese context for these stories to highlight values of traditional continuity and familial interconnectedness, these concerns are, I argue, directly related to his own relationships with writing and with family. The tension between these two contexts lies at the very center of this chapter. We began with an analysis of how a foundational trauma was reconfigured within "Emma Zunz" in a way that reframed it as a condition for the emergence of storytelling: fiction came into being—as an alibi, as a story—in a way that empowered and, also, transformed its author. This move into fiction soon provided a parallel literary connection with a character that shares his experiences and a reader that, perhaps, manages to intuit them. "La intrusa" functioned as a corrective to this somewhat triumphant narrative, emphasizing the violence and silencing that made the experience particularly difficult instead of drawing attention to the power of fiction and storytelling. The silence of Juliana Burgos and the alibi of Emma Zunz work in tandem: one is the function of the other.

"La secta del Fénix" and "Las ruinas circulares" take a step further by envisioning a kind of authorship crossed with a reconfigured procreative drive. In both, the act of creating another human being—procreative copulation—is overlapped or replaced with the act of fashioning a fictional text or literary character. The "penis" becomes a "pencil" (and vice versa) while women are conveniently excised. "Las ruinas circulares," to this specific end, borrows from Cervantes's 1605 Prologue to *Don Quijote* for the way it playfully suggests that while it might seem as though authors "create" their characters, it might be more accurate to suggest that they are born of textual antecedents. According to the "law of nature," like engenders like and a book's origins are therefore to be found in other books, in a textual tradition that parallels biological genealogy.[37]

The stories, in short, gesture beyond the act of sex—past the pleasure, intimacy, or connection that it might promise—in order to consider a new way to imagine how the possible result—a son, a daughter, a family—might emerge under the sign of fatherhood or under the sign of literature. Together, we sense that these stories emphasize a parallel set of ideals and possibilities that, respectively, inhabit the worlds of the literary and the everyday.

"El jardín de senderos que se bifurcan" continues Borges's meditation on writing, sex, and the concept of family by expanding the question of fatherhood to include a larger genealogical (and, thus, temporal) imaginary context: we read the account of a narrator subconsciously guided by two internal codes. Each is associated with a different work of art composed by his great grandfather. The first code guides the narrator into introspective ruminations about impermanence and ancestry. It echoes the logic of a garden of bifurcating life, a genealogical tree that grows with every birth (with every procreative sexual encounter), including that of the actual narrator. The second code directs the narrator to follow a plan to communicate a message (through an act of killing) that will result in the death of many. It is a code based on the logic of a book, composed in solitude, that is focused on diverse forms of death and killing.

Within the logic of the story, despite Albert's assertion to the contrary, the book and the garden are not just different works of art, they are diametrically opposed. Yet both of these opposing possibilities—the creation of life and the creation of death—depend on one another for logical sense. One sentence in particular, a refrain in the book written by Ts'ui Pên ("Así combatieron los héroes, tranquilo el admirable corazón, violenta la espada, resignados a matar y morir" [Thus fought the heroes, their admirable hearts at ease, their swords violent, resigned to kill and die (1:775)]), almost echoes the *Bhagavad-Gita* in its dispassionate approach to these facets of human life.[38] The violence of war, imagined from a faraway vantage point, can seem to recede into larger patterns of birth and death. As do, perhaps, the more hidden-away acts of procreative copulation.

In light of the first chapter in this book, it will likely not come as a surprise that Borges wrote about the doubled project of living everyday life and working within fiction while evoking theological ideas. In his essay "Del culto de los libros" (1951), he writes that while many traditions offer the idea of a book written by a God, it is also not uncommon to encounter the idea that there are, in fact, *two* divine texts. While the first is relatively easy to recognize as a book, the second—the *universe*—requires a more allegorical mind-set. He cites Francis Bacon who proposes that God "nos ofrecía dos libros, para que no incidiéramos en error: el primero, el volumen de las Escrituras, que revela Su voluntad; el segundo, el volumen de las criaturas, que revela Su poderío y que éste era la llave de aquél" (offered us two books, so that we would not err: the first, the volume of Holy Writ, which reveals His will; the second, the volume of earthly creatures, which reveals His power, and this one was the key to the first [2:98–99]). Thomas Browne, Borges continues, echoes the idea by writing that "[d]os son los libros en que suelo aprender teología: la Sagrada Escritura y aquel universal y público manuscrito que está patente a todos los ojos. Quienes nunca vieron en el primero, Lo descubrieron en el otro" (two are the books in which I tend to learn theology: the Bible and that universal, public manuscript that is available to all eyes. Those who never saw the first discovered It in the second [2:99]). Browne follows this idea with the suggestion that all things are artificial because Nature is the Art of God.

While the richness, variety, and possibility of a world of artifice deeply informed by theology is, as the first chapter of the book suggested, central to Borges's understanding of his relationship with literature, it is difficult not to see how the idea of an infinite, imagined family is precisely what is at risk for him as he contemplates his own inability to have a full sexual life. The artificial world created by *him* allows for an interconnectedness that bridges time and space with literary influence and reinvention, yet it is, ultimately, separate from the public world of earthly creatures evoked by Francis Bacon, Thomas Browne, and his own family.

Each of the stories encountered in this chapter is ultimately an attempt to balance, measure, and explore the possibilities of a set of relationships and connections within fiction that might take the shape of a different kind of genealogy, one made up of Borges's characters and narrators and, also, his readers and the readers of his readers. It includes the authors whom he has read and the authors who influenced them. The stories indicate that finding a sense of belonging within this kind of interconnection turns on his ability to reframe his own desire to construct a sense of "family" within literary terms. A growing, branching pattern of literary influences thus develops in a form akin to kinship. We might approach this potentially infinite set of possibilities as intimating a legacy handed down through generations of readers, one that—for Borges—stands next to the impossibility of creating generations of biological descendants.

We, if this is true, are walking in his textual garden.

The Risk of Death and the Possibility of Literary Salvation

Cuando el hombre se despoja del cuerpo etéreo, vive retrospectivamente su vida. Recorre todas sus experiencias, pero de un modo nuevo.

When man leaves behind his ethereal body, he lives his life retrospectively. He relives all his experiences, but in a new way.

—**Rudolf Steiner**, Las manifestaciones del Karma (from Borges and Bioy Casares, Libro del cielo y del infierno, 40)

Borges, in a short text titled "Diálogo sobre un diálogo" (1960), narrates a conversation (about a conversation) with a character based on Macedonio Fernández. The narrator, "A," describes how he and "Macedonio" had once spoken late into the night about the logic of immortality. "Macedonio" repeated, as he had many times before, that the soul is immortal and that death is insignificant, the least important thing that could ever occur to anyone.

So as to be able to continue the conversation without having to listen to a seemingly endless performance of the tango "La Cumparsita," "A" proposes that they both commit suicide. "Z," the listener of this story, comments jokingly, "Pero sospecho que al final no se resolvieron" (Well I suspect that in the end you decided against it [2:172]). "A" replies: "Francamente no recuerdo si esa noche nos suicidamos" (Frankly, I don't remember if we killed ourselves or not that night [2:172]).

The story might serve to remind us that the voices we are conjuring to create this dialogue are not coming from living beings: they emerge, like the whispers of ghosts, from somewhere else. To the degree to which they are associated with the living Borges or the living Macedonio Fernández, they hint at the kind of literary afterlife discussed within the narrated conversation. For characters, for narrators, death is rather insignificant.

Yet there is a crucial difference between the actual cessation of life and the playful evocation of "death" within a literary context. It might seem obvious to state, but the distinction is useful to keep in mind given the way Borges purposefully confuses everyday life and the imaginary world of the literary within his work. Death changes shape as it moves from place to place. When it is refracted by a prism of literary references and humorous quips, it often ends up referring to something very different from the actual end of a life.[1] Borges and Macedonio, for example, often associate a leap into death with a leap into a fictional existence. For them, suicide can be reframed as an act of faith in the literary afterlife. Elsewhere, of course, suicide might still register as the final act of someone who was profoundly ill and made a terrible mistake.

This final chapter focuses on an example of each kind of death. Two suicides are described. The first follows the tone and logic of Macedonio's philosophical humor: it involves a suicidal interpretation, in fact, carried out by a reader who is aware that if he or she discovers the answer to a particular riddle, they may be erased from the face of the earth. To pursue the answer, to read with an investigative, problem-solving mindset, is thus to risk death. And to risk death (in this literary context) is to welcome existence within another dimension, fully letting go of one's previous life (with its everyday concerns, norms, and rules). It is an act of freedom.

The second suicide is the actual suicide of a reader of Borges named José Luis Ríos Patrón. It is a death that registers within the small community of writers in Buenos Aires—Borges and Bioy find out about it almost immediately. It is not, by any means, treated as an act of freedom, of literary liberation. Yet years later, Borges finds himself returning to the suffering and suicide of his reader. By a twist of fate, they happen to be in similar situations, and he composes a story, with Bioy, that joins their lives together in a way that exposes a dark vein of anger, resentment, and cutting humor. I will argue that, even with its dose of cruelty, the story shows how Borges used fiction as a space of transformation through which his challenges could be reimagined in less threatening forms.

Viewing these two possibilities of approaching suicide alongside one another will hopefully point to the ways in which literature, for Borges, works in a register that is beyond the world of the everyday yet, inevitably and obscurely, connected to it. If this book begins with the description of a literary theology attuned to questions of fictive experience and existence, it is fitting that it ends with a contemplation of that which lies beyond the limit of these different varieties of death.

The story "La otra muerte" (1949) begins with "Borges" recalling a lost letter from "Patricio Gannon" (a character based on the actual writer). The letter, sent from Gualeguaychú, included Gannon's promise to share his translation of Emerson's poem "The Past." It had also mentioned that an acquaintance of "Borges"—an old man named Pedro Damián—had recently died. The letter stated that in the delirium preceding his death Damián relived his experiences at the Battle of Masoller. The narrator mentions that this was unsurprising: the battle was all that Damián wanted to talk about when they met in 1942. "Borges" adds that his only visual memory of the man was based on a photograph (now lost) that "Gannon" had once taken and sent to him. "Borges" states that he now refuses to look for the lost photograph, that he is too afraid to do so. The reason for this fear remains, initially, unexplained.

The next part of the story takes place in Montevideo. "Borges" recalls how, after deciding to write a story based on the experiences of Damián, he arranged to meet with a colonel named Dionisio Tabares, referred to him by "Emir Rodríguez Monegal" (once again, a character based on an actual person). At the meeting, the colonel describes the Battle of Masoller: the lack of munitions, the challenging conditions, and Aparicio Saravia, the leader of the revolutionaries, who could have entered Montevideo but demurred "porque el gaucho le teme a la ciudad" (because gauchos fear the city [1:874]). After being asked, he also recalls Damián and states that he had acted as a coward in the battle.

"Borges" is disappointed. He tries to convince himself that a cowardly man is more interesting than a courageous one, but is unsuccessful. The sense that the Argentinian Damián was less fierce than his Uruguayan compatriots does not sit well with him. He feels the echoes of a cultural "artiguismo" that holds Uruguay in higher esteem for its stronger, more "elemental" nature.

As the months pass, the story that he is writing refuses to take shape and "Borges" returns to speak with the colonel once again. Another veteran of Masoller, Juan Francisco Amaro, happens to be present at his house. As they talk about the battle, Amaro mentions Damián without prompting. He remembers him fondly as someone who fought heroically at the front lines before being caught with a bullet to the chest and, tragically, dying.

The colonel now strangely asserts that he has never heard of Damián before in his life, despite having described him in detail only months earlier. This odd sense of forgetfulness occurs again when "Borges" encounters "Patricio Gannon" in the basement of Mitchell's English Bookstore in Buenos Aires. "Gannon," with the complete works of Emerson before him, does not seem to remember the letter that he sent, stating that he has no plans to translate "The Past." When asked about Pedro Damián, "Gannon" does not recall the name.

"Borges" adds that he eventually received a letter from Colonel Tabares indicating that he finally remembered the heroic acts of Pedro Damián and his burial soon after the Battle of Masoller. "Borges" writes that he attempted to contact the man who saw Pedro Damián die but he, unfortunately, had just passed away as well. Even the narrator's own recollections are suspect; he notes that the photographic image he was associating with Damián corresponded, in fact, with that of the famous tenor Tamberlick playing the role of Othello.

The theory that "Borges" finally offers to explain all of the inconsistencies is suggested to him by a treatise written by Pier Damiani titled *De Omnipotentia*. It asserts that God, as an omnipotent being, has the power to change what once was, to alter the past. This idea—that the past can be altered from a point in the future—suggests a perfect explanation. Though Damián is indeed a coward at Masoller, he returns to live his life in Entre Ríos full of regret. Every day he quietly focuses on becoming a stronger version of himself so as to never fail in the same way again. Forty-two years pass until, in the moment of his death, a miracle occurs. He is, as he dies, allowed to return to the Battle of Masoller and act valiantly. In 1946 Damián is able to return to 1904 and die a hero.

The result of this heroic death is, however, an altered timeline: having died in 1904, the next 42 years of his existence had to be erased from the collective memory, replaced with new causes and effects that stemmed from his absence and from his heroic death. The alterations to reality—explains "Borges"—were not instantaneous. This is why Damián was, at first, recalled as the coward he originally was, later completely forgotten, and finally remembered as the hero that he was allowed to be. "Borges" suggests that Abaroa, the man who watched Damián die in 1946, passed away as a result of having too many memories of the now nonexistent older man. Abaroa, the man who knew too much, simply ceased to be within the second timeline.

"Borges" predicts, however, that he is now only at a moderate risk of being eliminated from the current timeline. He suspects that the story he has written, the story that he remembers, has been falsified by (importantly) himself. Names and circumstances have been altered, by him, so as to make the story appear to be a literary invention and not the historical record of a dangerous paradox. The similarity between the names "Pedro Damián" and "Pier Damiani" is what tips him off. "Borges" reasons that he chose to use "Pedro Damián" as a pseudonym in order to allow himself to believe, much later, that the character was an invention inspired by the theologian, that it did not correspond to a real individual. The protagonist, in other words, has a hidden name that the author (and his readers) are protected from. "Borges" adds that the mention of Emerson's poem in the letter by "Gannon" was almost certainly another fabrication on his part designed to convince himself that he was inspired by coincidence to create the story before us. We hear him explain that "[h]acia 1951 creeré haber fabricado un cuento fantástico y habré historiado un hecho real" ([a]round 1951 I will believe that I have created a fantastical story but in truth I will have described a historical fact [1:878]).

It is thus implied that "Borges," while writing the story, had seen the danger of the paradox. Noticing that the witness of Damián's death had lost his life, and that everyone else was losing their grasp of previous memories, the author decides to protect the essential characteristics of the paradox within the flexibility of a fictional form.

This is not, as we have seen, the first time that Borges has used this technique. "Emma Zunz" is published in 1948 while "La otra muerte" emerges one year later, in 1949. Both alter names, dates, and places in order to allow a fictional narrative to take on additional significance. Borges, in both examples, uses fiction as a protection, as a way of telling multiple stories at once. In "La otra muerte" the reader is protected, as is the writer (within the logic of the narrative), from potential erasure: everyone knows that there is another, dangerous story lurking behind the legible one, just out of view. This explicit sense of doubled narrative is harder to see in "Emma Zunz"; we might even imagine that Borges wanted to make this technical strategy more visible in the less emotionally vulnerable context of "La otra muerte."

Within the logic of "La otra muerte," "Borges" is not the only individual being protected by these fictions. We read about Pedro Damián (instead of about the true protagonist) so that we, too, might be protected from the obscured timeline. We do not run the risk of being eliminated like the unnamed, "true" protagonist's neighbor if we accept the protections that the narrator has offered us. Yet within this idea lurks a question: what might happen if we were to discover the truth? What would be our fate if we were to stumble across the historical paradox that we were being protected from? The story implies that we risk erasure, that we risk death. ("Borges," we should recall, was afraid to even see an image of "Pedro Damián" at the beginning of the story—any encounter with the truth is framed as dangerous from the very beginning.)

I argue, therefore, that it is not enough to understand the premise of the story, its central paradox, and the solution provided by Borges. The structure of the story requires us to approach it as a game that has not yet been played to completion. The simplest question that the story raises is: who is, truly, Pedro Damián? I will show that while Borges's story protects the reader from harm it also offers enough traces of the "original" true story to allow us to attempt to solve the riddle and, as we do so, experience a moment of peculiar concern regarding our own possible erasures. As in "Emma Zunz," the story allows for additional investigation to occur; doing so, however, requires that we do not remain satisfied with the answers provided to us in the story's conclusion.

It is useful to start with the narrator's assertion that the true protagonist—the man who fought as a coward at Masoller but was allowed to return and die as he wanted—would be remembered by us, by "Borges," as a *hero* within our shared time line. This individual would have died after performing valiantly at the Battle of Masoller. He would not, as the story notes, be named "Pedro Damián." Stating the problem in this way leads to an immediate possible solution: the story does, in fact, mention (twice) a man who fought in the Battle of Masoller who was, also, remembered as a hero. His name is Aparicio Saravia. It takes some outside historical knowledge to understand that Saravia—like the pseudonymous "Pedro Damián"—died heroically in the very same battle.

The first time that Aparicio Saravia appears in the text we read only that "[. . .] Pedro, a los diecinueve o veinte años, había seguido las banderas de Aparicio Saravia" ([. . .] Pedro, at the age of nineteen or twenty, had followed the flags of Aparicio Saravia [1:873]). The next mention comes from the colonel that "Borges" visits. Tabares speaks "de municiones que no llegaron y de caballadas rendidas, de hombres dormidos y terrosos tejiendo laberintos de marchas, de Saravia, que pudo haber entrado en Montevideo y que se desvió" (of munitions that never arrived and worn-out droves of horses, of exhausted men covered in dirt weaving marched labyrinths, of Saravia, who could have entered Montevideo but turned away [1:873–74]).

As we previously noted, Colonel Tabares explains that Saravia did not enter Montevideo in March of 1903 because "el gaucho le teme a la ciudad" (gauchos fear the city [1:874]). It is thus suggested that Saravia does not take Montevideo because he is afraid and, also, because he succumbed to this fear: because he was (at that moment) *a coward*. This is a very important detail. Courage and cowardice are the two possibilities that are at play within the heart of "Pedro Damián." The notion that Aparicio Saravia died heroically after a cowardly vacillation near Montevideo mirrors, precisely, the tension between the "two" versions of the obscured protagonist that we are presented with.[2] Both Saravia and Damián participate in the same transformation: a "coward" proves himself as a "hero" at a decisive moment.[3] It may be the case that they are the same character.

If "Pedro Damián" is a pseudonym designed to mask the identity of Aparicio Saravia, the story implies an alternate history in which *Aparicio Saravia* did not act heroically in 1904, one in which he was cowardly outside of Montevideo and equally cowardly in the Battle of Masoller. In this version of events he would have survived, grown old, and died in 1946. "Borges," in 1942, met this regret-filled man. His miraculous death, however, allows him to return to 1904 and die a hero, thus making the temporal distance between the "coward" outside of Montevideo and the "hero" who dies at Masoller 42 years instead of a year and a half.

One of the most direct clues that the story offers is the photograph that "Patricio Gannon" took of "Pedro Damián." The narrator tells us that he refuses to look for it and, also, that he erroneously had confused it in his memory with the image of the tenor Enrico Tamberlick. The image that Borges mentions is from a production of *Otello*. While *Otello* was an opera of Verdi's it was, first, an opera of Rossini's, an opera in which Tamberlick had the starring role.[4] An illustration of Tamberlick in the role of Othello (see fig. 7) should bear some resemblance to the image mentioned in the story. If, in fact, "Pedro Damián" is a literary pseudonym masking the identity of Aparicio Saravia, the popular images of Aparicio Saravia and Enrico

Tamberlick as Othello should appear somewhat similar to each other. If, however, they look radically different this would not support the notion that Aparicio Saravia is, indeed, the hidden protagonist. The image of Aparicio Saravia does, however, show a man who looks remarkably similar to the illustrated version of Enrico Tamberlick above (see fig. 8). Though finding similarities in appearance between Aparicio Saravia and Tamberlick as Othello is a subjective enterprise, both are presented in their disseminated images as austere, bearded men of battle. They look, in my opinion, alike enough to be confused.

It is unclear how much Borges knew of Aparicio Saravia. Borges explained to Emir Rodríguez Monegal in 1982 that he had never read the two detailed biographies on Saravia that came out in 1942 (one was written by Manuel Gálvez and the other by Monegal's father, José Monegal) and that his information on Saravia's life came mostly from his Uruguayan uncle, Luis Melián Lafinur (Rodríguez Monegal, *Jorge Luis Borges*, 370). It should be noted that this information seems to be contradicted, however, by Adolfo Bioy Casares's *Borges*, which describes a dinner in 1959 in which Borges ridicules Manuel Gálvez and his biography of Saravia in a fairly detailed manner (578). While we do not know about Borges' opinion of the other biography, Borges may have simply been trying to be polite in his conversation with its author's son.

As in "Emma Zunz," Borges has here introduced a literary puzzle in which certain details—proper names, places, descriptions—have been altered so as to create parallel, nested narratives. Precisely because of these purposeful alterations, the differences between the Pedro Damián described in the story and Aparicio Saravia are not sufficient to rule out the possibility that they represent the same individual. One potentially meaningful difference between Damián and Saravia in the story is that Damián is a young man from Argentina while Saravia is older, from Uruguay. This alteration, however, effectively gives the insignificant (invented) Argentinian the role of protecting the legacy of one of Uruguay's most heroic figures. The *artiguismo* mentioned by Borges is, in this way, turned on its head. The historical Uruguayan is represented as the true "coward" in the principal time-line while the fictional Argentinian is an invention designed solely

FIGURE 7 Illustration of Enrico Tamberlick in the role of Othello.
Photo: Bibliothèque nationale de France.

for our protection. By *posing* as a coward, the invented Damián is a
kind of fictional martyr; he is ridiculed while preserving the legend
of a hero who was not, in truth, particularly heroic prior to the fortu-
itous act of divine intervention. (This kind of reversal is particularly
attractive to Borges and can be seen in his story "Tres versiones de
Judas.")

It is important to underline the fact that the parallels (and even
the meaningful divergences) between Apararicio Saravia and Pedro
Damián that I have pointed to do not and cannot constitute "proof"
that Damián is in fact the pseudonymous mask of Saravia.[5] Yet instead
of placing the focus here on whether or not I have discovered the
"true" identity of Borges's protagonist, I would like to point, instead,
to the nature of the game of interpretation that makes this question

FIGURE 8 Aparicio Saravia.

possible. Borges has created a situation in which "knowing too much" is dangerous for the reader: the story is constructed as a safety mechanism that masks a dangerous paradox. Choosing to abandon the position of safety, risking "death" in the process, involves a mode of interpretation that, perhaps counterintuitively, requires a delicate balance between historical research and a literary "suspension of disbelief."

To read the story in this way necessitates that the everyday world (in which the illustration of Tamberlick as Othello does exist) be encountered through a logic that is plainly fictional (we seek out this image, ostensibly, for trace evidence of an erased historical figure). Borges facilitates this interpretive possibility by creating characters based on historical individuals. The "presence" of himself, Patricio Gannon, Aparicio Saravia, Pier Damiani, Emir Rodríguez Monegal, and others creates the sense that the story is engaged, to a degree, with our shared, everyday historical reality. If the narrator and characters had all been invented out of whole cloth the possibilities for investigation outside of the traditional limits of fiction would be fewer. It would not operate in (uncanny) conversation with our own sense of the everyday.[6]

While such an investigation is motivated by the possibility that Borges may have planted evidence about the obscured protagonist within his story, it is difficult to avoid recalling the warning from within the story: discovering the truth might result in a kind of death. As such, it is worth asking: what kind of death might this be? Macedonio Fernández may have suggested that as we search for the correct answer—the answer to the literary riddle—and consider our possible erasure, we are letting go of our traditional understanding of ourselves, allowing for other kinds of possibilities to enter our minds. To the degree to which we contemplate our literary deaths we become, almost, literary characters drawn into a logic that can be rewritten in diverse ways. Imagining this death, our death, from this perspective, is a kind of "sofocón" that places an everyday mindset in a state of crisis. Macedonio explains this idea in the following way:

> Si en cada uno de mis libros he logrado dos o tres veces un instante de lo que llamaré en lenguaje hogareño una "sofocación," un "sofocón" en la certidumbre de continuidad personal, un resbalarse de sí mismo el lector, es todo lo que quise como medio; y como fin busco la liberación de la noción de muerte: la evanescencia, trocabilidad, rotación, turnación del yo lo hace inmortal, es decir, no ligado su destino al de un cuerpo.[7]

If in each of my books I have created, two or three times, a moment that I might call an "asfixia," an "unease" within the certainty of personal continuity, a slipping away from the self of the reader, it is all that I desired in terms of a means; and as an end I seek liberation from the idea of death: the evanescence, transformation, rotation, and shifting of the self makes it immortal, which is to say that its destiny is not bound to that of a physical body.

Playing with the possibility of a deadly text might have the effect of freeing us, slightly or momentarily, from the idea that our identities and our experiences are exclusively tied to our bodies and to the logic of the everyday world.

One of the most peculiar aspects of this interplay between literary and historical realities involves the poem mentioned by "Patricio Gannon" at the beginning of the story. Emerson's "The Past" proclaims the immutability of history, stating that no one can reenter the past to "forge a name" or "alter or mend eternal fact." Not even the gods "can shake the Past."[8] The mention of the poem is a clear reference to an everyday understanding of historical truth and causality; the past remains inaccessible to alteration (though not, of course, to misrepresentation).[9]

A closer look at the context in which the poem is mentioned, however, provides other possibilities of interpretation. When "Borges" comes across "Patricio Gannon" in Mitchell's English Bookstore, he is sitting in front of Emerson's complete works. There are two possible editions that he could have been using: the 1883 edition or the 1903–4 Centenary edition. One of the features of the Centenary edition is that Emerson's son, Edward Waldo Emerson, wrote notes to accompany his father's texts. In the ninth volume, which features the collected poems, almost all of these notes are detailed and extensive. There is, however, one sole exception: the commentary included in the "Notes" section for Emerson's poem "The Past" (see fig. 9). Instead of providing concrete information, the note simply states, "no trace of the history of this poem remains." While Edward Waldo Emerson finds a tangentially related text to accompany this sentence, there is, clearly, nothing specific related to the text to share.[10] It may come as no small surprise that the preface to this volume, also written by

492   NOTES

Cupido.   *Page 257*. This, as well as the three poems
which precede it, was first published in *Selected Poems*. It
seems to have been written in 1843.

The Past. *Page 257*. No trace of the history of this poem
remains.
       Page 258, note 1. In the first pages of the essay on
Memory, in *Natural History of Intellect*, it is said of re-
morseful recollection of the Past: —
       "Well, that is as it should be. That is the police of the
Universe: the angels are set to punish you, so long as you are
capable of such crime. But . . . the day comes when you are
incapable of such crime. Then you suffer no more, you look
on it as heaven looks on it, with wonder at the deed, and with
applause at the pain it has cost you."

FIGURE 9 Edward Waldo Emerson, notes to his father's poem "The
Past," in the Centenary Edition of *The Complete Works of Ralph
Waldo Emerson*, 1903–4.

Edward Waldo Emerson, is dated March 12, 1904, the same year that
the volume was published and the same year, of course, as the death
of Aparicio Saravia and "Pedro Damián."

What is the significance of the fact that Borges includes a mention
of a poem about history that seems to *not have a history* in a volume
from 1904? Though the content of the poem seems to suggest that
the past is fixed, unalterable, the note at the end of the volume can
be read as expressing (within the context of Borges's story) that the
poem *itself* is without a past. Despite the fact that the poem states
that no one can "insert a leaf" into history, we can here be forgiven
for entertaining the possibility, especially given the context provided
by Borges's story, that this is precisely what has occurred. As a literary
(or as a literal) expression of the temporal contradictions that we have
been asked to contemplate, it can be read both as an antecedent for
the story and, paradoxically, as a result of it.

The title of "La otra muerte" (The Other Death) initially seems to
refer to the miraculous second death that Pedro Damián is allowed to
experience in 1904 (despite living until 1946). This death also belongs,
however, to the *hidden* protagonist of the story who, in fact, may be

"Aparicio Saravia." Whether or not this is true remains an open question and is, ultimately, not of the utmost importance. This is due to the fact that it is in the *search* for the identity of this protagonist and his obscured history (and not necessarily in its attainment) that the reader is placed in the contradictory position of reading historical documents through a literary logic, a logic that threatens death if the goal is finally met. It follows, accordingly, that one can reasonably ask whether it is *this* death, the death of the reader, that the title alludes to. By pointing always to "la otra muerte" Borges suggests a perpetually displaced center, a death that is always elsewhere. Assuring that the reader forms part of the cast of characters and historical figures that are threatened by nonexistence is a gift of inclusion, one that allows "la otra muerte" to be accessible to anyone willing to momentarily collapse the boundary between the world of fiction and the world of the everyday.

As a gift, however, this kind of death is circumscribed in very specific ways. It is situated between literary and historical contexts in a manner that allows it to function as a concept to be contemplated, an idea that bridges two different modes of thinking and being. Yet it does so without directly referring to the lived experience of dying or to the experience of witnessing a death close at hand. While it should be clear that this abstract death-of-the-reader is different in kind from the actual death of *any* living reader, it is useful to explore the limit between these two varieties of death in more detail. The best way of doing so is to closely examine a second set of enigmas that begin with the suicide of José Luis Ríos Patrón.

José Luis Ríos Patrón published his book *Jorge Luis Borges* in 1955. It is a general survey of Borges's work, glossing over his style, biography, and themes. It also includes short interpretations of many of his stories and some of his poems. In a section on the theme of "death" in Borges's work, Ríos Patrón writes the following:

> El futuro del hombre como conjunción de carne, huesos y espíritu, tiene un fin: la muerte. Vivimos sabiéndola un hecho inevitable, incoercible. Más que una presencia próxima a nosotros, la sentimos como un fluir misterioso. De ahí que Borges diga que la vida no es otra cosa que "muerte que anda luciendo."[11]

The future of mankind as a conjunction of flesh, bones, and spirit, has an end: death. We live knowing it as an inevitable, incoercible fact. More than just a presence alongside us, we feel it as a mysterious flow. Borges, as such, states that life is nothing more than "death on parade."

Ríos Patrón continues by differentiating between moments of existential death—in which one can feel the collapse of one's illusions, ideas, and hopes—and actual death, the permanent immobility of the body, mind, and spirit. He sees a connection between the two, imagining that the knowledge of death makes itself present when our mental attempts to construct permanence or safety collapse around their essential futility. Ríos Patrón also mentions the tendency of the spirit to recoil when contemplating the emptiness of its own death. He suggests that the conceptualization of the afterlife emerges as a reaction to this aversion, as a delusion masked as liberation. He notes, finally, that María Esther Vázquez explained to him that one of the principal aspects of deaths within Borges's fiction is that they are meaningful, pointing toward key ideas. They have significance.

About two years after the publication of the book, on September 13, 1957, Ríos Patrón shoots himself in front of a couple in a café. Borges finds out about Ríos Patrón's suicide almost instantly. Bioy writes that Borges had gone out with Silvina Ocampo for a walk. When Silvina returned she said to him: "¿Sabés lo que ha sucedido? Ríos Patrón se pegó un tiro. No sabemos si ha muerto. Cuando pasamos por Radio Nacional, en la calle Ayacucho, vimos el charco de sangre en la calle. Se pegó el balazo a las diez de la noche, delante de esa muchacha, que era su novia, y de Armani" (Do you know what happened? Ríos Patrón shot himself. We don't know if he's dead. When we walked by Radio Nacional, on Ayacucho, we saw the pool of blood in the street. He shot himself at ten o'clock at night, in front of that woman, who used to be his girlfriend, and Armani). Bioy Casares explains further: "La novia se llama María Esther Vázquez" (The girlfriend is named María Esther Vázquez).[12]

The next day, Bioy calls Borges, who informs him that Ríos Patrón died in the hospital the night before. Borges continues, explaining the situation in more detail:

> Los otros días trató de suicidarse en la Biblioteca. Clemente lo sujetó cuando ya estaba por arrojarse desde la galería alta que hay en el salón principal. Parece que celaba a María Esther. Cuando ella descubrió que la hacía seguir con un detective, rompió con él. [. . .] Entonces Ríos Patrón fue al café, los encontró allá y le dijo a María Esther que la pelea entre ellos era absurda, que debían casarse. María Esther le contestó que no, que la ruptura era definitiva. "Entonces no te voy a molestar más," dijo él, sacó el revolver y se descerrajó un tiro.[14]

> On other days, he tried to commit suicide in the library. Clemente grabbed him when he was about to throw himself from the high gallery in the main room. It seems as though he was spying on María Esther. When she found out that he was following her with a detective she ended it. [. . .][13] And so Ríos Patrón went to the café, found them there, and told María Esther that the fight between them was absurd, that they should get married. María Esther replied that no, the break between them was final. "In that case I won't bother you any more," he said, and took out the revolver and opened fire.

Bioy's journal goes on to describe how Borges learned that María Esther and Ríos Patrón had been romantically involved for a long time. They had fallen in love early and had been together for eleven years before the relationship ended. She had said that she wanted to marry him, a year earlier, in December, but he had rejected the idea, stating that he was too much of a womanizer, that he would make her suffer. Yet he had apparently changed his mind. One of the writers at the funeral commented that it was good material for a novel.

Where one might assume that the suicide of Ríos Patrón might inspire a degree of compassion, Borges and Bioy react to this suicide, initially, with ridicule. Borges states: "Esto es el arranque de mal humor de un desequilibrado; un acto contra María Esther; un acto de un muchacho vanidoso, presuntuoso, desagradable. Hasta el suicidio de las personas superficiales es superficial" (This is the fit of a mentally unstable person; an act against María Esther, the act of a vain, presumptuous, unpleasant young man. Even the suicides of superficial people are superficial). Bioy concurs: "Qué extraño que este muchacho tan trivial de pronto haga esta pirueta y quede dignificado por la muerte" (How strange that this completely trivial young man suddenly pirouettes and finds himself dignified by death).[15] The suicide of the reader, in this very real situation, is a stupid, offensive act that, for them, communicates nothing more than the ridiculousness of its author.

The story, however, soon becomes a bit more complicated. After the suicide of Ríos Patrón, Borges and María Esther Vázquez begin to see each other regularly; she helps him as an assistant and they eventually collaborate and travel together. Around 1963 Borges informs Bioy that he is in love with her. In 1964, María Esther Vázquez's book of stories *Los nombres de la muerte* appears with a prologue written by Borges; it closes by stating that she "ha sentido hondamente el central enigma de la muerte y cada uno de sus cuentos ilustra alguna de las formas inagotables de esa cotidiana acechanza" (has deeply felt the central enigma of death and each of her stories illustrates one of the inexhaustible forms of its daily stalking [4:162]).

According to Bioy, Borges told María Esther that he wanted to marry her, that he had lots of money in the bank and that they would be comfortable. She replied that there was someone else. Nevertheless, Borges believed that things could change, that there still might be hope. He suffered thinking about these possibilities and, every once in a while, opened up to Bioy about it. Once, he said: "Parece un destino circular al que estoy condenado. Esta situación se repite, cada tantos años. Para consolarme me digo que las otras mujeres, que olvidé, fueron tan importantes como ésta" (It is as though I am condemned to a circular destiny. This same situation repeats itself every few years. To console myself I say that the other women, whom I forgot, were just as important as this one).[16]

A few months later Bioy writes that, in a complete change of fortune, María Esther had asked Borges about the possibility of marriage. Borges rejoiced. The other man was still in the picture, but the shift that Borges has hoped for had seemingly come to pass. There was celebration and champagne. Yet everything, once again, fell apart. Bioy, recalling the night that Borges told him that the marriage would not take place, remembered that his friend described an anger building inside himself, a sense of being wronged. Borges told him that, under the right conditions, he could see his own capacity for cruelty. Before leaving that night, Borges stated that with impunity, we are all cruel: with the person who loves us, with our parents, with our brothers and sisters.[17]

Years later, Borges and Bioy write a story titled "La salvación por las obras," which was published in *Nuevos cuentos de Bustos Domecq* (1977). Its plot develops around a man named José Carlos Pérez who becomes increasingly frustrated due to a series of rejections by a female character. This man, referred to as "El Baulito," courts a woman that he is not attracted to in order to make someone else jealous. Yet she does not respond as expected: instead of being flattered by the attention she seems unmoved and demands better gifts. Flowers give way—per her demands—to jewelry and then, finally, to cash. She rejects him at every turn and yet he persists, perplexed that she is unaffected by his overtures. Eventually, through his entourage, El Baulito proposes marriage; his lawyer demonstrates that he has a lot of money in the bank, that they could live in comfort together. She rejects the offer but not without pocketing more money. The story ends with an explosion of superficiality and delusion and egomaniacal frustration: El Baulito, overwhelmed, shoots himself. The woman's name is María Esther.

One way of understanding the story is as a sarcastic, jarring parody of the violent suicide discussed by both authors above. Even at the funeral of Ríos Patrón writers had discussed the narrative possibilities of his demise.[18]

When Ríos Patrón had written about the theme of "death" in Borges, he had focused on the idea that the deaths narrated were all significant, that they had specific, accentuated meanings within their stories. María Esther Vázquez had, he wrote, helped him to understand this. It is disconcerting to consider that his own death—a suicide performed in front of María Esther Vázquez herself—became a death narrated within a story of Borges and that it, too, was given significance within the story's plot. Yet, in this particular case, the death of "El Baulito" seems to be highlighted for its absolute lack of meaning. It is very possible to come to the conclusion that Borges and Bioy wrote a story that culminates in a death significant for its lack of significance, its ridiculousness. Which, in a macabre sense, both substantiates and undermines Ríos Patrón's interpretation.

Upon closer examination, however, this idea changes shape. There are certain ways that the character El Baulito does not correspond with Ríos Patrón. For example, María Esther was not—according to Bioy—truly courted by him. Ríos Patrón stalked her, it seems, when their long relationship was coming to an end and she tried her best to distance herself from him. She did not continuously tell him that she was uninterested while sending him signals that she wanted more gifts, more social contact. Borges, on the other hand, persisted in his efforts to court María Esther for months while perceiving what he understood, at least, as conflicting messages. For this reason, I believe that it makes far more sense to read El Baulito as a composite character representing both Borges and Ríos Patrón. Both reside within this one fictional character. El Baulito is, in this sense, a small textual *baúl*: a memory trunk in which the author and his deceased reader somewhat uncomfortably share imaginary space.

The male protagonist, in any case, is protected pseudonymously, masked in a way that allows him to be potentially inhabited by multiple people. The story does not extend the same courtesy of anonymity, however, to María Esther Vázquez. On the contrary, she is readily identifiable to anyone in Borges and Bioy's social circle, which, given the traumatic event of witnessing her ex-partner's suicide, makes the decision to include her name especially jarring.

Borges stated to Bioy that, with impunity, anyone can be cruel, even to the people they love. While it is not possible to know the full social and personal context at work here, publishing a text that directly names María Esther while referencing Ríos Patrón's suicide and (less directly) Borges's own failed courtship is, at the very least, an act of callous disregard. The tone of the story—which is sarcastic and mocking—makes its connection to the real events described here even harder to understand. Borges may have found the impunity that he mentioned to Bioy within the ambiguities of fiction and shared authorship. The result is a text that, as best as I can tell, uses complex strategies of representation to cruelly exact a kind of literary revenge on a woman that Borges came to resent.[19]

Not entirely unlike Ríos Patrón, Borges seems to have displayed his anger publicly after figuring out how to avoid taking direct responsibility for it. Finding refuge in fiction is, nevertheless, a far safer escape than disappearing into suicide, which makes the title of the story, "La salvacíon por las obras," work in multiple registers. This title could be translated both as "salvation through deeds" and "salvation through works [of art]"; what separated Ríos Patrón and Borges in this instance is that one man chose to express his anger through a violent act of self-destruction and the other through the controlled, "virtual" violence of a work of fiction. "Actual" death (to use Ríos Patrón's terms) thereby meets "existential" death.

Turning back to Ríos Patrón's book on Borges we see that it carried the following dedication in its initial pages:

A MARÍA ESTHER VÁZQUEZ GRANDE
Siempre.

TO MARÍA ESTHER VÁZQUEZ GRANDE
Always.

Which means that the author dedicated both his suicide and his book to the very same person.

María Esther Vázquez eventually married Horacio Armani, the man she was with at the café the night of the suicide in 1957. She also wrote a book—*Borges: Esplendor y derrota* (1996)—in which she decided not to mention any of these events.

Borges, before he proposed marriage to María Esther Vázquez, dedicated a text to her titled "Poema de los dones."[20] Its first version was published in *Atlántida* in 1959.[21] In the poem, Borges writes about being blind and surrounded by books. He describes the out-of-reach paradise of the National Library, which he heads at the time, as a textual amalgam of East and West.

Enciclopedias, atlas, el Oriente
y el Occidente, siglos, dinastías,
símbolos, cosmos y cosmogonías
brindan los muros, pero inútilmente. (2:198)

Encyclopedias, atlases, the Orient
and the Occident, centuries, dynasties,
symbols, cosmos and cosmogonies
offer by the walls, but in vain.

The poem is known for describing the irony of being awarded the directorship of the National Library while being unable to read any of its books. Yet it also points to another experience: the sense of closeness that Borges is able to feel with an earlier director of the library who was, also, blind.

In this case a profound connection emerges from, interestingly, the *inability* to read. Instead of encountering an author by interpreting their published texts, Borges joins his uncertain footsteps with those of Groussac, who he imagines tracing a similar path through the inaccessible library. I am not sure if Borges ever read anything by Ríos Patrón but it is difficult to encounter these verses without thinking of the way in which they both also travelled, for a short time, a similar path.

Al errar por las lentas galerías
suelo sentir con vago horror sagrado
que soy el otro, el muerto, que habrá dado
los mismos pasos en los mismos días. (2:199)

Wandering through the slow galleries
I tend to feel the vague and sacred horror
that I am the other, the dead man, who would have walked
the same steps in the same days.

The poem's dedication to María Esther Vázquez makes it possible to consider the very real possibility that Borges, in addition to thinking of Groussac, thought also of Ríos Patrón while writing this poem. After hearing of his suicide, after all, Borges immediately recalled how Ríos Patrón tried to kill himself in the National Library. Clemente, Borges had said, prevented Ríos Patrón from throwing himself off of

FIGURE 10 Photograph of the interior galleries of Argentina's Biblioteca Nacional on calle México.

one of the "slow galleries" mentioned above (see fig. 10). Writing that verse and dedicating it to María Esther Vázquez *without* thinking of her deceased partner seems highly improbable, all the more so if he was beginning to feel attracted to her.

Yet if Jorge Luis Borges and José Luis Ríos Patrón travelled a similar path—of infatuation, suffering, rejection, anger, and cruelty—they walked it in two radically different ways. Borges invented a fictional suicide for himself to inhabit; Ríos Patrón took out a gun, and pulled the trigger.

The two deaths described in this chapter—the death refracted within "La otra muerte" and the death narrated in "La salvación por las obras"—are, as we have seen, multiple. Each refers to multiple bodies, possibilities, and concepts that complicate the divisions between reality, imagination and fiction.

In "La otra muerte," death is offered as a gift, as a way for the reader (any reader) to travel deeper within the text. The story asks us if we are willing to take the internal logic of the story seriously enough to contemplate our own risk of dying as a result of our interpretation. To answer in the affirmative is to refuse a passive relationship with the text and turn toward the everyday world with a literary logic (and therefore, one could also say, within a fictional identity). Doing so opens up possibilities of discovery and inquiry, mirroring Borges's invention of "Borges" with the creation of a "reader" whose life is truly at risk. The story, in this way, reframes the act of interpreting literature. Instead of presenting it as the act of encountering an invented text from the stability of the everyday world, it inverts the process, allowing the reader to act as one who has been altered, transformed by fiction. Readers are turned into writers, into (at least) participants in a game that continues outside of the limits of the story. By asking us to contemplate our own "deaths," by momentarily loosening our unstated beliefs in the limits of our identities as readers, Borges indirectly gestures to the kinds of freedom that fiction can offer. To imagine oneself dying a literary death is also to imagine a literary life that exists outside the desires and constraints of the everyday.

"La salvación por las obras" also points to the literature as a tool that allows a reader or a writer to experience invented parallel lives, to die without dying, to transform the limits of reality at its most difficult or restrictive moments while, also, sharing this path with others. Yet there is a way in which its sarcastic, parodic tone combines with an obscured cruelty directed against María Esther Vázquez to remind us that these literary possibilities, such as they are, do not correspond to the logic of sacred texts. Each is provisional, imperfect. While they might lead to revelations, to glimpses of what might lie beyond the visible order of things, they all inevitably remain in the complex, often disconcerting realm of the human.

Epilogue
In Case of Emergency, Burn Your Books

Ya basta amigo. Si quieres seguir leyendo, transfórmate
tú mismo en el libro y en la doctrina.

Enough, my friend. If you want to continue reading,
transform yourself into the book and into the teachings.

—**"Del viajero querubínico,"** Angelus Silesius (from Borges
and Bioy Casares, *Libro del cielo y del infierno*, 126)

While I was working on the final version of this book I visited the
Harry Ransom Center in Austin, Texas. It houses a unique set of original documents related to Borges, including several of his journals.

As I went through the material, reading his drafts and scattered
thoughts, adjusting my eyes to peculiarities of his tiny script, I noticed
that I was, for the first time, seeing Borges working with (and working
through) the incomplete, the fragmentary, and the unresolved.

It was as though Borges had discovered Cortázar's exaltation of
playful disarray, his appreciation of the messiness and disjointedness
of being. Careful notes on astrological triads accompanied sets of
evocative quotes whose fragmentary nature resisted incorporation
within the three chapters of this book. One page described an imaginary book in terms of its capacity to function as a prism, as food, as

a mode of transportation, as clothing. A draft of an outline of a film suggested that astrology (with its triads?) might provide an underlying structure for the plot. On one page of "Místicos del Islam," Borges scrawls: "Lo diré burdamente: Nadie ha sido devorado, ni corrido, por la definición correcta de un tigre y no daríamos fe al caso de un buen lexicógrafo que quedara encerrado en su definición de una cárcel" (I will say it crudely: No one has ever been devoured, nor chased, by the correct definition of a tiger and we will not accredit the tale of a good lexicographer who found himself trapped inside his definition of a prison [3, obverse]).

It was possible, in a number of cases, to relate the material in Borges's journals to lines of inquiry within this book. Far more often, however, the most compelling fragments that I encountered floated along their own idiosyncratic trajectories. While they might one day intertwine with other related texts and ideas, becoming the seeds for future projects, they could also just as easily remain disconnected and incomplete.

There was one section in Borges's journals, however, that provided a more developed and contextualized set of ideas that was clearly relevant to my research. It was a handwritten draft of an unpublished essay titled "Místicos del Islam" (Mystics of Islam) that was, also, the main reason that I had made the trip to Austin. While I was able to utilize some of its content within the first chapter of this book, I realized that its real value does not exactly reside in what it reveals about Borges's knowledge of Islam or Islamic mysticism. Instead, I believe that the manuscript is important for the specific way that it falls apart at its conclusion. The essay begins confidently, with a strong, coherent structure but, after a few pages, dissolves into a set of disconnected asides related to Buddhism. As it loosens and frays, it reveals—I suggest—a crucial idea that Borges was trying (and failing, perhaps) to weave into his essay, an idea that is relevant to his larger literary project.

I want to share this abandoned attempt at closure, here, at the end of this book, because of the rebellious, disobedient spirit that it struggles to give voice to. Beginning this project with the claim that Borges imagined and invented a "literary theology" makes it especially appealing to end by highlighting the irreverence that I believe made such a project possible. Concluding with a borrowed, frayed conclusion is, also, a way for me to acknowledge the essential incompleteness of this project: it is clear that no work of interpretation can ever aspire to the fullness of a satisfactory resolution. This book offers what it can while awaiting the corrections, rejections, and critiques that it hopefully inspires in other readers and writers.

The draft of "Místicos del Islam" begins with Borges describing Islam in general terms. We read Borges note that Chesterton viewed Islam as a Christian heresy, that Dante similarly understood it as a rupture, an internal division within the larger context of Christianity. The essay, as one might expect after having read the first chapter of this book, describes the split between Christianity and Islam, in large part, as a war on images. It states that "el Islam fue una guerra contra los ídolos, un odio encarnizado de las imágenes, que llevó a sus prosélitos a proscribir todo arte representativo y a descubrir / idear el arte austero y abstracto de los arabescos" (Islam was a war against idols, a fierce hatred of images, which caused its followers to outlaw all representative art and discover / imagine the austere and abstract art of the arabesques [1]).

Despite this bellic language, Borges does not seem to imagine Islam as a religion in deep conflict with Christianity. Instead, underneath their differences, they echo one another. He writes:

> Una religión que proclama un Dios personal, un Dios único, una religión cuyos artículos fundamentales enseñan un Juicio Final, en el término de la historia, y después un infierno eterno o un cielo eterno, con demonios o ángeles, no difiere excesivamente de la cristiana—salvo en que falta el Cristo.[1]

> A religion that proclaims a personal God, a solitary God, a religion whose fundamental articles teach of a Final Judgment, at the end of history, and afterwards an eternal hell or an eternal heaven, with demons and angels, does not differ excessively from that of Christianity—save in terms of the absence of Christ.

Borges, in this sense, follows in the footsteps of Chesterton and Dante without, however, a religious interest in heresy or its absence.[2] Borges emphasizes a shared history and a shared set of discourses that he soon uses to bridge Christian and Islamic mysticism.

The essay traces Islamic mysticism back to the story of Muhammad's ability to channel divine language in the creation of the first written incarnation of the Qur'an. Borges suggests that Islam, from the very beginning, is interested in direct contact with the divine, with a kind of sacred intimacy that goes beyond the enactment of specific rites and the obedience of a set of rules. As Islam expanded to more urban areas—Baghdad and Cairo—he writes that different groups sought distinct ways of achieving such transcendence. He cites the diverse practices of Sufi orders and various monastic orders of dervishes.

Borges then turns his attention to *poetic* strategies of transcendence, seeking a counterpoint with examples from Spain and the Americas. We read how poets such as Mansur al-Hallaj ("Soy El que amo y El que amo es yo; somos un cuerpo dos almas" [I am the He whom I love and He whom I love is I; we are one body two souls]) and Bayezid Bastami ("De Dios fui a Dios, hasta que Estos gritaron de mí en mí: ¡Oh Tú / Tú Yo!" [From God I went to God, until They cried from me in me: Oh Thou! / Thou I!]) communicate ecstatic wholeness with strategic poetic confusions of an "I" and a "Thou" that echo the poetry of San Juan de la Cruz.[3]

As the essay builds in intensity, it suggests that this sense of transcendent union (between the poet and divinity) is often expanded in a pantheistic identification that involves a radical unification of all things and beings. Emerson and Walt Whitman thus conceptually join poets such as Rumi, who (in Borges's essay) exclaims:

> Soy el mástil, el timón, el timonal, el barco, el escollo; . . . soy la imagen, el espejo, el grito y el eco; . . . soy el Árbol de la vida y, en sus ramos, el papagayo; . . . soy el médico, el mal, el veneno, el contraveneno . . . ; la rosa y el ruiseñor que la rosa embriaga; . . . soy el cimiento y el tejado, el muro y su caída; . . . soy el ciervo, el león, el cordero y también el lobo; . . . soy la cadena de los seres creados, soy el anillo de los mundos. Soy lo que es y lo que no es.[4]

I am the mast, the helm, the helmsman, the ship, the reef; . . . I am the image, the mirror, the cry and the echo; . . . I am the Tree of life and, in its branches, the parrot; . . . I am the doctor, the illness, the venom, and the antidote . . . ; the rose and the nightingale that it intoxicates; . . . I am the foundation and the roof, the wall and its destruction; . . . I am the doe, the lion, the lamb and also the wolf; . . . I am the chain of created beings, I am the ring of worlds. I am what is and what is not.

This shift away from a direct encounter with an abstract God and toward a reappraisal of both one's own identity *and* one's relationship with perceived reality as a whole is clearly important to Borges. One can hear echoes of conversations between him and Macedonio Fernández in the ecstatic identifications of Rumi; the use of building repetition easily recalls the techniques Borges used to describe the alluring wonders of the Aleph.

At this point in the essay, Borges is working in a feverish counterpoint, leaping back and forth between Christian and Sufi mystics. They share, he suggests, the idea that the divine can be known through its relationship with its opposite (just as light is understood only in terms of darkness, the color red in relation with colors that are not red). Borges writes that this relationship between the everyday and the divine leads to the (Neoplatonic) idea that all of the essential aspects of worldly things and beings exist, in their ideal forms, within God. We read that this perspective often implies that everything and everyone desires to return to this ideal state, to return to their divine origin.[5] He provides examples of this impulse in Fray Luis de León and, also, Hafez.

The essay underlines the idea that, from the perspective of Sufi mystics such as Rumi, all of creation can be thought of as a text. The world is seen as a missive, as the authored representation of a God who simply wishes to be (imperfectly) known by (imperfect) beings. These beings wish, in turn, to know the perfect versions of themselves and their own divine origins. Borges writes: "Dios es la única realidad; también se dice que es la realidad esencial de cada una de sus creaturas. Una famosa tradición atribuye estas palabras a Dios: 'Yo era un tesoro oculto y quería ser conocido y por esa razón hice el mundo"

(God is the only reality; it is also said that he is the essential reality of every one of his creatures. A famous tradition attributes these words to God: "I was a hidden treasure and I wanted to be known and for that reason I made the world").[6]

Sufi mysticism is thus presented as a mode of interpretation, as a hermeneutic applied to a world-text (and to oneself) that stands between the reader and the divine Author (who contains, also, the essential reality of this reader). To learn how to properly *read* the world breaks down the everyday categories of the self, of others, and of known reality, replacing them with a perfect transcendent unity.

The relationship between this specific understanding of mysticism and Borges's own literary work is difficult to avoid. Especially, of course, given the carefully engineered transgressions of everyday concepts of identity, time, and mortality described throughout this book. Yet if Borges borrows from the transgressive capacity of theology in his writing, challenging these traditional limits within fiction, it is crucial to point out that he does so without offering a *perfectly resolved sacred truth* in exchange. Borges's stories are provisional, not holy. Instead of pointing toward divine perfection, Borges directs us to the capacities of the active, creative mind, suggesting new possibilities of being to enact and explore and break apart within literature. His project is thus set in perpetual motion; there is no consecrated wholeness (no symbol of consecrated wholeness) for his readers to revere. The Aleph, precisely due its entrancing allure, comes with a warning label. It is a trap.

After a paragraph about the imagery used in Sufi poetry, which mentions the poetic intertwining of eroticism and mysticism and lists some commonly used symbols, the essay begins to deteriorate. It mentions a mysterious man, the Qutb (El Eje), who wanders the earth unaware of his divinity. This figure is hastily linked to a version of the Jewish story of the Tzadikim Nistarim: thirty-six men whose collective virtue justifies the universe to God and who die, to be instantly replaced, if they ever discover that they are members of the group. The connections between ideas soon become looser, less coherent. Pivoting on the Sufi term "fana" (Borges describes it as the idea of an experienced "extinction" of the self) and its similarity to the idea of nirvana, the essay suddenly veers into Buddhism, describing two short anecdotes that seem to have almost nothing to do with the "Mystics of Islam."

The first anecdote involves a conversation between a Chinese emperor, in Nanking, and Bodhidarma.[7] The emperor describes the great works that he has done, the buildings that he has built and the temples that he has founded. Bodhidarma listens but ultimately shares the opinion that all of the emperor's contributions belong to the world of appearances—which is as insubstantial as a simple dream—and as such are ultimately worth nothing.[8] Nirvana, he says, is the result of the extinction of will and is not the result of any one purposeful act. He states further that "no hay una doctrina sagrada, porque nada es sagrado, o fundamental, en un mundo ilusorio. Los hechos y los seres son momentáneos y ni siquiera podemos afirmar si son o no son" (there is no sacred doctrine, because nothing is sacred, or fundamental, in an illusory world. Occurrences and beings are momentary and we cannot even affirm whether they exist or do not exist). The emperor asks who the man replying to him in this manner is and Bodhidarma, "fiel a su nihilismo" (faithful to his nihilism), says, "Tampoco sé quien soy" (Neither do I know who I am).[9]

It makes sense, I believe, to pause here to acknowledge the unusual move that Borges is making in this text. The essay began by tracing the origins of Islam, tying them to Christianity and demonstrating the parallel paths of each religion's mystical tradition. These traditions are then described—in my view—in a way that quietly highlights their parallels with Borges's own project (their mutual questioning of everyday reality and conventional ideas of selfhood through storytelling that imaginatively and strategically conjures a different dimension of experience). Yet the mystical traditions also diverge from Borges's project to the degree to which this different "dimension of experience" is *divine* as opposed to *literary*: his fiction and their theology stand on opposite sides of a chasm of belief, of sanctity. Just when it seems as though there is no way to resolve this distance, Borges finds a way to leap across (or into) the chasm by describing a mode of theological inquiry that eschews the very notion of the sacred.

The short anecdote that Borges utilizes preserves nearly all of the principles of mysticism that he had described (a radical questioning of reality, traditional social categories, perception, and identity through paradoxical, imaginative storytelling).[10] Yet it does so while refusing to offer a focal point for reverent belief. Borges's essay ends far away from Islamic mysticism, describing a theology without a concept of the sacred that is based, instead, on the cultivated awareness of impermanence and radical provisionality. The version of Buddhism that Borges describes approaches knowable reality and selfhood as, essentially, a set of overlapping fictions. Telling stories—especially unresolvable stories (such as Zen's famous koans)—is a way of bringing people closer to this mode of experience.

Beyond the visible representations of the divine (in text, or in art) lies a far more chaotic, unregulated dimension within which it is possible to create and recreate experience while acknowledging its essential provisionality, its chaotic flux and openness.

After providing an example of one of these unresolvable stories (Borges refers to it as an "enigma doctrinal"), the essay ends with what I can only describe as an act of liberating iconoclasm. When faced with texts and objects elevated above others as sacred, with objects that begin to exert a kind of power over those who value them, we read that one possible reaction is to take them off their pedestals, to burn them into ashes. "En los monasterios, arrojan al fuego las imágenes de madera del Buddha y destinan a usos innobles la Escritura sagrada, cf: 'La letra mata, pero el espíritu vivifica' [2 Corinthians 3:6]" (In the monasteries, the wooden representations of the Buddha are thrown into the fire and the sacred texts are used for ignoble purposes, cf: "The letter kills, but the spirit gives life" [2 Corinthians 3:6]).[11] With that, the essay ends.

The final reference to Christianity has the function of bringing the series of ideas back to the first concepts that Borges expressed: Christianity was positioned as the origin of Islam, which broke from it within an iconoclastic war on images. In his final move, Borges unites this iconoclasm with the Bible by way of Buddhism. The destruction of a sacred image (or a sacred text) is, here, no longer an act motivated by orthodoxical belief. Rather, it is intended to cut against orthodoxy, to challenge any notion of the sacred that fixes meaning in place. Holding tightly on to books or to objects can, we read, piously impede the freedom of the spirit.

As much as literature might lead to a kind of provisional liberation from the everyday limits we struggle against, when it is revered instead of simply read it can become its own kind of prison. In these cases, when fiction becomes sacred, Borges seems to suggest that we must be willing to set it alight. Without irreverence, rebellion, and resistance we become caught in repeating the gestures of others, pantomiming and reciting their orthodoxies. Many have told versions of the story of Witold Gombrowicz's departure from Argentina after his 24 years living there: asked as he was departing about any advice that he might have for Argentinian writers, he is alleged to have said "Maten a Borges" ("Kill Borges") before turning away from the crowd. Here, Borges seems to agree. In case of emergency, he says, burn your books, destroy your idols. And begin, then, to write in the direction of your own freedom.

Notes

INTRODUCTION

1. Unless otherwise specified, all direct quotations from Borges's work are from Borges, *Obras Completas* (with volume and page numbers given in parentheses after the quotation), and all English translations of Borges's writings are by the author.

2. In an interview in the magazine *Raíces* (February 1971, p. 37) cited by Saúl Sosnowski, Borges comments that the Kabbalists are interesting to him because it is as though they wrote not to facilitate understanding, to directly communicate, but instead, to insinuate truth and stimulate the search for it (*Borges y la Cábala*, 16).

3. Sylvia Molloy writes that there is a tendency in some scholars to read Borges's references without any serious consideration of the ways in which they are reframed and significantly altered within their literary contexts: "As the stability of the narrator, the character, and the rewritten text are questioned, so should the erudite quotes and literary allusions. Unfortunately, this is not always the case. Erudition in Borges is read to the letter, as a guarantee of textual authenticity and authority" (Molloy and Montero, *Signs of Borges*, 33).

4. Borinsky, *Theoretical Fables*, x, 133. Ronald Christ also draws attention to the way in which references must be read in the context of their position in the literary text and not on their own independent terms. He writes: "by allusion Borges introduces into his work other literary and philosophical writings which, by their very appearance in a new and often unexpected context, create that disturbing quality of novelty and unreality which Borges understands as the source of our sense of the fantastic" (Christ, *Narrow Act*, 34–35). Daniel Balderston reminds us that while a literary context is important, this does not mean that Borges's fiction is *only* interested in fictionality. He writes that "the interest of the stories is considerably heightened by attention to the historical and political elements, elements that can then be put in counterpoint to the others" (Balderston, *Borges*, 5), while acknowledging that all the elements involved are often quite unstable (17).

5. This sense of Borges's project is shared by many scholars, including Ana Barrenechea, who wrote the following in 1957: "Para socavar nuestra creencia en un existir concreto, Borges ataca los conceptos fundamentales en que se basa la seguridad del propio vivir: el universo, la personalidad y el tiempo" (To

undermine our belief in a concrete existence, Borges attacks the fundamental concepts on which certainty of life itself is based: the universe, identity, and time [Barrenechea, *Expresión de la irrealidad*, 19]). In this book, I draw special attention to the importance of a literary context for this sense of transformation, often making a distinction between the everyday sense of unreality that Barrenechea points to and the kind of unsettledness that is specific to the experience of reading literature.

6. Evelyn Fishburn writes that "Borges's stories are not simply fictionalized intellectual propositions of an abstract nature, but are rooted in expressions of human emotion which reveal a concern for human individuality hitherto rarely identified with his fiction" (*Hidden Pleasures in Borges's Fiction*, 133). This emotional foundation of Borges's work is an important part of the interpretations offered in this book and I agree with Fishburn with regard to the role that his own personal life plays in his literary work. John Sturrock offers a contrasting opinion, writing in *Paper Tigers* that "the circumstances of Borges's life intrude only in small ways on his fiction, and should not be dwelt on" (9).

7. Jaime Alazraki writes that in Borges's work "the apparent ambiguity is produced by the conjunction of several intuitions, by the overlapping of several motivations and sources that, like thin layers, were masterfully pressed into one tight and limpid fabric. One can simply enjoy the product in its outward result, or one can attempt to strip off those layers in order to comprehend fully the hidden richness embedded in the whole" ("Kabbalistic Traits in Borges' Narration," 84). The suggestion is that when one encounters indeterminacy and ambiguity in Borges's fiction, they are often simply the *effects* produced by overlapping, complex layers of meaning before they are understood. When these layers are investigated more closely, they can offer a legible set of ideas and gestures. Synonyms for "ambiguous" that frequently appear in literary criticism can, for this reason, include adjectives such as rhizomatic, paralogical, palimpsestic, etc.

8. Sylvia Molloy writes that it is common for scholarly readers of Borges to "hastily incorporate" difficulties "in order to get rid of them as quickly as possible," "underscoring a voracity that no longer recognizes its true appetite" (Molloy and Montero, *Signs of Borges*, 1). To begin to rediscover the hunger that one has for literature, she recommends reading with an appreciation of slowness, pausing in anticipation of both the pleasant and the difficult, while resisting the impulse to find an easy, reassuring solution.

CHAPTER I

1. Borges and Bioy Casares, *Crónicas de Bustos Domecq*, 116. All translations in the book are mine unless otherwise indicated. It is important to note that this statement about the Qu'ran is not true in the context of everyday historical reality. Finbarr Flood notes that the tradition of prohibiting the representation of living beings stems from the Hadith, not the Qu'ran ("Between Cult and Culture," 643). He additionally writes that the use of these proscriptions varied widely: there was no monolithic, static "policy" with regard to visual representation. The restrictions, he states, were based on "a concern with not usurping

divine creative powers and a fear of shirk, a term that came to mean polytheism and idolatry but originally meant associating other gods with God. Both suggest a concern with the materialism of worship in non-Islamic traditions" (643).

2. Finbarr Flood writes that exhibitions or essays that juxtapose "premodern Islamic art with modern Euro-American abstract art" often involve the assumption that "Islamic art is an art of abstraction," with no attention paid to historical or regional differences or to the "theoretical parameters of 'abstraction'" ("Picasso the Muslim," 43). The motivation behind these comparisons, Flood writes, is often to "illuminate the rehabilitation of perceived values of aniconism and antinaturalism in (and even *as*) modernism, if not modernity tout court" (43). The connection between abstract art (in the present) and Islamic art (of the past) is suggested within a pairing that remains relatively unquestioned. In this story, Borges and Bioy fabricate a set of ironic distances that complicate this enthusiastic juxtaposition—Tafas has only a tenuous connection with the Islam of his ancestors and is creating art that, while explicitly serving to respond to the limitations imposed by his understanding of aniconism, seems to grow out of the context of modern abstract art with or without the artist's explicit awareness. Instead of articulating an emphatic connection between modern art and premodern Islamic art, the story sarcastically hints at the tension between superficiality and sublimity that Flood observes in different Euro-American writers who become interested in the relationship between premodern Islamic art and the art of their day. It does so while directing the reader to a third destination that lies outside of the dichotomy of ornamental superficiality and mystical depth: the interpretive capabilities of a reader relying on their imagination over their ability to simply see.

3. Walid Sadek's installation "Love is Blind" (2006) uses a set of parallel ideas, presenting only the textual labels of paintings composed by Moustafa Farroukh, "a forbear of Lebanese painterly modernism and the artist responsible for one of Lebanon's first public exhibitions of easel painting in 1927" (Lenssen and Rogers, "Articulating the Contemporary," 1321). The piece was reimagined by Walid Raad, who eliminated the actual labels, replacing them with trompe l'oeil painted-on reproductions as part of his *Scratching on Things I Could Disavow: A History of Art in the Arab World* installation (2007).

4. The stories are listed according to the order in which they appear in this chapter.

5. I will use quotes to differentiate between "Borges" (the narrator) and Borges (the author) throughout the book.

6. These interpretations recognize the evocative power, reach, and scope of Borges's literary invention and positively associate it with his capacities as an author. John T. Irwin, for example, asks how it could be possible to understand the Aleph as anything other than "an evocation of the metaphysical (i.e., metaphorical) space of thought?" (*Mystery to a Solution*, 16). Similarly, Maurice Jean Lefebve (cited in English within Christ, *Narrow Act*, 11) writes: "Who does not see that each of Borges's stories, each of his short essays is an Aleph of the dream world? In concentrating an indefinite multiplicity of acts, suggestion and sensation onto a narrow textual surface, in pursuing enumeration with a taste

for the eternal, as well as in making each story capable of reflecting itself (in the way facing mirrors do), the author opens our minds to vertigo, to a problematic and inexhaustible magic, which is what one properly calls literature" (Roux and Milleret, *Jorge Luis Borges*, 224).

7. These questions are further echoed in Borges's 1951 essay "La esfera de Pascal," which traces the history of a specific idea: the metaphorical use of an infinite sphere "whose center is everywhere and whose circumference is nowhere" to represent God (at first) and, eventually, the natural universe that, devoid of divinity, terrified Pascal. The first version of the geometrical metaphor is attributed to the philosopher Xenophanes, who criticizes the way in which the Gods are portrayed through the use of anthropomorphic icons. In this anachronic Ancient Greek echo of Islam's aniconicity, Borges offers a vision of one God through the figure of an eternal sphere. Borges notes, further, that the very notion of an infinite sphere is a "*contradictio in adjectio*" (2:17) given the impossibility of visualizing it in a way that does not fix it into place. Yet he also suggests that its capacity to allow people to "intuit" a sphere that resists visual or even mental representation is a crucial part of its effectiveness as a metaphor, given our inability to behold or even easily define words like "God" or "universe."

The connection between the essay and "El Aleph" is buttressed by Borges's text "[La belleza no es un hecho extraordinario]," which states that

> El anillo es la forma de la eternidad, que abarca todo el espacio, y al abarcar todo el espacio abarca también el pequeño espacio que ocupa, y así en "El Aleph" hay un "Aleph"; porque esa palabra hebrea quiere decir círculo, y en ese Aleph otro Aleph y así infinitamente pequeño, esa infinitud de lo pequeño que asustaba tanto a Pascal.

> The ring is the form of eternity, which contains all space, and in doing so it contains, also, the small space that it occupies, which means that in "El Aleph" there is an "Aleph," because this Hebrew word means circle, and in that Aleph there is another Aleph and so on in the direction of the infinitely small, that microscopic infinitude that so terrified Pascal. (72)

This infinite and internally nested vision of the universe is also found at the end of Borges's essay "Pascal" (1952).

8. As Guillermo Martínez notes, "Borges" here references the idea that within the concept of infinity, one can imagine a particular set of infinite numbers (all natural numbers, for example) that logically contains another, nested group of numbers (all even numbers). Both of these sets (the natural numbers and the even numbers) are infinite in overall quantity but we can see that the even numbers represent only a part of the whole represented by the natural numbers . . . a part that is nevertheless not *less* than the whole given that both are, of course, infinite (*Borges and Mathematics*, 8). This internally nested quality was present in the description of the Aleph; in showing all points from all possible perspectives, it contained infinite views of the Aleph, all of which led to other (embedded) infinite lenses.

9. In "El Aleph," "Borges" describes this biblical angel whose four faces look out toward the East and the West, the North and the South, as an example of a composite, multiple figure used to represent divinity. Laura Rosato and Germán Álvarez, in *Borges, libros, y lecturas* (292-93), show that Borges's handwritten notes within his copy of August Rüegg's *Jenseitsvorstellungen vor Dante* demonstrate that he associated this angel with the angels described in Miguel Asín Palacios' *Dante y el Islam* (1927). Asín Palacios, in this book, describes how Muhammad and Gabriel encounter multitudes of angels whose bodies are covered in faces, each one singing divine songs of praise (51). Further, the idea that there was a significant connection between Dante and Islam may be a useful way to approach the connections between "El Aleph" and Dante's *Divine Comedy* suggested by scholars such as Roberto Paoli (*Borges: percorti si significato*), Jon Thiem ("Borges, Dante, and the Poetics of Total Vision") and Humberto Núñez-Faraco ("In Search of the Aleph"), among others. Rosato and Álvarez's book confirms that Borges possessed and read a copy of Asín Palacios' *Dante y el Islam* (1927) as well his *Huellas del Islam* (1941).

10. In an essay that predates the story ("Historia de los ángeles," 1926), Borges, citing Stehelin's *Rabbinical Literature* (1748), suggests that the variety of possible meanings of the word Aleph in the Kabbalah is illustrative of a system of belief that combines rationality with theology in a way that leads to a "fanatical" proliferation of meaning:

> Así la letra *alef* mira al cerebro, al primer mandamiento, al cielo del fuego, al nombre divino *Soy El Que Soy* y a los serafines llamados Bestias Sagradas. Es evidente que se equivocan de medio a medio los que acusan a los cabalistas de vaguedad. Fueron más bien fanáticos de la razón y pergeñaron un mundo hecho de endiosamiento por entregas que era, sin embargo, tan riguroso y tan causalizado como el que ahora sentimos. (1:214)

> In that way, the letter aleph gestures toward the brain, the first commandment, the heavens of fire, the divine name I Am That I Am and to the seraphim called Sacred Beasts. It is clear that those who accuse Kabbalists of being vague are mistaken. They were, rather, fanatics of reason and they created a world composed of serialized deification that was, nevertheless, as rigorous and causal as the one that we feel in the present.

11. Beginning the second-to-last paragraph of the story with the succinct pronouncement "[d]oy mis razones" (These are my reasons [1:932]) is a particularly direct and confident manner of preparing the reader for an explanation that never truly arrives.

12. The reference to Merlin's crystal ball, as the narrator suggests, can be found in Edmund Spenser's poem *The Faerie Queen* (1596). An illustrated manuscript of the Indian poet Amir Khusrow (1253–1352) currently at the Walters Art Museum shows a representation of "Alexander the Great's mirror," which is portrayed mounted on a tower in such a way as to allow him to see great distances. The mirror of Tarik Benzeyad, the general who led the conquest of

Visigothic Spain, can be found, according to the narrator, in Burton's *The Book of the Thousand Nights and a Night* (1885). The Cup of Kai Khosrow forms part of Persian mythology; it was the possession of a mythical king described in the *Shahnameh*, a poem by Ferdowsi (940–1020), that, when peered into, could reveal special visions. The "lanza especular" (mirrored lance) that the narrator asserts forms part of Capella's *Satyricon* is a bit puzzling. It seems to refer, in fact, to a magical sphere that is placed in front of the thrones of Jupiter and Juno. The text states that

> [. . .] they saw placed on a celestial platform before the throne a sphere with a great variety of carved figures; it had been so made out of a compound of all the elements that nothing that is believed to be in nature was missing from it. On it were all the sky, air, the seas, all the different things on earth and the barriers of Tartarus: cities, crossroads, every kind of living thing, in species and in genus, could be counted there. This sphere seemed to be an image and model of the world. The daily actions of each and all the people of all nations appeared in this as in a mirror which the Pythian used as he shaped the affairs of men. There Jupiter traced with his own hand those whom he wished to raise up or lay low, to be born or to die. (*Martianus Capella and the Seven Liberal Arts*, 2:26)

Lucian's mirror is (as the narrator explains) from his *Vera Historia*, which describes a trip to the moon during which he finds the mirror in a palace: "Moreover, I beheld another wonderful sight in the Palace. A vast mirror lies over a somewhat shallow well. Any one who descends into the well, hears all that is said amongst us mortals on earth; and any one who gazes into the mirror, beholds all the cities and nations as plainly as if he were present on the spot. On looking, I saw my friends and all my own country, but whether or not they saw me I cannot say for certain. The incredulous person who refuses to credit my statement will learn the truth of it if he will only some day visit the place himself" (*Lucian's Wonderland* [trans. Willson], 43).

13. The narrator's assertion that the Aleph of Daneri is "false" has been dealt with in a variety of ways. Humberto Núñez-Faraco, for example, interprets this statement as a judgment about Daneri's poetry. He writes that the poor quality of his poetic project leads the narrator to see him as a false poet and analogously call the Aleph false as well ("In Search of the Aleph," 622). Gordon Brotherston refers to this section of the story as a set of proofs that he dismisses as "erudite to the point of silly" ("Borges and Aleph," 235). Luce López-Baralt writes that the Aleph in the basement of Daneri is labelled as false "porque quedó inscrito en el lenguaje sucesivo, mientras que el 'verdadero' Aleph, oculto en el pilar de una mezquita del Cairo [. . .] nunca fue 'falseado' por la palabra" (because it was left inscribed in successive language, while the "true" Aleph, hidden within the pillar in a mosque in Cairo, [. . .] was never "falsified" by the word ["Jorge Luis Borges y el Islam," 188]). This logic sidesteps the visual or "optical" register presented by the narrator given that the labels of "true" or "false" no longer have to do with the Alephs themselves but rather, retroactively, with how they have been represented:

if one were to describe what was heard or felt at the Aleph in Cairo (in language), it would, according to this argument, also be rendered equally false.

14. One way of reading Borges's *Atlas* (1984) is as an indirect reply to the premise of Daneri's *La Tierra*. *Atlas*, as a series of poems and meditations based on the author's experiences travelling as a blind man accompanied by his partner through different countries, stands in direct contrast with *La Tierra*, a poem fashioned through a device that grants perfect sight only if one stays at home.

15. When Borges publicly praised the work of Ramón Gómez de la Serna in 1925, he described it, metaphorically, with the idea of an "Alef":

> ¿Qué signo puede recoger en su abreviatura el sentido de la tarea de Ramón? Yo pondría sobre ella el signo del Alef, que en la matemática nueva es el señalador del infinito guarismo que abarca los demás o la aristada rosa de los vientos que infatigablemente urge sus dardos a toda lejanía. Quiero manifestar por ello la convicción de entereza, la abarrotada plenitud que la informa. [. . .] Ramón ha inventariado el mundo, incluyendo en sus páginas no los sucesos ejemplares de la aventura humana, según es uso de poesía, sino la ansiosa descripción de cada una de las cosas cuyo agrupamiento es el mundo. Tal plenitud no está en la concordia ni en simplificaciones de síntesis y se avecina más al cosmorama o al atlas que a una visión total del vivir como la rebuscada por los teólogos y los levantadores de sistemas. (1:132)

> What sign might be able to communicate in its brevity a sense of Ramón's work? I would place upon it the sign of the Aleph, which in the new mathematics signals the infinite figure that contains the rest, or the compass rose that indefatigably urges its darts toward every horizon. I want to thus express the conviction of completeness, the bustling fullness that informs it. [. . .] Ramón has inventoried the world, including in his pages not the exemplary events of human adventure, as is poetry's tendency, but rather the eager description of each of the things that come together to form the world. This fullness is not found in harmony or in synthetic simplifications and it is closer to the cosmorama or the atlas than to a total vision of life like those sought after by theologians and the engineers of systems.

The book that Borges was praising is *La sagrada cripta de Pombo* (*The Sacred Crypt of Pombo*). The title refers to a café in which Gómez de la Serna would discuss his literary ideas with his group of friends and collaborators—the book itself is a collection of miscellany related to both café culture in general and Gómez de la Serna's set of associates. Leaving aside the actual text, reading Borges's review of it gives the impression of a project nearly identical to that of Carlos Argentino Daneri. One that, in private, Borges would mock. To Bioy Casares, Borges confessed: "Ramón es un buen escritor. Pero qué horror vivir en esa casa llena de postales, con la cripta sagrada de Pombo y con la muñeca de cera. Qué horror vivir en un mundo tan detallado y, como si eso fuera poco, duplicarlo aún en los libros" (Ramón is a good writer. But how horrible it must be to live in that house full of postcards, with its sacred crypt of Pombo, and with the wax doll.

How horrible to live in such a detailed world and, as if that weren't enough, to duplicate it further in one's books [Bioy Casares, *Borges*, 648]). Seeing this earlier Aleph-in-a-basement/crypt as a literary enterprise that Borges both praised and mocked is helpful to the degree to which it contextualizes the original Aleph as a less-than-glorious object constructed in the ridiculous (for Borges) aim of creating an inventory of the known world.

It is also useful to note that Borges has a similar set of reservations about James Joyce. Borges praises Joyce in a way that explicitly echoes his writing on Gómez de la Serna, writing that

> en las páginas del Ulises bulle con alborotos de picadero la realidad total. [. . .] La dualidad de la existencia está en él: esa inquietación ontológica que no se asombra meramente de ser, sino de ser en este mundo preciso, donde hay zaguanes y palabras y naipes y escrituras eléctricas en la limpidez de las noches. En libro alguno—fuera de los compuestos por Ramón—atestiguamos la presencia actual de las cosas con tan convincente firmeza.

> in the pages of Ulysses all of reality teems with the commotion of a circus ring. [. . .] The duality of existence is there; that ontological unease that is not awestruck by mere existence, but rather by being in this exact world, where there are hallways and words and playing cards and electric writing in the clarity of the night. In no other book—save those composed by Ramón—can we witness the actual presence of things with such a convincing tenacity. (1:73)

In private conversations with Bioy, however, Borges remarks: "qué error el de Joyce haber escrito un libro tan detallado" (what an error of Joyce's to have written such a detailed book [Bioy Casares, *Borges*, 298–99]). In his "Fragmento sobre Joyce" (1941), Borges deepens his critique: "A falta de la capacidad de construir (que los dioses no le otorgaron y que debió suplir con arduas simetrías y laberintos) gozó de un don verbal, de una feliz omnipotencia de la palabra" (Lacking the capacity to construct [which the gods did not grant him, forcing him to make up for it with arduous symmetries and labyrinths] he enjoyed the gift of language, a felicitous omnipotence of the word [*Borges en SUR*, 169]). Yet even this "gift of language" is mocked in "Joyce y los neologismos" (1939) for relying on "portmanteau words" (*Borges en SUR*, 164-166) that, when encountered on their own, often reveal themselves to be relatively uninspired puns or empty linguistic riffs: wordplay that does not ask very much of the reader or lead to any particular insight.

Joyce, then, emerges (for Borges) as a writer without a strong sense of how to construct a narrative who leans on verbal wordplay and a vague, vast, intense project of communicating a sense of the complex simultaneity of being in one's particular corner of the world. Daneri—as Thomas Rice has also suggested ("Subtle Reflections," 55)—embodies these criticisms (though, he points out, so might the younger Borges who sought to describe Buenos Aires, instead of Dublin, by drawing out some of its everyday surprises in poetry). Borges's complaints about Joyce's neologisms especially come to mind when Daneri, celebrating his own poetry, exclaims: "¿Y qué me dices de ese hallazgo, *blanquiceleste*? El pintoresco neologismo *sugiere* el cielo, que es un factor importantísimo del paisaje australiano" (And what do you have to say about that discovery, *celestivory*? The eccentric neologism *suggests* the sky, which is an extremely important factor in the Australian landscape [1:925]). Daneri also references Homer and Odysseus several times while pompously explaining the value of his own poetry, seemingly as a way of giving it more importance (echoing, perhaps, Borges's lack of enthusiasm when it came to the possible connections between Joyce's *Ulysses* and *The Odyssey* ["Fragmento sobre Joyce," *Borges en SUR*, 168). Other writers have found potential echoes between Daneri and Leopoldo Lugones (Franco, *Utopia of a Tired Man*, 354) as well as Oliverio Girondo (Williamson, *Borges*, 203).

16. Making the connection between the Aleph of Daneri and the mesmerizing devices of the Internet age is almost inevitable given the way in which Borges evokes the technological tools of his day. The ways in which smartphones are currently being used—in concert with Facebook, Twitter, Instragram, and Google—seem to strongly echo many of Borges's concerns.

17. When the Aleph is framed critically as one of Borges's greatest literary gifts to his readers, its negative connotations are often brushed aside. Borges, on the other hand, in an interview with Antonio Carrizo, refers to the Aleph as "un objeto mágico que solo sirve para producir la desdicha o la locura" (a magical object that only serves to produce misfortune or insanity [*Borges, el Memorioso*, 232]). Evelyn Fishburn brings both of these possibilities together, however, by suggesting that Borges both ridicules and elevates the Aleph in Daneri's basement so as to critique "humanity's persistent attempts to seek the truth of a universe known to be unfathomable" (*Hidden Pleasures in Borges's Fiction*, 117).

18. Evelyn Fishburn draws attention to this shift toward the aural in a way that suggests that Borges is treating each of the senses as opening toward a different universe. She writes that "the distinguishing feature of this latest microcosm is that it is a *sound*, thus adding the aural to the verbal and the visual, a move that can be seen as an imaginative interpretation of the possibilities of Cantor's Set Theory regarding the plurality of universes, with each of the senses representing not simply another manifestation of the universe but a completely different one. What is a believable proposition for the theoretical mathematician is satirized by Borges" (*Hidden Pleasures in Borges's Fiction*, 116). While I do not read this moment in the story as a satire of Cantor's ideas or their possible connection to a "many worlds" theory, I do find that the shift from seeing to listening is significant for the way it opens to a different version of the "world" that does not arrive without the effort of imagination. One that, further, the author was anticipating in his own life given the likelihood of his future blindness.

19. Ortega, Parra, and Borges, *"El Aleph,"* 39.

20. Lisa Block de Behar mentions the crossed-out mihrab in the manuscript copy of "El Aleph" without giving Islam much consideration as a source of specific and potentially relevant discourses for Borges. Instead, for her, the erased word "evokes the return to a primordial unity, to an archetype that engages the particularity of a place in a universal vision, of historical times in an eternity"

("Rereading Borges's 'The Aleph,'" 185). This interpretation forms part of an argument for the importance of "despatialization" in Borges, a process that renders geographical, national, and cultural discourses irrelevant. She writes, for example, that "it is the same to him whether a deed occurs in the territory that the geographers and literati call the pampa, or in the unnamed expanses of an unknown region of whose existence one learns only by way of the inclusion in an encyclopedia. That one comes from Cairo, Egypt, or Cairo, Illinois [. . .] does not alter the question" (173). While it is clear that Borges is interested in questions that transcend that which might be described as "exclusively" local, and is openly disdainful of the tendency to fashion "local color" so as to appeal to the tastes of a reader-tourist, I have found that Borges directly engages with discourses from other cultures, often transforming them in strategic ways that are specific to their contexts. This chapter suggests that it can matter, in short, whether something occurs in Illinois or in Egypt in Borges's stories.

21. Corbett describes the original structure as "a simple oblong room [. . .] ; the low roof no doubt supported by a few columns, which were easily stolen from the nearest villages, or from the ruins of Memphis, a few miles south on the other bank of the Nile; the walls probably of baked, but very possibly only unbaked bricks, and unplastered; the floor pebble-strewn; the light probably supplied, as in the great colonnade at the present day, through square apertures in the roof. It possessed no minarets, or other attractive outside feature; no niche, nor any other internal decoration; the very pulpit was destroyed after a short time" ("Art. XV.," 767).

22. Julio Ortega points in the direction of this history in the following footnote in his article "El Aleph y el lenguaje epifánico": "Vale la pena recordar que la mezquita de Amr es bien conocida por su mihrab" (It is worth remembering that the mosque of Amr is well known for its mihrab [464]).

23. Whelan, "Origins of the Miḥrāb Mujawwaf," 209–10.

24. Ibid., 210; Corbett, Art. XV., 773.

25. Borges mentioned in an interview with Ronald Christ that he would often look through this edition at the Biblioteca Nacional when he was younger, out of shyness, since it was a reference book and did not require interaction with the librarian ("Art of Fiction," 148). In 1929, he bought a second-hand set of the eleventh edition with a portion of the money from the Premio Municipal awarded to his *Cuaderno San Martín* ("An Autobiographical Essay," in *Aleph and Other Stories*, 233).

26. The more common spelling of the English version of the historian's name is "Al-Maqrizi."

27. Di Giovanni points out that the mentioned title of Burton's book is erroneous: the actual book by Burton is *The Lake Regions of Central Africa* (*Lesson of the Master*, 202–3). I will argue that Borges may have alluded to Burton's actual text toward the end of this chapter.

28. In Lane's version, the individual performing the ceremony asserts that only "a boy not arrived at puberty, a virgin, a black female slave, and a pregnant woman" were able to actively participate in the ceremony" (*Account of the Manners and Customs*, 369).

29. Borges's word choice here is potentially relevant given the manner in which the term "aborrecible" is also used to describe the "artificial" reproduction of living beings in "El tintorero enmascarado Hákim de Merv" and "Tlön, Uqbar, Orbis Tertius." These stories will be discussed later in this chapter.

30. The art historian Estelle Whelan suggests that the representational restrictions of Islam were closely related to the use of the mihrab. She argues that the mihrab serves as an empty space designed to "represent" the presence of Muhammad in prayer facing Mecca. In lieu of an iconographic portrayal, the mosque uses a framed absence that allows followers to contemplate the "intangible presence" of the Prophet. She also writes that the mihrab likely altered a tradition of iconic representation in a way that conformed to the prohibitions of representation in Islam: "as for the choice of the niche form, it should occasion no surprise: as Diez remarked, the semicircular niche was a cliché of late antique architectural decoration. Evidence from later periods does suggest, however, that uninhabited niches were sometimes used in public settings as substitutes for direct representation of princes, which would have been considered inappropriate. It is possible that similar considerations influenced the choice of the semicircular niche, widely used in the period as a frame for statuary, in a context in which a reference to Muhammad was to be understood" ("Origins of the Miḥrāb Mujawwaf," 215).

31. David Ling also points to the way in which Yakub sees (mostly) what he desires and not, importantly, what an external author has created ("Manners and Customs of Literary Appropriation," 91). This supports the notion that the allegory is not meant as a direct reference to the literary experience but rather, in a negative sense, as a clarification of what it cannot do.

32. From this point forward, as a way of emphasizing the notion that Borges is using the word "Islam" to refer to an altered theology designed to reinforce his own literary ideas (and not to the historical religion), it will appear within quotes as "Islam" wherever the distinction is appropriate.

33. Abós, *Macedonio Fernández*, 100.

34. Ibid.

35. Isaacson, *Macedonio Fernández*, 71–72.

36. Álvaro Abós writes that these café conversations involved, among others, Julio César and Santiago Dabove, Carlos Ruiz Díaz, Enrique Fernández Latour and, later, Xul Solar (*Macedonio Fernández*, 100). Abós reminds us that their relationship was not limited to conversations and debates; Borges and Macedonio worked together within *Proa* and *Martín Fierro*, literary magazines that Borges launched with other collaborators.

37. Fernández, *Teorías*, 236.

38. Borges's essay "Después de las imagenes" was published in 1925, the same year as José Ortega y Gasset's "La deshumanización del arte." Ortega is interested in finding connections between the different forms of Modernist artistic expression, joining Debussy, Pirandello, Joyce, and Picasso (among others) under his category of "dehumanized art," art that works at a distance from the immediate, common experiences of life and its intuitive pleasures in order to represent ideas, internal feelings, and concepts to an elite audience. Cubism and Expressionism,

in his view, break away from the aims of representational art to (in fact) *attack* reality as it is intuitively experienced.

> Lejos de ir el pintor más o menos torpemente hacia la realidad, se ve que ha ido contra ella. Se ha propuesto denonadamente deformarla, romper su aspecto humano, deshumanizarla. Con las cosas representadas en el cuadro nuevo es imposible la convivencia; al extirparles su aspecto de realidad vivida, el pintor ha cortado el puente y quemado las naves que podían transportarnos a nuestro mundo habitual. ("La deshumanización del arte," 365)

> Far from going toward reality in a somewhat ineffectual manner, one sees that the painter goes directly against it. The proposal is to purposefully deform it, break its human aspect, dehumanize it. It is impossible to live among the objects represented in the new painting; by uprooting their connection to lived reality, the painter has destroyed the bridge and burned the ships that might have transported us to our habitual world.

Borges, we should note, is not interested in maintaining the rigid dichotomy between "reality" and "unreality," between the "human" and the "inhuman" that Ortega articulates here. Following Macedonio Fernández, he suggests that reality includes fiction, and that literary experience is but one mode of being in the world.

Ortega's essay is potentially significant (at least as a foil for Borges) in that it then draws a parallel to religious traditions of rejecting visual representation in a brief section titled "Iconoclasia" (Iconoclasm). Here art is presented as an expression of "asco," of disgust, toward living forms and living beings.

> No parece excesivo afirmar que las artes plásticas del nuevo estilo han revelado un verdadero asco hacia las formas vivas o de los seres vivientes. [. . .] La revolución contra las imágenes del cristianismo oriental, la prohibición semítica de reproducir animales [. . .] tiene, sin duda, junto a su sentido religioso una raíz en la sensibilidad estética. [. . .] En el arte nuevo actúa evidentemente este extraño sentimiento iconoclasta y su lema bien podía ser aquel mandamiento de Porfirio: *Omne corpus fugiendum est.* Y claro es que se refiere al cuerpo vivo. ¡Curiosa inversion de la cultura griega, que fue en su hora culminante tan amiga de las formas vivientes! ("Deshumanización del arte," 3:377-378)

> It does not seem excessive to assert that the plastic art of the new style has revealed a true disgust for living forms or living beings. [. . .] The revolution against images of Eastern Christianity, the Semitic prohibition of representing animals [. . .] has, without a doubt, a grounding in aesthetic sensibility, along with its religious significance. [. . .] In the new art this strange iconoclastic sentiment is evidently operating; its slogan could very well be that commandment of Porphyry: *Omne corpus fugiendum est.* And it

is clear that he is referring to the living body. A curious inversion of Greek culture, which at its height was such a friend of living forms!

While Islam is not mentioned, the iconoclasm and aniconism that Borges associates with it are given special emphasis.

As Peter Earle has noted ("Ortega y Gasset in Argentina," 475), Borges did not express, in general, very much affinity with the ideas of Ortega y Gasset. "La deshumanización del arte," in fact, was criticized (rather reductively, as Judith Podlubne points out ["Borges contra Ortega," 172]) by Borges in his 1940 prologue to Adolfo Bioy Casares's *La invención de Morel*. Nevertheless, in 1925, both Borges and Ortega turn toward their contemporaries' practices of artistic expression and consider the degree to which a theological framework might be useful. The fact that Borges, years later, encounters the perceived aniconism and iconoclasm of Islam as a way to "enter" into the complex visuality of literature suggests a possible link between the ideas expressed in these two essays. It is speculative, but one can imagine Borges deciding to take on iconoclasm and aniconism not as a way to "dehumanize" his art, but, instead, as a tool to render it more attentive to the human capacities of imagination and artificial invention.

39. In conversation with Antonio Carrizo, Borges says that he often approaches theological texts with the same set of intentions that he uses to read fiction.

> Eso quiere decir, que si yo he leído la *Dogmática*, del teólogo lutherano Rothe, la he leído, yo creo, con el mismo impulso que me ha llevado a leer y releer *Las mil y una noches*, o el *Orlando furioso*, de Ariosto: buscar lo maravilloso. Salvo que es mucho más maravilloso lo maravilloso de la teología que lo maravilloso de la mera literatura, o de la poesía. (Borges and Carrizo, *Borges, el Memorioso*, 252)

> It means that, if I have read *Zur Dogmatik*, by the Lutheran theologian Rothe, I have read it with the same impulse that compelled me to read and reread *The Thousand and One Nights*, or Ariosto's *Orlando Furioso*: to search for the marvelous. Except that the marvelous of theology is far more marvelous than the marvelous of mere literature, or of poetry.

40. See Francine Masiello's essay "Lenguaje e ideología" for a description of some of these contradictions. She writes that

> Macedonio afirma y niega alternativamente el yo como principio organizador de la realidad. A veces defiende al Ego en su rol de agente estructurador de las percepciones; en forma contradictoria, admite la libertad ilimitada de un Ego fragmentado en juego. Como lo sugiere el título de su libro [*No toda es vigilia la de los ojos abiertos*], la conciencia no puede relacionarse con solo el estado de vigilia. (522)

> Macedonio alternately affirms and negates the self as the principal organizer of reality. At times, he defends the Ego in its role as a structuring agent of

perception; in a contradictory sense, he admits the unlimited freedom of a fragmented Ego at play. As the title of his book [*Not Everything is Wide-Eyed Vigilence*] suggests, consciousness cannot solely be associated with the state of wakefulness.

41. Borges's reliance on "Islam" to create this literary theology involves a specific, targeted set of purposes: to allow his literary characters to insinuate, encounter, or even reject the artificiality of their provisional existence through a critical encounter with the sensory (and especially the visual) register of their perceived reality. This is done in a way that brings the textuality of the story (and the active imagination of the reader) to the forefront. Other theological traditions—Judaism, Christianity, Hinduism, Buddhism, etc.—have also been referenced and reframed by Borges in myriad ways. While these theological traditions (especially Judaism and early Christianity) each have their own relationships with divine texts and aniconism, Borges nevertheless draws principally from "Islam" for this part of his literary project, perhaps because of the way he associates it with a stronger iconoclastic approach more appropriate for his intended critique (an idea he expresses in his manuscript essay draft "Místicos del Islam").

42. In the broadest sense, Borges found that certain aspects of religious belief corresponded well with the nature of literary "existence." For example, he states that while the practice of looking for prophetic signs tends not to bear much fruit in the context of the everyday world, it is a practice that corresponds perfectly with the norms of literary texts. After commenting on José Antonio Conde's *Historia de la dominación de los árabes en España* in "El arte narrativo y la magia" (1932), he writes:

> Ese recelo de que un hecho temible pueda ser atraído por su mención, es impertinente o inútil en el asiático desorden del mundo real, no así en una novela, que debe ser un juego preciso de vigilancias, ecos, y afinidades. Todo episodio, en un cuidadoso relato, es de proyección ulterior. (1:512)

> The worry that a feared event might be encouraged to come to pass by its very mention is inappropriate or useless in the Asiatic disorder of the real world, but not in a novel, which should be a precise game of observations, echoes, and affinities. Every episode in a carefully crafted story relies on future projection.

The fact that his chosen example also involves Islam does not limit the idea, of course, to this religion. Borges notes at the end of the essay that he has mentioned two causal processes: one belonging to the everyday (which is the "resultado incesante de incontrolables e infinitas operaciones" [incessant result of uncontrollable and infinite operations, 1:512]) and the other to the "lúcido y limitado" (lucid and limited, 1:512) context of magic, "donde profetizan los pormenores" (where details are prophetic, 1:512). The story closes with two crucial sentences: "En la novela, pienso que la única posible honradez está con el segundo. Quede el primero para la simulación psicológica" ("In a novel, I believe that the only honorable possibility lies with the second. May the first be left for psychological simulation," 1:512). Fiction is, in this way, positioned far above the 'mere' mimetic representation of a psychological, subjective inner world; it, instead, involves a new set of rules, expectations, and possibilities that participate in a magical logic wholly appropriate to its unique ends.

43. Finbarr Flood writes that individual acts of iconoclasm should ideally be interpreted within their specific contexts, especially given the manner in which they are often misleadingly framed in journalistic or historical accounts ("Between Cult and Culture," 641).

44. Where the book of Genesis has the beginning of human language arise from the mind of Adam, the Qur'an asserts that language is divine. Adam is quite literally faced with the choice of being true to the divinity of language or to corrupt it with his lies. The book of Genesis states that "out of the ground the Lord God formed every beast of the field, and every fowl of the air; and brought them unto Adam to see what he would call them: and whatsoever Adam called every living creature, that was the name thereof" (Gen 2:19). Comparing this with the Qur'an, one finds: "He taught Adam the names of all things. Then He displayed them to the angels and said: 'Tell me the names of these things, if you are truthful.' They said: 'Glory be to You! We have no knowledge except what You taught us. You! You are All-Knowing, All-Wise!' God said: 'O Adam, reveal to them their names.' When Adam revealed their names, God said: 'Did I not tell you that I know the Unseen of the heavens and the earth? That I know what you make public and what you hide?'" (2:31–33).

45. It is also worth pointing out that while the link between divinity and language exists also within Judaism, Borges draws a distinction between the two belief systems along these terms in his 1932 essay "Una vindicación de la cábala." He writes that the interpretive methods of the Kabbalah are based on the idea that human beings can become impersonal secretaries of God through mechanical inspiration, allowing for the expressed perfection of the divine to enter into the text. There is, in this sense, a chronologically intuitive process of divine author-scribe-text. The followers of Islam, however, "pueden vanagloriarse de exceder esa hipérbole, pues han resuelto que el original del *Corán—la madre del Libro*—es uno de los atributos de Dios, como Su misericordia o Su ira, y lo juzgan anterior al idioma, a la Creación" (can take pride in exceeding this hyperbole, as they have asserted that the original *Qur'an—the Mother of the Book*—is one of the attributes of God, like His mercy or His anger, and they see it as preceding language, antedating Creation [1:489]). While Judaism and Christianity rely on the concept of divine language, in Islam (according to Borges) the sacred text is temporally situated in a dimension outside of history and even causality, prior to the development of the language in which it is written and the events that it narrates. It is possible that this paradox allegorically underscores, for Borges, the inherent contradictions within the relationships between a fictional reality, the reader, the text itself, and the author's intentions (especially when the "perspective" of a fictional character is given primacy). Avoiding the intuitive author-text-interpreter-interpretation causal progression, in other words, better communicates the disorientation that would accompany

a literary character's paradoxical interrogation of their reality. See the analysis of "La busca de Averroes" in the following pages for a sense of how this works in a specific context. Similar ideas about Islam are also referenced in the 1952 essay "Del culto de los libros." While Borges's references to Judaism are far too extensive and complex to summarize in a footnote, it is worth pointing to the scholarship of Saúl Sosnowski (*Borges y la Cábala*), Jaime Alazraki (*Jorge Luis Borges*), Edna Aizenberg (*Aleph Weaver*), Evelyn Fishburn (*Hidden Pleasures in Borges's Fiction*), and Ilán Stavans (*Borges, the Jew*).

46. Luce López-Baralt explains that this text was a refutation of the Persian Al-Gazzali's *Tahafut al-falasifa* (*Destruction of the Philosophers*), an attack by the mystic on rationalist theology. "Algacel considera que la razón humana era incapaz de abordar la experiencia trascendente, y defendió en cambio el método cognoscitivo de la 'ciencia directa de Dios'" (Algacel holds that human reason is not capable of grasping transcendental experience and defended, in turn, the method of knowledge referred to as the "direct science of God" ["Jorge Luis Borges y el Islam," 182]).

47. The word "sustantivo" here provides a sly wink to the reader; meaning both "noun" and "substantive" it playfully joins the idea of a pure abstraction (a word) and a solid, substantial thing. It is a game continued within the story "Tlön, Uqbar, Orbis Tertius."

48. Erika Spivakovsky writes that Averroes was working from "an Arabic version of a Syrian translation of the Greek text; the Arabic version of the *Poetics* says *madih* (panegyric) instead of the Greek *tragoidía*, and *hidja* (invective, satire), instead of the Greek *komoidía*" ("In Search of Arabic Influences," 231). This would mean that the observation about Averroes's translation offered by Renan (Borges's source) would not, in the context of historical reality, be traced to a difficulty originating in Averroes's "struggle to understand."

49. Peter Chelkowski notes that "despite the strong and consistent objections of Islamic theologians to the representational arts, indigenous theatrical forms such as puppetry, shadow plays, improvised comedies, traditional storytelling and even passion plays have not only existed but thrived in Islam for centuries" ("Islam in Modern Drama and Theatre," 45). See his "Islam in Modern Drama and Theatre" for more on the historical relationship between the theater and Islam.

50. I found no evidence to suggest that this is a citation of work of the historical figure Ibn Qutaybah. It may be a reference to Sa'di's *Gulistan* (Rose Garden), which compares the ephemerality of the rosebush with the more lasting pleasure of the book that carries its name.

51. An alternate spelling of the writer's name is "Al-Jahiz."

52. The character is likely a reference to Abd al-Rahman I (756–788), the founder of the Muslim dynasty that ruled in Spain for over two centuries. However, it is also possible that it refers to Al-Hurr ibn ʿAbd al-Rahman al-Thaqafi, the ruler of Al-Andalus from 716–718 who built "the emiral residence in Córdoba, facing the Guadalquivir bridge" (Mahmoud Makki, "Political History of Al-Andalus," 12). The verses that the story mentions appear to be inventions of Borges.

53. This moment can be read as a response to the author's own call, in "Después de las imágenes," for the creation of a being who could metaphorically enter the "frame of the mirror" to experience the contradictions of literary existence.

54. Ian Almond sees a chronological progression in Borges's references to Islam that builds toward more complexity and nuance, drawing from a diverse set of Orientalist texts until "Borges finally breaks free of his dependence on the Orientalists and sees through the illusion of their claim to knowledge" ("Borges the Post-Orientalist," 438). This moment in "La busca de Averroes" is, for Almond, when this breakthrough occurs. I would offer a sense of caution with regard to the decision to directly link the author's thoughts to those expressed by his narrators and characters, though I would agree that the text explicitly points here to the limited kinds of knowledge that are possible to obtain through the writings of Orientalists such as Lane and Renan. Almond reminds his readers that though Borges's literary evocations of Islam encompass "a wide number of its varied differences—not just geographical variations (Persia, Egypt, Spain), but also its theological differences (Ismailis, exotericists) and philosophical disputes (between commentators of Aristotle such as Averroes—falsafiyah—and 'anti-philosophers' such as al-Ghazali)" (436), his reliance on Orientalist texts places his writing, to a degree, within that tradition. With regard to the applicability of Edward Said's "charges of ignorance and cultural blindness" against the European canon, Almond writes that everything hinges on the question of "seriousness" in terms of Borges's intent to represent the "Orient," perhaps "as a Western style for dominating, restructuring, and having authority over the Orient" (Said, *Orientalism*, 3). While I believe that the question remains very open, in this chapter I present Borges's seriousness as extending mostly to "Islam's" capacity to represent a mode of inquiry for his characters to enact an exploration of his literary ideas, especially as they relate to the allure of visuality in fiction.

55. In "El escritor argentino y la tradición" (1932) Borges writes, however, that descriptions that situate characters within a recognizable foreign milieu inevitably serve to mark the entire scene as the fantasy of an outsider: "un falsario, un turista" (a liar, a turist [1:553]). As easy as it is to imagine Averroes surrounded by doves and gardens, this narrative approach is, for many readers familiar with Borges's ideas, marked as suspect from the start.

56. Finbarr Flood notes that the very notion of Islamic iconoclasm is often utilized as an essentialist construct that ignores the diverse historical and political moments that correspond to acts of altering figurative representations in secular and religious contexts throughout the history of Islam ("Between Cult and Culture," 641). While this essay is principally concerned with the manner in which ideas (even essentialist ideas) of Islam and Islamic iconoclasm are transformed within Borges's literary strategies, it is nevertheless important to note that the historical realities associated with the moments of Islamic iconoclasm are complex and diverse.

57. Another erasure of a face tied to Islam is found within the very brief story "Los espejos velados" (1960); it begins with a description of Islam and its prohibitions of visual representation:

El Islam asevera que el día inapelable del Juicio, todo perpetrador de la imagen de una cosa viviente resucitará con sus obras, y le será ordenado que las anime, y fracasará, y será entregado con ellas al fuego del castigo. Yo conocí de chico ese horror de una duplicación o multiplicación espectral de la realidad, pero ante los grandes espejos. (2:174)

Islam holds that on the unappealable Day of Judgment every perpetrator of the image of a living being will be resuscitated with his works of art to be commanded to give them life, and he will fail, and he will be sent with them into the fires of punishment. I knew as a child this horror of the spectral duplication or multiplication of reality, only for me it was before large mirrors.

The story that follows describes a wide-eyed woman who, after meeting Borges and hearing of his fear of mirrors, sees his face instead of her own within the mirrors of her house. She has them "veiled" in order to protect herself from her own facial erasure.

58. This character is based on the life of Al-Muqanna (sometimes spelled Al-Mokanna), who was represented in fiction within Thomas Moore's *Lalla Rookh*. Edwin Williamson relates that Borges was frightened by Moore's poem when he was young and associated it with Alexandre Dumas's *The Man in the Iron Mask* (*Borges*, 41).

59. In a 1983 interview with Julia Kushigian, Borges makes the connection between the erasure of Averroes' face and the reader's encounter with fictional artifice explicit. He notes that the Averroes of his story disappears because he suddenly understands that he is a fictional character (*Crónicas orientalistas*, 65–66). This moment of realization (or even self-realization) draws the nature of the fictional text into the story, warping traditional tools of realism as the text collapses.

60. Hákim could, in this sense, almost be read as the antithesis of Don Quixote, whose belief that he is, in fact, a literary character, allows him to *see* a new reality that he celebrates and wishes to participate in.

61. In his essay "La cábala" (1980), Borges notes that the Gnostics believed that "el universo es obra de una Divinidad deficiente, cuya fracción de divinidad tiende a cero. Es decir, de un Dios que no es *el* Dios (the universe is the work of a deficient Deity, whose fraction of divinity approaches zero. Which is to say, of a God that is not *the* God [3:298]).

62. Viewing oneself as a redundant and flawed fiction, in a pejorative sense, is different than simply understanding one's existence as artificial. Borges, in his essay "Del culto de los libros" (1951), describes how some approaches to theological artificiality involve a degree of peace and acceptance:

Sir Thomas Browne hacia 1642, confirmó: "Dos son los libros en que suelo aprender teología: La Sagrada Escritura y aquel universal y público manuscrito que está patente a todos los ojos. Quienes nunca vieron en el primero, lo descubrieron en el otro" (Browne, *Religio Medici*, 1:16). En el mismo párrafo se lee: "Todas las cosas son artificiales, porque la Naturaleza es el Arte de Dios."

Around 1642, Sir Thomas Browne confirmed: "Two are the books in which I tend to learn theology: the Bible and that universal and public document that is accessible to all eyes. Those who never saw it in the first, discovered it in the second" (*Religio Medici*, 1:16). In the same paragraph one reads: "All things are artificial, because Nature is the Art of God." (2:98–99)

It may be the case that Borges needed to fashion a literary theology that could create a degree of conflict between literary characters and the sources of visuality or theatricality that he was interested in subverting; "Islam," more so than early Christianity or Judaism, seems to have offered this kind of emphatically iconoclastic gesture.

63. Sylvia Molloy writes that "for Borges's characters (and even for their author), reading is more than a circumstantial activity, it is an emblematic representation, expressly referring to their own texture" (Molloy and Montero, *Signs of Borges*, 34). Many of Borges's stories, in this view, allegorically align represented moments of interpretation with the act of interpretation actually being carried out by the reader.

64. Arturo Echevarría Ferrari also identifies a connection between this statement and the nature of language. For him, however, Tlön is not related to a literary context as much as it is to language in general. He writes:

> Descubrimos muy pronto que ese mundo es "sucesivo, temporal, no espacial" como lo es también el lenguaje. Aún más. La vertiginosa verdad es que Tlön es un planeta hecho, constituido exclusivamente por el lenguaje, puesto que la doctrina idealista de Berkeley—según le entiende Borges—niega la existencia objetiva de la materia. Sin referentes externos el mundo se convierte en una serie de ideas y sensaciones cuyo único referente es el lenjuaje mismo. ("'Tlön, Uqbar, Orbis Tertius,'" 404)

> We soon discover that this world is "successive, temporal, non-spatial" as is, also, language. Yet there is more. The vertiginous truth is that Tlön is a planet made and constituted exclusively by language, as the idealist doctrine of Berkeley—according to Borges's understanding—denies the objective existence of matter. Without external referents, the world becomes a series of ideas and sensations whose only referent is language itself.

While I concur that the story makes an explicit connection between this form of philosophical idealism and Tlön, I would add that all of the claims of Berkeley highlighted here are *literally* true in the case of fiction. By shifting to a literary context, philosophy becomes subordinate to Borges's own ideas about his medium.

65. It is worth recalling here that the deceptively stable description of Averroes's surroundings in the first paragraph of "La busca de Averroes" culminated in a vision of a space in which "hay pocas cosas, pero donde cada una parece estar de un modo sustantivo y eterno" (there are few things, but where each seems to be present in an eternal and substantive sense [1:885]). The adjective "sustantivo" is important, signaling that the illusory realism that collapses in Borges's other story was populated by seemingly substantive objects that soon revealed themselves

to be mere nouns (sustantivos). Here, on the other hand, is a space that has the opposite characteristics: it lacks both physical objects and the nouns to describe them. As the obverse of the realism that Borges imploded, the literature of Tlön emerges as a kind of extreme alternative: a version of "literary reality" that corresponds not to the everyday norms of lived experience but, instead, to the norms of interpretation and textuality.

66. John Sturrock also points to the way in which this story allegorically communicates about the nature of fiction. He states that "as an author, Borges gladly and logically affiliated himself to the Idealists because he wishes to demonstrate the true nature of fiction: the immateriality of fictional objects, the distinction between succession and causation, the juxtaposition on an equal footing of the possible with the impossible, and the provisional but complete authority of the fiction-maker over the fictions he makes" (*Paper Tigers*, 24).

67. Within the context of Tlön, the principles of "realism" are reintroduced as the "materialistic" ideas of a heretical sect. This group believes, for example, that when a particular object is left unmentioned (by a literary text, in my reading) it *continues* to exist. This set of expectations (everyday expectations for us, as living embodied individuals) within the world of Tlön provokes problems that are resolved only when a brilliant thinker conceives, essentially, of the possibility of a reader/author who imagines all of the individuals and objects in Tlön into existence, giving them a conditional permanence: "Esa conjetura feliz afirma que hay un solo sujeto, que ese sujeto indivisible es cada uno de los seres del universo y que éstos son los órganos y máscaras de la divinidad" (That happy conjecture affirms that there is only one subject and that this indivisible subject is each one of the beings in the universe and that they are the organs and masks of the deity [1:731]). Objects in literature, in this view, have permanence insofar as they are recalled by the reader or the author: a reasonable idea, which, contemplated from within fiction by fictional characters, takes on a religious form.

68. Mercedes Blanco notes that the "1947" postscript was included in the 1940 editions of the story, in *SUR* 68 and in *Antología de la literatura fantástica*. Each of these editions paradoxically also contained a note in the postscript referencing the very publication that they appeared in (*SUR* 68, for example) as the source material for the story ("Arqueologías de Tlön," 21–22). One might read this as yet another incursion of the seemingly paradoxical Tlön into the world of the everyday, which in these cases would include the text that one is holding.

69. The other book mentioned from the bibliography is by a "Silas Haslam." This author does not correspond to a historical figure—though it does involve a transformation of the name of Borges's paternal grandmother, Fanny Haslam. Interestingly, a similar transformation of an ancestral name is a key aspect of Andreä's invention of "Christian Rosycross" and the order of the Rosicrucians. Borges, in this sense, places an additional emphasis on Andreä while directly relating his own name (and capacities for invention) to that of the creator of Rosicrucianism.

70. De Quincey, *Collected Writings of Thomas De Quincey*, 410 (italics mine).

71. Evelyn Fishburn notes that the history of Rosicrucianism echoes within the internal logic of the story given the ways in which Tlön begins as a fiction and then erupts into the everyday (*Hidden Pleasures in Borges's Fiction*, 38).

72. This idea counterintuitively both tempers and bolsters a critique of Borges's work written by Jean Franco. Franco argues that the author's popularity partially lies in the manner in which he manages to eschew difficult political and social positions within his fiction while also creating intricate, but ultimately legible, games that flatter egos within academic circles. She writes that "the fictions conceal nothing. As in tightrope-walking the skill is visible to all. Any reader (any reader with "competence") can pick up some of the clues, for they are meant to be deciphered" ("Utopia of a Tired Man," 328). Borges, here, seems to agree with at least the spirit of this critique, acknowledging that a certain kind of approach to his work—especially one focused on the most visible aspects of his writing—can in fact have the effect of making ethical and moral problems fade from view while offering, instead, the challenges and pleasures of interpretation. Yet by offering this critique, this warning, he does engage with a political context, especially as it relates to Nazi Germany in particular and to anti-Semitism more generally. Other stories ("Deutches Requiem" is a frequently cited example) take on political and social issues of justice even more directly. Borges's engagement with politics—and the way critics have at times avoided it, most notoriously in the De Man case—is detailed by scholars such as Edna Aizenberg (see "Deutsches Requiem" and *Aleph Weaver*) and Evelyn Fishburn ("Hidden Pleasures in Borges' Allusions").

73. This also shows an important difference between Borges's and Macedonio's respective approaches to emphasized literary artificiality. Macedonio's understanding of the experience of altering one's selfhood (as a reader or as an author) within the abstraction of literary existence was always presented as uniformly positive: as a transformative experience that could only enlighten the participant, freeing them from the restrictions of everyday life. Borges here expresses a degree of skepticism: transforming oneself within artifice, he points out, can have both liberating and terrifying results.

74. Aizenberg, *Aleph Weaver*, 34. Aizenberg also notes that Victoria Ocampo wrote an essay in the same magazine decrying the dictatorship of Hitler and its promotion of hate (34).

75. Mercedes Blanco writes convincingly about the adjective "Quevedian," suggesting that both the style and thematic content of Quevedo match well with Browne's *Urn Burial* ("Arqueologías de Tlön," 43-44). I can add that in Borges and Bioy's actual translation they cite Quevedo in one of their footnotes:

Quevedo, Epístolas a imitación de las de Séneca, XXXIX:
Por mucha riqueza que gastemos en cubrir este polvo, siempre seremos el asco, y el edificio el precio; disfrazar en palacio la sepultura engaño es, no confesión. (*SUR* III: 23)

Quevedo, Epistles in the style of Seneca's, XXXIX:
For all the riches we spend in covering over this dust, we will always be wretched, and the edifice is the price; disguising in a palace one's grave is delusion, not faith.

James Crosby suggests, however, that it is likely that Quevedo did not in fact write this text ("Última prisión de Quevedo," 115).

76. Alan White writes that "seeking Uqbar, the narrator should have found Ur: in Borges's favorite edition of the *Britannica*, it occupies precisely the spot held by Uqbar in Bioy's copy of the *Anglo-American Cyclopaedia*, and on our earth, it occupies the geographical spot where the *Cyclopaedia* locates Uqbar" ("Appalling or Banal Reality," 52). White observes that the 11th Edition of the Encyclopedia Brittanica explains that the word "ur" means simply "the city." He also points out that Borges makes use of the fact that "ur" is a German prefix meaning "originary" by using the word "urspracht." As the word "ur" is used in the story to also refer to certain strange objects within Tlön that are brought into existence solely by the power of hope, White suggests that Borges is insinuating the idea that any concept of the origins of civilization is nothing more than a product of wish fulfillment. I would offer another possibility: that Borges is creating a riddle that is, also, a joke. Any reader that would actually look in the 1911 *Encyclopedia Britannica* to find "Uqbar" (as Alan White and I did) would be principally motivated by the *hope* that Borges's nonexistent country might lead to another "clue" useful for the interpretation of the story. Ur is thus in the category of ur, arising out of the desires of the reader.

77. Evelyn Fishburn points out that "the real Borges, in collaboration with the real Bioy, did publish a joint translation of a chapter of Urn Burial in Sur 111, January 1944" (*Hidden Pleasures in Borges's Fiction*, 72). This translation (of the fifth chapter) is not present in Emecé's *Borges en Sur*, though it can be accessed online through the Biblioteca Digital Trapalanda of the Biblioteca Nacional.

78. Within the story, Borges, did in fact quietly insert an object—a shining cone about the size of a dice that is almost too heavy to lift—that exists on the boundary between Tlön and the "everyday" world of "Borges" and "Bioy." The story informs us that these heavy cones are images of divinity in some religions of Tlön. Arturo Echavarría Ferrari ("Tlön, Uqbar, Orbis Tertius," 408) points out that Borges, in his essay "Pascal," includes a footnote stating that "que yo recuerde, la historia no registra dioses cónicos, cúbicos o piramidales, aunque sí ídolos" (as far as I can recall, history registers no conical, cubical, or pyramidal gods, though there are such idols [2:87]). The cone, as opposed to the notion of the infinite sphere "whose center is everywhere and whose circumference is nowhere" described as a contradictory expansion of space in Borges's essay, can be approached as the miraculous (for Tlön) representation of the meeting of a point and the plane of a circle in three dimensions. This particular distinction between an idol and a representation of God suggests that idols are designed to be easily comprehended while representations of divinity tend to challenge the imagination with a certain degree of contradiction. (For Tlön, a simple cone would indeed represent a contradiction given the inability to conceptualize physical space and object permanence.)

79. 1929 is here marked as an important year. It appeared earlier, in "El Aleph," as the date of the death of Beatriz Viterbo. While there are surely many ways of approaching this date and its significance, Borges himself drew attention to 1929 as the year he was able to purchase the eleventh edition of the *Encyclopedia*

Britannica in his text "An Autobiographical Essay" (*Aleph and Other Stories*, 233). Whether or not the repetition of 1929 refers to this acquisition or not, the encyclopedia, as a stand-in for the human attempt (and failure) to create an object that reveals total knowledge of the world, is inevitably in conversation with these magical, world-constituting lenses.

80. The "vein within a marble pillar" may subtly point to the "true" unseen Aleph within the Amr Mosque as does, perhaps, the blind man in the mosque.

81. Luce López-Baralt writes that "si bien *Teo* nos refiere a Dios, *delina* (del griego delo, 'aclarar,' 'hacer visible o evidente') nos devuelve al sentido principal de la raíz árabe z-h-r, hacer 'notorio' o 'visible'" (if Teo refers to God, *delina* [from the Greek *delo*, "to make clear," "to make visible or evident"] returns us to the principal sense of the Arabic root z-h-r, "to make known" or "visible" ["Lo que había del otro lado," 75]). She also writes that "Borges leaves nothing to chance, and he was fully aware of the multivalent and opalescent character of the three-letter z-h-r root, judging from the masterly way with which he plays upon this device throughout his narration. . . . Let there be no doubt, Borges will pluck all the strings of the three-letter lyre from which, linguistically speaking, gives rise to his ever evasive Zahir" ("Borges, or the Mystique of Silence," 31). Despite these assertions, I have found no evidence to suggest that Borges knew Arabic and have found other explanations for Borges's references to visuality and interpretation. López-Baralt, in fact, points out that Borges took a few beginner Arabic classes in Geneva toward the very end of his life, which to me indicates that he was not particularly familiar with the language earlier in his life ("Jorge Luis Borges y el Islam," 180). Nevertheless, she also asserts that Borges knew the "corresponding diacritical and contextual alterations" of the root of the word zahir, allowing him to use several other "simultaneous meanings" such as "back, rear, side, rear part, rear side, reverse"; "memory," "eye," "mirador," "vantage point," "esoteric or literal meaning," and particularly "followers of the sect of the zahiriyya [dahriyya], who profess the esoteric or literal interpretation of the Koran and tradition" ("Borges, or the Mystique of Silence," 30–31).

With regard to the scholarly opinion about Borges's understanding of Arabic, López-Baralt writes that "scholars have been unanimous in admitting that Borges knew somewhat more Arabic than what he might have picked up from the translations of the *Thousand and One Nights* by Mardrus, Lane, Galland, Burton and Cansinos Assens, which he passionately commented on during his life" ("Borges, or the Mystique of Silence," 32). It is difficult to evaluate what it means, exactly, to know *somewhat more* Arabic that what one *might* have picked up from English translations of the *Thousand and One Nights*, though I feel confident in stating that there is no chorus of scholars "admitting" that such a nonstatement is true.

With regard to these English translations of the *Thousand and One Nights*, Borges wrote that

> he tenido siempre la impression de que todas las versiones que he leído son
> traducciones de la de Lane, porque la de Lane, simplemente, fue la primera

> que leí, de modo que para mí, la version árabe (no conozco el árabe) tiene
> que ser una traducción más o menos buena de la traducción inglesa de Lane.
> ("Belleza no es un hecho extraordinario," 67)

> I have always had the impression that all the versions that I have read are
> translations of Lane's text, because Lane's was, simply, the first that I read,
> which is to say that for me, the Arabic version (I do not know Arabic) must
> be a passable translation of Lane's English translation.

While one might be tempted to attribute this direct statement admitting full
ignorance of Arabic to the author's humility, I am more inclined to take Borges
at his word.

 82. After describing his struggle with being caught by the coin and the *idea* of
coins, "Borges" explains that he discovered the term "Zahir" in a [nonexistent]
book titled *Urkunden zur Geschichte der Zahirsage* (1899). Borges's actual source
of the term is still uncertain. The wording of the story seems to refer indirectly
to verse 57:3 in the Qur'an, which states that "He is the First and the Last, the
Apparent and the Hidden, / And has knowledge of all things." (Az-Zahir is
translated as "Apparent" and Al-Batin is translated as "Hidden.") It seems likely,
however, that he encountered the term from another text given the emphasis on
Zahir being one of the attributes of God.

 Some Borges scholars have offered the opinion that there is a meaningful
opposition in the story between Zahir and Batin (the Visible and the Hidden).
Humberto Núñez-Faraco, for example, suggests that this alluded-to opposition
is a way of signaling the hidden layers of meaning in the story (*Borges and Dante*,
162). Nada Elia writes that "the zahir and the batin are as inseparable as two sides
of a coin, and the Zahir is indeed a coin in the short story by this title" ("Islamic
Esoteric Concepts," 131). Luce López-Baralt, in numerous essays, builds on the
same idea by suggesting not only that Borges was aware of the opposing terms
but that he was referencing different schools of interpretation. She writes that:

> Borges hace gala una vez más de su *expertise* en la mística islámica: la escuela
> ortodoxa Zahirita, adepta a la interpretación literal ("visible") del Corán y
> atada, por lo tanto, al lenguaje exterior de la teología, tenía su contrapartida
> en la secta Batiniyya, que desvelaba el sentido esotérico oculto bajo la letra
> del Corán. (*"Ultra Auroram et Gangem,"* 125–26)

> Once again Borges shows off his expertise in Islamic mysticism: the orthodox
> Zahirite school, adept at the literal ("visible") interpretation of the Qur'an
> and tied, as such, to the exterior language of the theology, had its counterpart
> in the Batiniyya sect, which revealed the esoteric meaning hidden beneath
> the text of the Qur'an.

 I would suggest that the opposition between the visible and the hidden operates almost as a constant in Borges's work and that, while it would be intriguing

to find that Borges was aware of these opposing terms and even the opposing hermeneutical schools associated with them, there is no direct evidence to support these claims. They might seem to be inseparable, but it is, of course, possible that Borges was not familiar with both words. I have found no evidence of Borges using the term "batin" at all. The closest I was able to get was to find that Borges and Bioy, in their *Libro del cielo y del infierno* (1960), cite from Thomas Patrick Hughes's *Dictionary of Islam*. This dictionary, holding definitions for "Zahir" and "Az-Zahir" that mention the idea of batin, also states that Az-Zahir is one of the ninety-nine attributes of God and defines zahir as "outward, exterior, manifest" (698). This, it would seem, comes close to a possible source for Borges if he had access to the 1935 text when he was writing "El Zahir." In his manuscript draft "Místicos del Islám," however, Borges does not mention these schools of interpretation or the zahir/batin opposition at all. With that being said, any emphasis on the "visible" or the "apparent" would immediately suggest the obverse, the obscured, and the hidden. This is especially true given Borges's relationship with seeing and the allure of the visual; as someone aware of approaching blindness he would not require the word "batin" to explore the other side of the term. What we can state with confidence, regardless, is that Borges associates the word "zahir" with a theologically inflected approach to the visible within his constructed "Islam."

While the connection is also very speculative it is also worth noting that the word "zahir" is used in Lane's *An Account of the Manners and Customs of the Modern Egyptians* (a book that Borges did possess and use at the time in which he was writing "El Zahir") in reference to a tradition of publicly reciting "romances." Lane describes a group referred to exclusively as "Mohadditeeen" or "story-tellers": "There are said to be about thirty of them in Cairo. The exclusive subject of their narrations is a work called 'the Life of Ez-Zahir' ('Seerect Ez-Záhir,' or 'Es-Seereh es-Záhireeyeh'). They recite without book" (*Account of the Manners and Customs*, 114).

83. Luce López-Baralt, interpreting the inscription on the coin, comes to the conclusion that "NT apunta al *Noli Tangere* bíblico—'no oses tocarme'" (NT points to the biblical *Noli Tangere*—"do not dare touch me" ["Jorge Luis Borges y el Islam," 189–90; "*Ultra Auroram et Gangem*," 124]). It strikes me as a peculiar warning, however, given how one would have to *already* be touching the coin in order to read the inscription. Also, as a matter of some urgency, the hidden command would not be the most effective means of communicating danger given the many possibilities of interpreting the letters—warnings are usually issued with clarity in mind. If one wants to stay with Latin it could just as easily be read as "Noli timere"—"Do not fear." Luce López-Baralt also writes that Borges "conoce la numismática Islamica, y sabe que hay monedas que tienen inscrito el Zahir en un lado y a Dios en el otro" (is familiar with Islamic numismatics, and knows that there are coins that have the Zahir on one side and God on the other ["Jorge Luis Borges y el Islam," 192; "*Ultra Auroram et Gangem*," 126]). She is referring to certain coins that contain the last name of a particular sultan (Al-Malik al-Zahir) on one side and a religious inscription on the other. While

the possibility is an intriguing one, I did not see any evidence for this claim provided in the article.

84. A similar idea is expressed within Borges's short text "Paradiso, XXI, 108," first published in *SUR* 231 (1954), which describes a desire to see the actual face of Jesus (in the context of countless representations of it). The text states:

> Los hombres han perdido una cara, una cara irrecuperable, y todos querrían ser aquel peregrino (soñado en el empíreo, bajo la Rosa) que en Roma ve el sudario de la Verónica y murmura con fe: Jesucristo, Dios mío, Dios verdadero, ¿así era, pues, tu cara?
>
> [...]
>
> Perdimos esos rasgos como puede perderse un número mágico, hecho de cifras habituales; como se pierde para siempre una imagen en el calidoscopio. Podemos verlos y ignorarlos. El perfil de un judío en el subterráneo es tal vez el de Cristo; las manos que nos dan unas monedas en una ventanilla tal vez repiten las que unos soldados, un día, clavaron en la cruz.

> Mankind has lost a face, an irrecoverable face, and everyone would like to be that traveler (dreamt in the Empyrean, under the Rose) who in Rome sees Veronica's shroud and murmmers with faith: Jesus Christ, my God, the True God, was this, then, your face?
>
> [...]
>
> We lost these features as one might lose a magic number composed of everyday digits; as one loses forever an image in kaleidoscope. We can see them without realizing it. The profile of a Jew in the subway is perhaps that of Christ; the hands that give us a few coins in a stall window might repeat those that some soldiers, one day, nailed to the cross. (1)

The narrative voice then wonders if the true physical form of Jesus is denied to mankind so that it might be democratized, associated with the features of anonymous strangers, with everyone. From this perspective, the parade of iconography can free the mind to contemplate other possibilities if and when it is understood to be artificial, fictional, and provisional. This rather iconoclastic possibility is supported by Borges's reference, earlier in the text, to a section in Frazer's *The Golden Bough* that describes how Osiris's body, after being "rent . . . into fourteen pieces" and "scattered" by Typhon, was sought out by Isis, who recovered every part except for the genitals, which had been eaten by fish. She then created an image of his sex and, to ensure that he would be worshipped throughout the land, also created fourteen human figures out of wax and spices, each one containing one of the fourteen true parts of Osiris. Each artificial body was entrusted to the priest of a different family, who was told that it was the true body of Osiris and that they should bury it and worship him as a god (Frazer, *Golden Bough*, 365). In the story, the mannequins that Osiris creates are deceptive works of art and yet, also, (in combination) all that is left of the true body of Osiris. Borges relates this idea of a broken-apart and dispersed god with the ways in which not having access to a perfect image—only imperfect icons—makes the notion of divinity less rigid and more inclusive.

85. This structured tension between literary approaches can be seen as one of Borges's most powerful tools. Alicia Borinsky writes, for example, that Borges is far less interested in occupying one specific theoretical position (and creating a coherent argument for it) than he is focused on setting multiple theories against one another to create doubt, unease, and an active, questioning mindset.

> Was Borges interested in building a theory of literature? He certainly spoke and wrote with admiration about his friend and predecessor, Macedonio Fernández, who says in his *Museum of the Novel of the Eternal* that he is not sure whether he has written a novel or a theory of the novel. Unlike Macedonio, though, Borges was not bound by the limitations that a protracted, coherent, theoretical language implies. He was indeed inclined to take his texts to their ultimate conclusions and make them spin against their own certainties, but the quality that dominates his writing is the sense that theory may be the best of fictions. (Borinsky, *Theoretical Fables*, 29)

Borinsky also emphasizes that Borges, as opposed to Macedonio, was able to work with heterogeneous voices and approaches that avoided theoretical purism in order to create a more dynamic complexity that ultimately relies on the reader's ability to navigate intertextual possibilities ("Borges en nuestra biblioteca," 610).

86. It may be useful, as well, to point to the ways in which Borges was wary of the allure of blindness for the sighted in terms of its associations with "wisdom" and "insight." Emir Rodríguez Monegal recalled that Borges "told me that they greatly exaggerated his blindness, that newspapermen had transformed him into a pathetic figure because a nearsighted man sells less copy than a blind one" ("In the Labyrinth," 22). Aravinda Bhat has emphasized that Borges expressed a wide range of thoughts and reactions with regard to his relationship with his blindness ("Corporeal Refractions," 85–87). Bhat finds that while disability is often correlated with compensatory gifts in Borges's literary work, the author's own experience with blindness (and the anticipation of blindness) can subtly influence his relationship with the experience of time, identity, and embodied experience (114). Kevin Goldstein concurs, writing that Borges's multifaceted approach to blindness unsettles simplistic narratives while pointing in the direction of blindness as an artistic process that involves "a new sense of time, a greater dependence on memory, as well as a new kind of social life" ("'La cara que me mira,'" 56).

87. It is perhaps worth mentioning that Borges was well aware that James Joyce was blind late in life. The last two sentences of a short biography for *El Hogar* emphasize it, in fact, in stark terms: "James Joyce, ahora, vive en un departamento en París, con su mujer y sus dos hijos. Siempre va con los tres a la ópera, es muy alegre y muy conservador. Está ciego. (James Joyce, now, lives in an apartment in Paris, with his wife and two children. He always goes to the opera with the three of them, is very happy and very conservative. He is blind [4:261]). While the Homer-Borges-Joyce triangle, joined at the vertices by blindness, might not hold together under serious scrutiny, some have

commented about its possible relevance. I turned toward the possibility of a connection between the three authors after reading the following section from Joyce's *Ulysses:* "He crossed Townsend street, passed the frowning face of Bethel. *El, yes: house of: Aleph*, Beth. And past Nichols's the undertaker. At eleven it is. Time enough. Daresay Corny Kelleher bagged the job for O'Neil's. Singing with his eyes shut. Corny. Met her once in the park. In the dark. What a lark" (58, emphasis mine). To encounter "El . . . Aleph" in the middle of a section that seemed to lead to a playful reference to blindness was a strange surprise. My sense is that it is more of a coincidence than an actual link between the texts, though Suzanne Jill Levine ("Notes to Borges's Notes on Joyce," 349) and Patricia Novillo-Corvalán (*Borges and Joyce*, 145) express more confidence in the connection. I do believe, as previously mentioned, that Joyce does make an appearance elsewhere in "El Aleph" (alongside Ramón Gómez de la Serna) within the parodic figure of Carlos Argentino Daneri. It should be mentioned that Borges seemed to offer skepticism about the depth of the connection between Homer's *Odyssey* and Joyce's *Ulysses*. In conversation with Bioy, he said: "Se habla de la construcción del *Ulysses*, de sus paralelos con la *Odisea*. Esta construcción, estos paralelos no sirven para nada, o solo sirven para el crítico, que escribirá sobre el libro" (People talk about the construction of *Ulysses*, its parallels with the *Odyssey*. This construction, these parallels are worthless, or at least they are only valuable for the critic, who will write about the book [Bioy Casares, *Borges*, 681]). For this reason, I am reluctant to place too much emphasis on the possible connection between the three authors. Borges does not need Joyce, of course, to be influenced by the idea and myth of Homer.

88. The buried Aleph is, also, an object that requires a degree of intimacy and quiet for it to be beheld and, crucially, *interpreted* within an individual mind. This kind of attention, and the way it can lead to a unique context of imagination, was also the subject of a story that Borges wrote much later, in 1975, titled "Ulrica." While many of its attributes have already been explored in this chapter via other stories, it stands alone by virtue of having been written when Borges was completely blind. It is also important as an example of the ways in which "Islam" is replaced by another iconoclastic religious tradition.

The narrator, a Colombian professor named Javier Otárola, first sees a woman named Ulrica in England's walled city of York, next to the "Five Sisters": a set of stained-glass windows in the York Minister that are nonfigurative. He describes them as "esos vitrales puros de toda imagen que respetaron los iconoclastas de Cromwell" (those windows, pure of all images, which were respected by Cromwell's iconoclasts [3:20]). It is worth emphasizing that the narrator only *sees* Ulrica in this particular place (they do not actually meet); Borges has chosen an aniconic backdrop for this purely visual encounter, as well as a theological architectural feature that survives the demands of an iconoclastic religious authority. (For more on the topic, see Spraggon, *Puritan Iconoclasm*.) Even in this different theological context, several of the essential characteristics of Borges's "Islam" reappear in a different guise—we are cued to mistrust this initial visual representation with aniconic and iconoclastic allusions.

On the following day, the narrator once again emphasizes the sight of Ulrica.

Fue entonces cuando la miré. . . . Era ligera y alta, de rasgos afilados y de ojos grises. Menos que su rostro me impresionó su aire de tranquilo misterio. . . . Hablaba un inglés nítido y preciso y acentuaba levemente las erres. No soy observador; esas cosas las descubrí poco a poco. (3:20–21)

It was then that I saw her. . . . She was slight and tall, with fine features and gray eyes. More than her face it was her air of peaceful mystery that struck me. . . . Her English was clear and precise, and she lightly accentuated her r's. I'm not observant; these things I discovered bit by bit.

In this second visual encounter, we are further disoriented—while it seems initially as though he is meeting her for the first time (thought he is not), when we reach the end of his description, it apparently arises not from the first or second meetings but from an accumulation of later impressions. The simple act of seeing or describing her is made unusually complex.

After following their conversation on a walk through the woods, the story ends in the room of an inn that is wallpapered in an arabesque style that emphasizes, also, the literary, textual character of the what we are reading. (As Alice Petersen points out, the florid wallpaper design is that of William Morris, who is also the translator of a text referenced throughout the story and quoted for its epigraph: *The Saga of the Volsungs* ["Borges's 'Ulrike,'" 329].) Here, when the characters are making love, we read the narrator asserting that "secular en la sombra fluyó el amor y poseí por primera y última vez la imagen de Ulrica" (secular in the shadows love flowed, and I possessed for the first and last time the image of Ulrica [3:22]).

The notion that the narrator would focus on possessing the *image* of Ulrica (it, specifically, and not her), can be disorienting. However, the story of this possession is set up—as we have noted—by a series of descriptions that challenges the expectations associated with everyday sight and traditional visual representation. Beyond the aniconic framing of his first glimpse of Ulrica and the arabesque-esque room for this final scene (Morris drew heavily from Persian designs [Sasso, *Pre-Raphaelites*, 68]), there is also a gradual shift away from sight, with the white snow accumulating outside and, inside, the shadows taking the place of the inn's interior. Even when we are given a traditional description of Ulrica's appearance earlier in the story, the narrator complicates it, muddying the origin of its creation. Finally, the concluding assertion of Otárola invalidates this previous, rather formulaic visual description—the first account is not, we are told, the actual, true image of Ulrica. The true image is, strikingly, *nonoptical*: a mental figure composed in darkness, informed by touch, intimacy and a shared sensibility discovered through conversation. It is also ephemeral; if it is possessed, then this possession lasts only for a moment (Ulrica asks, at one point in the story, if anything can truly be possessed, or lost). Perhaps one final aspect of the story deserves mention: it is difficult to sense whether or not the Spanish word "secular" in the last sentence is principally intended to signify "secular" or "ancient," yet for a story that draws, as this chapter shows, from a longstanding practice of reshaping theological traditions, the idea that the true image of Ulrica arises in a secular and ancient context of human relation is, I believe, worth special mention.

89. Examples of this desire to be the invisible man include an interview with María Esther Gilio published in *Crisis* in 1974 (46) and, more noticeably, a public letter that he wrote weeks before dying at the age of 86 in Geneva, Switzerland (*La Gaceta*).

CHAPTER 2

1. Borges and Carrizo, *Borges, el Memorioso*, 260.

2. Brodzki, "'She Was Unable Not to Think,'" 331.

3. Bioy Casares, *Borges*, 89.

4. Grínor Rojo observes that Emma *assumes* that her father committed suicide, that the letter does not explicitly present this information. His essay describes this as a "mala lectura" ("Sobre 'Emma Zunz,'" 91), a bad reading, with serious consequences. Beatriz Sarlo echoes this point in a later essay, which refers to the protagonist's interpretation as a "lectura en exceso" (excessive reading ["Saber del cuerpo," 233]). Another way to approach Emma's interpretation of the letter is to suggest that it involves the use of an extratextual understanding of her father, his experiences and his mental state. In other words, she interprets the letter with the knowledge that it was likely altered by its author (Fein or Fain) in a way that corresponded to a hidden, underlying truth that was not easy to express. Fain, from her perspective, *feigns* in order to simultaneously express and obscure the truth. This (as will become apparent later in the chapter) is a mode of interpretation that is especially important for the story and thus may not deserve to be simply classified as "bad" or "excessive." There may, in other words, be unmentioned contexts in play.

5. Silvia Dapía and Grínor Rojo both suggest that Emma Zunz's storytelling should be read as referencing Borges's own act of fiction-creating. Dapía writes that the story's "partially omniscient narrator, with his lack of certainty, reminds us of the precarious status of our verbal constructions. He reminds us that 'because a word is there,' this does not mean that 'something real must correspond to the word'" ("Why Is There a Problem," 175). She views Emma's story as a work of literary realism than echoes Borges's own work of realism and, as such, is intended to remind the reader of the constructed nature of all stories. Rojo points to the possibility that the narrator of the story is representing Emma in fraudulent ways, with interpretations and assumptions that should be questioned. He sees the text as a possible echo of Emma's self-serving story: an untrustworthy representation of a nonexistent crime paired with a careless set of interpretations.

6. Edwin Williamson writes that letters between Borges and his friend Roberto Godel indicate that, at the time, he had feelings for a woman named Emilie (*Borges*, 63). It is not clear, however, to what degree the relationship existed.

7. Beatriz Sarlo, in "El saber del cuerpo," describes the ways in which Emma's body is activated by her plan in a way that supersedes the capacities of any mind to plan, order, and act. In her view, the story narrates this movement *away* from control—in which the body is following its own logic of memory, associations,

sensations, and emotions. I agree that this gesture exists in the story and would add that it can be read contextually as an acknowledgement of the way in which the body (Borges's and Emma's) is possessed by the memory or echo of pain. While this movement away from control is important to notice, this chapter draws more attention to the way in which control is (later) reinstated in the story through the act of narration and invention.

8. Grínor Rojo also draws attention to the inclusion of Emma's name within the name of her father. This observation is used, however, to suggest that she is "una Electra judía y porteña, quien, poseída por una abrasadora sed de justicia, se cobra en nombre de su padre lo que su padre mismo no se pudo o no se quiso cobrar" (a Jewish, porteña Electra, who, possessed by a burning thirst for justice, takes in the name of her father what he himself was not able or willing to attain ["Sobre 'Emma Zunz,'" 93]). The gender of the character, read through the psychological cues posed in the story, leads Rojo to an interpretation that reinforces the divide between "male" and "female" psychologies while also drawing from the Jewish context of the story. Miguel Rivera-Taupier offers a similar, parallel interpretation by suggesting that Emma Zunz is a retelling of the biblical story of Judith in "Emma Zunz y sus precursoras." It is worth mentioning that Josefina Ludmer, working in the opposite direction, explores the possibility that Emma Zunz is meant to be understood as a non-Jewish, anti-Semitic character that, in killing Loewenthal, is intended to point in the direction of the Holocaust ("Justicias de Emma," 478).

9. Another possible interpretation related to the protagonist's name is provided by Evelyn Fishburn who connects it to that of Leopoldo Zunz, "one of the leading nineteenth-century Jewish scholars of Hasidism." She explains further: "This popular religious movement arose in Poland, as a reaction to what was considered an excessive adherence to the letter of the law, and which encouraged among its followers a more direct approach to God, one based primarily upon direct prayer and intuition. Emma's decision to become the personal interpreter and executor of Divine Justice [. . .] can be read in this light" ("Borges, Cabbala and 'Creative Misreading,'" 403–4). This potential connection is especially relevant to my reading of the story for the way in which it points to a form of interpretation that requires a degree of flexibility with regard to the text. In seeking out the secondary context for the story that I outline here, one first has to trust in the intuition (helped along by doubts raised at end of the story) that there is another level of meaning operating in the background.

10. Brodzki, "'She Was Unable Not to Think,'" 331.

11. Borges and Montenegro, *Diálogos*, 67.

12. Demetrio Anzaldo is the only scholar that I have been able to find that takes this idea at face value. In his essay "Mito(s) en la Argentina, ¿Emma Zunz o Borges?," Anzaldo plays with the notion that since all of Borges's characters reflect and offer literary variations of Borges's own identity, this same principal should apply to Emma Zunz. His text is an expansive, ludic exploration of the echoes between Borges the historical and literary figure, on the one hand, and the multiple interpretations of Emma Zunz offered by the scholarly tradition, on the other. His text suggests that Emma Zunz, for Borges, opens up possibilities

of representation that reconfigure his own relationships with storytelling, sexuality, honor, and personality while also conjuring myriad stories associated with women in historical and literary contexts (9).

13. Brodzki, "'She Was Unable Not to Think,'" 347.

14. This is especially true given Borges's and Macedonio's shared interest in creating literary texts that alter the identity of their readers and authors, converting them into literary characters that no longer behave according to the rules and norms of everyday life.

15. A copy of this manuscript is housed in the Harry Ransom Center. It is also referenced in Daniel Balderston's article "Una lógica simbólica: Manuscritos de Jorge Luis Borges en la Biblioteca Nacional." The note reads: "Querida Cecilia: Aquí está, a la espera de su dictamen, el primer borrador de *Emma Zunz* (que también podría titularse *El castigo*). Toda mi amistad. Borges" (Dear Cecilia: Here, awaiting your judgment, is the first draft of *Emma Zunz* [which could also be titled *The Punishment*]. In friendship. Borges [15]).

16. In "Las justicias de Emma," Josefina Ludmer also connects José Ingenieros with "Emma Zunz," arguing that his ideas about the farcical nature of the state's claims to truth resonate within the story given the various ways in which Emma utilizes strategic falsehoods to establish legitimacy in terms of the languages of the state, the company she works for, and her family.

17. Ingenieros, *Simulación en la lucha*, 80–81.

18. In conversation with Bioy, Borges in 1963 describes the daughters of Ingenieros in the following manner: "Todas esas chicas están muy preocupadas porque son hijas de Ingenieros. Como si temiera que eso las borrara. No sé si Delia o Cecilia, una me dijo: 'No hija de Ingenieros, ¡hija de nadie!'" (All of those girls are very concerned because they are daughters of Ingenieros. As if they feared that this might erase them. I don't know if it was Delia or Cecilia, one of them told me: "Not the daughter of Ingenieros, the daughter of no one!" [957]). It may be relevant to consider that, from Borges's perspective, at least, Cecilia's own relationship with her father was fraught. He may have approached the story that she suggested to him (given its central father-daughter relationship) with this in mind; it would have been natural to then consider the relationship with his own father as he imagined how to make the story his own.

19. Corbatta, *Borges y yo*, 93.

20. This is the interpretation advanced by Gregorio Santiago Montes in "La intrusa en la vida de Borges" (93–96).

21. An intriguing secondary possibility is the relationship between Cristián Nilson and Christine Nilsson, a Swedish singer who appears in Borges's 1911 *Encyclopedia Britannica*. Her encyclopedia entry notes that she was married twice but later retreated from the stage after one of her marriages. Reading the silence of Juliana Burgos alongside this far more public silence is tempting, though doing so would require more supporting evidence. One can, however, imagine Borges deciding to use the name of Leopoldo Torre Nilsson and then consulting the encyclopedia for additional context (or, rather, additional material).

22. Borges commented on the relationship between his last name and the last name "Burgos" on several occasions. See, for example, *Jorge Luis Borges: Conversations*, 227.

23. Rodríguez Monegal, *Jorge Luis Borges: A Literary Biography*, 458.

24. See Silvia Magnavacca (*Filósofos medievales*, 97–99) for a careful analysis of these references. She points to their connection with the mythical temple of the Phoenix (in the case of the Egyptian references) and the use of the phoenix as a metaphor for resurrection (in the case of the Germanic ones).

25. Anders Johansson notes that this story is nearly always approached in a way that reduces it to a riddle whose answer is sex. He argues, instead, that it should be read as a text that, after suggesting an apparent solution, resists it, defending itself "against every attempt at interpretation and analysis through its formal constitution" ("Borges Beyond Interpretations," 199). Johansson describes the materials of the rite in the story as both "insignificant" (178) and, also, as important parts of the author's strategy to create a story about a secret that remains pure and unreachable (given that there is, in Johansson's view, no actual secret being referred to). They are, in this way, presented as significant tools of insignificance. (He also offers the idea that contingency and extraneousness are inevitably part of the text, and every text, and do not necessarily require such intentional moves.)

I would argue that this conclusion—which asserts that (first) the materials in the rite are insignificant and that (second) there is no secret—is, also, a definitive interpretation that has the function of "solving" the story as an illustration of the power of aporia, or language's indeterminacy. This is an interpretation that, moreover, forecloses the possibility of other viable approaches. I should state, however, that Johansson seems to be aware of the risk of championing an approach to reading literary texts that leads, in every case, to the same conclusion—a celebration of contingency and ambiguity (183). He frames his interpretation as a more descriptive, process-oriented approach. On the one hand, he recognizes that Borges's stories call out for interpretation with their puzzles, allusions, contradictions, and references. On the other, he senses that every attempt to discover a discrete, specific explanation or solution runs the risk of drawing attention away from how Borges's stories expertly cultivate a sense of possibility, curiosity, and bewilderment. He proposes that it is a worthwhile project to describe how stories such as "La secta del Fénix" *unsettle* the interpreting mind *without* offering any kind of interpretation that succumbs to the temptation to arrive at a specific meaning. I wholeheartedly agree with the aims of this kind of descriptive, process-oriented interpretation. However, for it to be viable, I believe that it has to allow for the possibility that, in truth, there are some solutions to be found (just as there are, even in his approach, words with meanings that are intelligible, if not completely fixed and static). The line between unintelligibility and meaning, in other words, shifts and fluctuates without ever fully disappearing. More concretely, with regard to this story one cannot be too attached to the idea that there is no Secret (since this also threatens to fix the text in place). Otherwise there is the risk of simply exchanging "procreative copulation" for Adorno's "aporia" in terms of the solution to the implied riddle.

With this being said, I am very sympathetic to the idea that it is not sufficient to rely solely on Borges's own statements about his stories and their meaning. I also agree that it is important to be aware of how interpretations built upon one's own initial preferences and impressions can ignore or explain away aspects of a text that provide contradiction (though a preference for aporias should also be included among the list of possible roadblocks). Finally, as will be apparent later on in the chapter, I believe that Johansson's sense of the resistant indeterminacy in the text—the way in which it fights against the coherence of an interpretation that equates it to a simple riddle—is principally the result of two different discourses that, in being overlayed on each other, create a kind of "oscillation" or "constant alternation" (to borrow his terms) that produces a complexity superseding the structure of a riddle and its answer. One of these discourses does, in my opinion, refer to procreative sex. The other involves the materials described within the rite at its center, which, in my view, are not insignificant (or significant for their insignificance). Johansson's essay does an excellent job of critically approaching existing interpretations—bringing up the textual information they avoid or how they fail to provide convincing arguments. I would suggest that this critical mindset is far more valuable than the certainty that there is no Secret to discover, especially since this claim *also* lacks coherent evidence (how does one prove that there is no secret, that the materials in the rite are insignificant?).

The interpretation offered in this chapter is not, I should restate, intended to be read as the only way to approach the story; it (like any story) functions in a way that is always beyond our capabilities of description or interpretation. While it can at times be helpful to speak to this indeterminacy, as Johansson does, in order to evoke that which cannot be contained in a work of interpretation, positioning indeterminacy as the "solution" or "secret" of a text can, unfortunately, render it incapable of communicating. This approach also rather problematically transfers the capacity to communicate to the literary theorists writing *authoritatively* on undecidability. (Why is Johansson so certain about the intentions of Adorno or the meaning of 'aporia' or 'contingency'?) I prefer, instead, to position indeterminacy as a possible place to begin a process of investigation, especially given the way in which doing so can allow for new discoveries to take place. I do not believe that the fruits of investigation neutralize literary texts since this idea implies that the ideal reader should know and learn as little as possible so as to remain in an empty state of evocative openness. I would suggest that Borges, to the contrary, was interested in inviting readers into an active process of interpretation that, with every discovery, leads deeper into questions that, by their very nature, resist simplistic approaches. For more on the nature of indeterminacy in Borges's work, see Borinsky, *Theoretical Fables*, xi.

26. In 1920, Borges published a prose poem in *Grecia* titled "Paréntesis personal" that describes an erotic encounter between the narrator and a woman. It echoes the connection between sexual reproduction and divine creation:

> Bésame. Bésame. . . . Ya las dudas han muerto. Ya las penas han muerto y contigo a mi lado me siento fuerte como un Dios. Yo soy un Dios. Yo puedo crear la Vida.

El borroso zaguán. La escalera indecisa. Luego la Alcoba. La Alcoba es íntima y discreta. Hay profundos espejos y Alcatifas de Persia y hondos Divanes y un amplio Lecho sumiso. (Borges and Carril, *Textos Recobrados*, 35)

Kiss me. Kiss me. . . . Now the doubts have all died. Suffering has died now and with you by my side I feel strong, like a God. I am a God. I can create Life.

The blurred hallway. The hesitant staircase. Then the Bedroom. The Bedroom is intimate and discrete. There are deep mirrors and Persian Rugs and ample Divans and a large, submissive Bed.

Some of this imagery (together with Arabic-origin words such as alcoba, zaguán, alcatifa, divan) recalls the beginning of "Tlön, Uqbar, Orbis Tertius," in which a large mirror, copulation, and Islam are all thematically combined.

27. Also worth considering is a text alluded to by both stories: Browne's *Religio Medici*.

The whole World was made for man, but the twelfth part of man for woman: Man is the whole World, and the Breath of God; Woman the Rib, and crooked piece of man. I could be content that we might procreate like trees without conjunction, or that there were any way to perpetuate the World without this trivial and vulgar way of coition; it is the foolishest act a wise man commits in all his life, nor is there anything that will more deject his cool'd imagination, when he shall consider what an odd and unworthy piece of folly he hath committed. I speak not in prejudice, nor am averse from that sweet Sex, but naturally amorous of all that is beautiful. (2:160–61)

Borges repeats some of this wording in "La secta del Fénix," describing the "rite" at its center as both *trivial* and *vulgar*. Additionally, the main idea being expressed by Browne—that it would be desirable to procreate botanically, without copulation (and without the need for women)—reappears within "Las ruinas circulares."

28. Christ agrees that this list of materials for the rite suggests that the sexual interpretation of the story is not sufficient. Yet his solution to the puzzle also seems to avoid these very materials. He writes: "Those readers I have talked with all suggest that the answer is propagation by sexual intercourse, a way of guaranteeing the immortality of the species rather than that of individuals. . . . Then there are those perplexing ingredients of cork, wax, gum arabic and, sometimes, slime or mud. One chooses to stop short of seeing a sexual implication in those. I think Borges has a rather more typically metaphysical answer in mind. The rite which is celebrated by the sect of the Phoenix is the last rite, that of death. We die in order to be reborn" (*Narrow Act*, 155–56). Christ does not explain how the specific materials are connected to any rites of death.

29. Carolyn Fornoff writes that the general tendency to accept the obvious answer to the riddle in the story (copulation) at face value is the reason that it has not received as much critical attention as other stories. Echoing the ideas of

Anders Johansson, Fornoff suggests that things are not quite as simple as these responses would indicate, that the text's style of circling around the mystery is an important part of its structure. "Solving" the riddle is in this view a way of shutting down the text and turning one's gaze away from the "ambiguity" and "multiplicity" that are essential to its form. For Fornoff, the project of deciphering the mystery is futile, since language itself functions as a system that constantly defers meaning and maintains an aura of undecidability ("Descifrar el Secreto," 137). "Para Derrida, la literatura depende de la atracción del secreto, pero de un secreto incognoscible, porque detrás del texto no hay nada" (For Derrida, literature depends on the attractiveness of the secret, but of an unknowable secret, because behind the text there is nothing [137]). While I strongly agree with Fornoff in terms of the limiting tendency to accept the *visible* solution provided by the text without engaging in a deeper way with the story's contradictions, I have attempted to show that it is possible to find an answer to the riddle that oscillates between two possibilities (the act of procreative sex and the act of writing) that, through their interaction, open toward a new field of meaning that does not necessarily complete and close the interpretation in a simplistic manner. Doing so, in my view, suggests that pursuing an interpretation of the story and, even more narrowly, a solution to the riddle, is not futile. Instead, it can be a way to respect the internal lucidity of the text. On the contrary, by deciding that the secret of the text is a secret that *all literary texts* contain (the unknowable secret of literature), once can homogenize the story; it only reveals to us what every story reveals. As Alicia Borinsky has written, collapsing all literary texts into "undecidability" creates a context in which only literary theory—and those who wield it—have the capacity to communicate (*Theoretical Fables*, xi). It is reasonable to ask how it is possible for Fornoff, above, to be confident regarding Derrida's intentions (or the meaning of "his" words) given her assertion that behind language one finds only ambiguity and unknowability. While I agree with Fornoff's observation that the apparent "answer" to the story has prevented closer readings of the text, I also suspect that when literary texts are exalted as unknowable mysteries, they are placed out of reach in a way that leaves us only with the orthodoxies of literary theory.

30. Cordero, *El lápiz*, 64.

31. *Encyclopedia Britannica*, 21:86.

32. John T. Irwin offers the possibility that Yu Tsun is at least partially derived from the protagonist of *Dream of the Red Chamber*, a book mentioned within the story that its editor claimed to have finished after the death of the author left it in fragments. Irwin notes that a scene from the book is included within Borges's *Anthology of Fantastic Literature* (*Mystery to a Solution*, 88).

33. See, for example, Barrenechea, "Tiempo y la eternidad," and Sasson-Henry, *Borges 2.0*. Daniel Balderston has lamented that it often seems as though the story "has not left its critics any option except to speak of games with time: to repeat, that is, Stephen Albert's position in the story, deprived of its dialectical punch" (*Out of Context*, 40).

34. If one sees the book as infinite due to the unlimited possibilities of interpretation, this would apply equally well to any novel, fragmentary or otherwise.

Even the idea that this novel might contain multiple timelines or uninterrupted timelines cannot mean that it is infinite in a way that differentiates it from other texts. Every literary text—by virtue of its endings or omissions—can suggest infinite, unstated courses of action in precisely the same way.

35. Another example is provided in which every bifurcation pivots around death and killing:

> Fang, digamos, tiene un secreto; un desconocido llama a su puerta; Fang resuelve matarlo. Naturalmente, hay varios desenlaces posibles: Fang puede matar al intruso, el intruso puede matar a Fang, ambos pueden salvarse, ambos pueden morir, etcétera. En la obra de Ts'ui Pên, todos los desenlaces ocurren; cada uno es el punto de partida de otras bifurcaciones. (1:774)

> Fang, let's say, has a secret; a stranger knocks on his door; Fang decides to kill him. Naturally, there are various possible outcomes: Fang can kill the intruder, the intruder can kill Fang, both can survive, both can die, etcetera. In Ts'ui Pên's work, all of the outcomes occur; each is a point of departure for other bifurcations.

36. Daniel Balderston points out that the story seems to reference *The Art of War* by Sun Tzu (*Out of Context*, 42–43). Its title would definitely be appropriate for Ts'ui Pên's text.

37. Laraway writes that "one of the morals of 'Las ruinas circulares' might be expressed in this way: questions of identity are by their nature open-ended and indeterminate, for the concept of identity is contingent upon other concepts and perspectives that are made available only through the mediation of an Other" ("Generations," 29). While his interpretation turns more toward an evocation of ambiguity and open-endedness, our approaches both take notice of the "genealogical" metaphor and share an interest in the relationship between literary influence and identity.

38. Borges wrote a prologue to an edition of the Bhagavad-Gita that states that it was considered, by some, to be written by a God. Viewed from the perspective of immortal, divine beings, war becomes illusory. "La derrota o la victoria no importan; lo esencial es cumplir con su deber y lograr la Nirvana" (Defeat or victory are unimportant; what is essential is to do one's duty and achieve Nirvana [4:521]).

CHAPTER 3

1. While Macedonio often wrote that death was an insignificant event, this did not necessarily correspond with his personal relationship with death and dying. In conversation with Adolfo Bioy Casares, for example, Borges stated: "Padre tardó un mes en morir y Macedonio nunca fue, porque sentía horror a la muerte y no quería tener imágenes de una agonía" (My father took a month to die and Macedonio never came to visit him, because he was terrified of death and did not want to have any mental images of him dying [Bioy Casares, *Borges*, 1056]).

2. Daniel Balderston mentions the similarity between the heroic aspirations of Pedro Damián and the story of Aparicio Saravia, writing that, "la figura de héroe que el protagonista se afana por crear es claramente una construcción y se vincula con el suicidio heroico de Saravia en el campo de batalla" (the figure of the hero that the protagonist attempts to create is clearly a construction and it is connected to the heroic suicide of Saravia in the field of battle [*Borges*, 91]).

3. In the essay "Historias de jinetes," Borges emphasizes Aparicio Savaria's reaction of fear (and cowardice) stemming from his unfamiliarity with the city. The text echoes Luis Melián Lafinur's statement that Saravia would not enter the city "porque el gaucho le teme a la ciudad" (1:428).

4. Julio Crespo pointed out the existence of Rossini's *Otello* to me after reviewing a draft of this chapter, also noting that Tamberlick performed in Buenos Aires. He in fact participated in the inauguration of Buenos Aires's original Teatro Colón in 1857, starring as Alfredo Germont in Verdi's *La traviata*.

5. Additionally, Juan Francisco Amaro, in the story, uncannily mentions that Pedro Damián cried out "¡Viva Urquiza!" in the battle (1:875), words that correspond with an even earlier historical context. Once one begins playing with time travel and identity transformation, it becomes possible to imagine an unending series of conflicts and temporal alterations. Maybe Aparicio Saravia was delivered even further into the past, to gain experience in another conflict before being able to return to his battle. Perhaps it is Justo José de Urquiza, not Aparicio Saravia, that is at the center of the riddle. One is tempted to think that the riddle has no fixed center, that it is designed to initiate an inquiry that repeats into the past in decidedly unstable terms.

6. Evelyn Fishburn, similarly, finds that the allusions (to Pier Damiani, to Emerson, to Bertrand Russell) in the story create a counterpoint of perspectives with regard to memory, history, and valor that stimulate an internal dialogue in the reader that demands further thought and interpretation (*Hidden Pleasures in Borges's Fiction*, 40).

7. Fernández, *Museo de la novela de la Eterna*, 33–34.

8. Lois Parkinson Zamora notes that Borges seems unimpressed with Emerson's traditional stance with regard to the past, reminding us that in his poem titled "Emerson," Borges "makes his 'tall New Englander' dissatisfied with his own progressive, unrepeatable history: 'No he vivido. Quisiera ser otro hombre'" (*Usable Past*, 228).

9. Naomi Lindstrom approaches "La otra muerte" as a parable that dramatizes the way in which history is altered through the process of being observed, recorded, and manipulated. She writes that this manipulation is especially common when it comes to the "accounts of the last moments of any much-celebrated combatant" (*Jorge Luis Borges*, 77). Evelyn Fishburn, similarly, suggests that the story reminds us that history itself is composed of memories and not acts and, as such, can be easily altered and transformed ("Lecturas recónditas," 57). I agree that, on one level, the story takes on questions of memory and history, though my approach here takes the paradoxical intervention in the historical timeline more seriously as a central aspect of the story's structure.

10. This footnote was discovered by David Howlett, a participant in a seminar on *El Aleph* that I taught at Chicago's The Newberry Library in 2011. After our discussion of "La otra muerte," he consulted his own copy of this edition of Emerson's complete works and brought the note to the seminar's attention.

11. Ríos Patrón, *Jorge Luis Borges*, 37.

12. Both quotes are from Bioy Casares, *Borges*, 359.

13. It is possible that this is a typo and that he was following her "like" ("como") a detective and not "with" ("con") a detective.

14. Bioy Casares, *Borges*, 359.

15. Both quotes from ibid.

16. Ibid., 959.

17. Ibid., 1024.

18. Ibid., 360.

19. This story from 1977 should be read, however, alongside another text published in the same year: Vázquez, *Borges: Imágenes, memorias, diálogos*. The book is offered under a sign of friendship between the two writers and consists mainly of interviews with Borges conducted by María Esther. None of the events described in this chapter are mentioned in the text and the tone of the conversations is collegial. The public politeness contrasts, clearly, with the underlying tone of the story.

20. The dedication to María Esther Vázquez is, in my view, an important part of the poem. It is worth mentioning that this dedication does not appear in Sudamericana's *Obras Completas*. It appears as though some other recently published editions of the poem lack the dedication, though it is present in others, such as Tapscott, *Twentieth-Century Latin American Poetry* (146).

21. I am basing this on Adolfo Bioy Casares's entry on September 2, 1959: "En *Atlántida* leo, de Borges, el admirable 'Poema de los dones.' Admirable, aunque un tanto previsible" (In *Atlántida* I read Borges's admirable "Poema de los dones." Admirable, if a bit predictable [Bioy Casares, *Borges*, 545].)

EPILOGUE

1. Borges, "Místicos del Islam," 1.

2. Borges's interest, as I have argued in the first chapter, is aesthetic, literary, and personal. As he created literary texts designed to foster unease around the allure of visuality, Islam became an important source of theological material for his "literary theology." Its war on images was similar to his own war on the primacy of visual allure—the fact that he carried out his project with the knowledge that he would one day be unable to see makes stories such as "El Aleph" and "El Zahir" all the more resonant.

3. Borges, "Místicos del Islam," 2.

4. Borges, "Místicos del Islam," 2.

5. Elsewhere in Borges's notebooks, some of these ideas are associated strongly with Blake. "Man is all imagination. God is Man and exists in us and we in him," reads one of Borges's handwritten citations. Next to it is a note reading "Keynes

820," referring to the scholar Geoffrey Keynes. Another states: "El Dios cruel de este mundo ha atado nuestros cinco sentidos y ellos fabrican este falso mundo cruel" (The cruel God of this world has bound together our five senses and they create this cruel, false world). This second statement carries the note Saurat 123; Denis Saurat was another scholar of Blake. Another related quote of Blake that Borges copied by hand reads: "If the doors of perception were cleansed every thing would appear to man as it is, infinite," which is from "The Marriage of Heaven and Hell." In his journal, it is accompanied by the note "Keynes 187." For another example of the intertwining of Blake, Buddhism, and Islamic and Christian mysticism, see Borges's short book, coauthored with Alicia Jurado, *¿Qué es el budismo?*, 73–74.

6. Borges, "Místicos del Islam," 3.

7. Bodhidarma, the text later informs us, is the monk who brought Buddhism to China at the beginning of the sixth century, which led, in turn, to the development of Zen in Japan.

8. This anecdote reappears in Borges and Jurado, *¿Qué es el budismo?*, 63–64, within a section on Buddhism in China. While this book was published in 1976, manuscripts presented in 2016 at the Mariano Moreno National Library suggest that its content was written at the beginning of the 1950s, at around the same time that Borges's "Místicos del Islam" was created. Both are written in a similar script that Borges was no longer able to produce after 1955 due to his blindness.

9. Borges, "Místicos del Islam," 4.

10. In Borges and Jurado, *¿Qué es el budismo?*, Borges compares the affinities between the mystical traditions in Buddhism, Christianity, and Islam, noting that they all involve a disdain for rational schemas and an emphasis on intuitive perception and experience. They also share, Borges notes, a faith in the possibility of perfect understanding and the annihilation of the self that is associated with a vision of universal unity and sensations of profound happiness.

11. This anecdote reappears in Borges and Jurado, *¿Qué es el budismo?*, 72, within a section dedicated to Zen Buddhism.

Bibliography

Abós, Álvaro. *Macedonio Fernández: La biografía imposible*. Buenos Aires: Plaza & Janés, 2002.

Aizenberg, Edna. *The Aleph Weaver: Biblical, Kabbalistic and Judaic Elements in Borges*. Potomac, MD: Scripta Humanistica, 1984.

———. "Deutsches Requiem 2005." *Variaciones Borges* 20 (2005): 33–57.

Alazraki, Jaime. *Jorge Luis Borges*. New York: Columbia University Press, 1971.

———. "Kabbalistic Traits in Borges' Narration." *Studies in Short Fiction* 8, no. 1 (1971): 78–92.

Almond, Ian. "Borges the Post-Orientalist: Images of Islam from the Edge of the West." *Modern Fiction Studies* 50, no. 2 (2004): 435–59.

Anzaldo, Demetrio. "Mito(s) en la Argentina, ¿Emma Zunz o Borges? Las (in)creíbles invenciones de la palabra y del pensamiento confeccionadas en el cuento 'Emma Zunz.'" *Narrativas* 31 (2013): 3–19.

Balderston, Daniel. *Borges: Realidades y simulacros*. Buenos Aires: Editorial Biblos, 2000.

———. "Una lógica simbólica: Manuscritos de Jorge Luis Borges en la Biblioteca Nacional." In *Borges el mismo, otro*, 13–18. Buenos Aires: Biblioteca Nacional Mariano Moreno, 2016.

———. *Out of Context: Historical Reference and the Representation of Reality in Borges*. Durham: Duke University Press, 1993.

Barrenechea, Ana Maria. *La expresión de la irrealidad en la obra de Jorge Luis Borges*. Buenos Aires: Paidos, 1967.

———. "El tiempo y la eternidad en la obra de Borges." *Revista Hispánica Moderna* 23 (1957): 28–41.

Bhat, Aravinda. "Corporeal Refractions: Narrativising the Visually Impaired Subject in Selected Writings by Jorge Luis Borges, John Hull, and Stephen Kuusisto." Ph.D. diss., The English and Foreign Languages University, Hyderabad, 2016.

Bioy Casares, Adolfo. *Borges*. Buenos Aires: Ediciones Destino, 2006.

Blanco, Mercedes. "Arqueologías de Tlön: Borges y el Urn Burial de Browne." *Variaciones Borges* 15 (2003): 19–46.

Block de Behar, Lisa, and William Egginton. "Rereading Borges's 'The Aleph': On the Name of a Place, a Word, and a Letter." *New Centennial Review* 4, no. 1 (2004): 169–87.

Borges, Jorge Luis. *The Aleph and Other Stories, 1933–1969: Together with Commentaries and an Autobiographical Essay*. Edited and translated by Norman Thomas di Giovanni. New York: E. P. Dutton, 1970.

———. "La belleza no es un hecho extraordinario." *Cuadernos Hispanoamericanos* 505 (1992): 51–72.

———. "Blak." The Jorge Luis Borges Collection, The Harry Ransom Center at the University of Texas, Austin, Container 1.2.

———. *Borges en SUR, 1931–1980*. Buenos Aires: Emecé, 1999.

———. *Macedonio Fernández*. Buenos Aires: Ediciones Culturales Argentinas, 1961.

———. "Místicos del Islam." The Jorge Luis Borges Collection, The Harry Ransom Center at the University of Texas, Austin. Container 1.14.

———. *Obras Completas*. 4 vols. Buenos Aires: Sudamericana, 2011.

———. "Paradiso, XXI, 108." *SUR* 231 (November and December 1954).

Borges, Jorge Luis, and Adolfo Bioy Casares. *Crónicas de Bustos Domecq*. Buenos Aires: Losada, 2003.

———. *Libro del cielo y del infierno*. Buenos Aires: SUR, 1975.

———. *Nuevos cuentos de Bustos Domecq*. Paris: Ediciones Librería La Ciudad, 1967.

———. "Quinto capítulo de la *Hydriotaphia* (1658) por Sir Thomas Browne (1603–1682)." *SUR* 111 (January 1944).

Borges, Jorge Luis, and Richard Burgin. *Jorge Luis Borges: Conversations*. Jackson: University Press of Mississippi, 1998.

Borges, Jorge Luis, and Sara L. Carril. *Textos Recobrados, 1919–1929*. Barcelona: Emecé Editores, 2007.

Borges, Jorge Luis, and Antonio Carrizo. *Borges, el Memorioso: Conversaciones de Jorge Luis Borges con Antonio Carrizo*. México: Fondo de Cultura Económica, 1983.

Borges, Jorge Luis, and Ronald Christ. "The Art of Fiction." In *The Paris Review Interviews*, edited by Philip Gourevitch, 111–59. New York: Picador, 2006.

Borges, Jorge Luis, and María Esther Gilio. "Yo querría ser el hombre invisible." In *Crisis*, 40–47. Buenos Aires: Editorial Del Noroeste, 1974.

Borges, Jorge Luis, and Alicia Jurado. *¿Qué es el budismo?* Buenos Aires: Editorial Columba, 1976.

Borges, Jorge Luis, and Néstor Montenegro. *Diálogos: Jorge Luis Borges*. Buenos Aires: Nemont, 1983.

Borinsky, Alicia. "Borges en nuestra biblioteca." *Revista Iberoamericana* 43, no. 100 (1977): 609–14.

———. *Theoretical Fables: The Pedagogical Dream in Contemporary Latin American Literature*. Philadelphia: University of Pennsylvania Press, 1993.

Brodzki, Bella. "'She Was Unable Not to Think': Borges's 'Emma Zunz' and the Female Subject." *MLN* 100, no. 2 (1985): 330–47.

Brotherston, Gordon. "Borges and Aleph." *Variaciones Borges* 31 (2011): 233–38.

Browne, Thomas. *Religio Medici*. 1 vol. in 2 parts. London: George Bell and Sons, 1898.

Burton, Richard Francis. *The Lake Regions of Central Africa: A Picture Exploration.* 2 vols. London: Longman, Green, Longman and Roberts, 1860.

Canto, Estela. *Borges a contraluz.* Madrid: Espasa Calpe, 1999.

Capella, Martianus. *Martianus Capella and the Seven Liberal Arts.* Translated by William Harris Stahl and Richard Johnson. 2 vols. New York: Columbia University Press, 1977.

Cervantes, Miguel de. *Don Quijote de la Mancha.* Edited by Francisco Rico. Madrid: Punto de Lectura, 2007.

Chelkowski, Peter. "Islam in Modern Drama and Theatre." *Die Welt des Islams* 23, no. 1 (1984): 45–69.

Christ, Ronald. *The Narrow Act: Borges' Art of Allusion.* New York: New York University Press, 1969.

Corbatta, Jorgelina. *Borges y yo / Borges y los otros.* Buenos Aires: Corregidor, 2014.

Corbett, Eustace K. "Art. XV.—The History of the Mosque of Amr at Old Cairo." *Journal of the Royal Asiatic Society of Great Britain and Ireland* 22, no. 4 (1890): 759–800.

Cordero, Tulio Febres. *El lápiz.* Caracas: Instituto Autónomo Biblioteca Nacional, Sala Tulio Febres Cordero y el Consejo de Publicaciones de la Universidad de los Andes, 1888.

Crosby, James. "La última prisión de Quevedo: Documentos atribuidos, atribuibles y apócrifos." *La Perinola: Revista de investigación quevediana* 1 (1997): 101–24.

Dapía, Silvia G. "Why Is There a Problem About Fictional Discourse? An Interpretation of Borges's 'Theme of the Traitor and the Hero' and 'Emma Zunz.'" *Variaciones Borges* 5 (1998): 157–76.

De Quincey, Thomas, and David Masson. *The Collected Writings of Thomas De Quincey.* London: A. & C. Black, 1896.

Di Giovanni, Norman Thomas. *The Lesson of the Master: On Borges and His Work.* New York: Continuum, 2003.

Earle, Peter G. "Ortega y Gasset in Argentina: The Exasperating Colony." *Hispania* 70, no. 3 (1987): 475–86.

Echavarría Ferrari, Arturo. "'Tlön, Uqbar, Orbis Tertius': Creación de un lenguaje y crítica del lenguaje." *Revista Iberoamericana* 43, no. 100 (1977): 399–413.

Elia, Nada. "Islamic Esoteric Concepts as Borges Strategies." *Variaciones Borges* 5 (1998): 129–44.

Emerson, Ralph W., and Edward W. Emerson. *The Complete Works of Ralph Waldo Emerson.* Boston: Houghton Mifflin, 1903–1904.

Encyclopedia Britannica. 11th ed. New York: Encyclopedia Britannica, 1910.

Fernández, Macedonio. *Museo de la novela de la Eterna.* Buenos Aires: Centro Editor de América Latina, 1967.

———. *Teorías.* Buenos Aires: Corregidor, 1974.

Fishburn, Evelyn. "Borges, Cabbala and 'Creative Misreading.'" *Ibero-Amerikanisches Archiv* 14, no. 4 (1988): 401–18.

———. "Hidden Pleasures in Borges's Allusions." In *Borges and Europe Revisited.* London: University of London, Institute of Latin American Studies, 1998.

————. *Hidden Pleasures in Borges's Fiction.* Pittsburgh: Borges Center, University of Pittsburgh, 2015.

————. "Lecturas recónditas en las alusiones de Borges." *Cuadernos Americanos* 4, no. 64 (1997): 195–203.

Flood, Finbarr B. "Between Cult and Culture: Bamiyan, Islamic Iconoclasm, and the Museum." *Art Bulletin* 84, no. 4 (2002): 641–59.

————. "Picasso the Muslim: Or, How the *Bilderverbot* Became Modern (Part 1)." *Res: Anthropology and Aesthetics* 67, no. 8 (2017): 42–60.

Fornoff, Carolyn. "Descifrar el Secreto: 'La secta del Fénix' y el acertijo literario." *Variaciones Borges* 39 (2015): 125–42.

Franco, Jean. "The Utopia of a Tired Man: Jorge Luis Borges." Edited and with an Introduction by Mary Louise Pratt and Kathleen Newman, 327–65. *Critical Passions: Selected Essays.* Durham: Duke University Press, 1999.

Frazer, James G. *The Golden Bough: A Study in Magic and Religion.* New York: Macmillan, 1935.

Goldstein, Kevin. "'La cara que me mira': Demythologizing Blindness in Borges's Disability Life Writing." In *Libre Acceso: Latin American Literature and Film Through Disability Studies*, edited by Susan Antebi and Beth Jorgensen, 46–62. New York: State University of New York Press, 2016.

Harvard Art Museums. "Description of Object Number 2005.115.91, Denarius of Augustus, Lugdunum." October 27, 2017, https://www.harvardartmuseums.org/art/21041.

Holy Bible: Authorized King James Version. Introduction and notes by C. I. Scofield. Oxford: Oxford University Press, 1967.

Hughes, Thomas P. *A Dictionary of Islam, Being a Cyclopædia of the Doctrines, Rites, Ceremonies, and Customs, Together with the Technical and Theological Terms of the Muhammadan Religion.* London: W. H. Allen, 1885.

Ingenieros, José. *La simulación en la lucha por la vida.* Buenos Aires: Spinelli, 1903.

Irwin, John T. *The Mystery to a Solution: Poe, Borges, and the Analytic Detective Story.* Baltimore: Johns Hopkins University Press, 1994.

Isaacson, José. *Macedonio Fernández, sus ideas políticas y estéticas.* Buenos Aires: Editorial de Belgrano, 1981.

Johansson, Anders. "Borges Beyond Interpretations: Changeability and Form in 'La secta del Fénix.'" *Variaciones Borges* 9 (2000): 177–201.

Joyce, James. *Ulysses.* Edited by Hans W. Gabler. London: Vintage, 1993.

Khalidi, Tarif. *The Qur'an.* New York: Penguin Books, 2009.

Kushigian, Julia A. *Crónicas orientalistas y autorrealizadas: Entrevistas con Jorge Luis Borges, Carlos Fuentes, Juan Goytisolo, Elena Poniatowska, Severo Sarduy y Mario Vargas Llosa.* Madrid: Editorial Verbum, 2016.

Lane, Edward W. *An Account of the Manners and Customs of the Modern Egyptians.* London: J. Murray, 1871.

Laraway, David. "Generations: Borges and His Progeny." *Latin American Literary Review* 28, no. 56 (2000): 27–42.

Lenssen, Anneka, and Sarah Rogers. "Articulating the Contemporary." In *A Companion to Islamic Art and Architecture*, vol. 2, edited by Finbarr Flood and Gülru Necipoğlu, 1314–48. Oxford: Wiley Blackwell, 2017.

Levine, Suzanne J. "Notes to Borges's Notes on Joyce: Infinite Affinities." *Comparative Literature* 49, no. 4 (1997): 344–59.

Lindstrom, Naomi. *Jorge Luis Borges: A Study of the Short Fiction*. Boston: Twayne Publishers, 1990.

Ling, David J. "Manners and Customs of Literary Appropriation: Mirrors of Ink from Borges, Burton and Lane." *Arabica* 59, no. 1 (2012): 87–108.

López-Baralt, Luce. "Borges, or the Mystique of Silence: What Was on the Other Side of the Zahir." In *Critical Essays on Jorge Luis Borges*, edited by Jaime Alazraki, 29-70. Boston: G. K. Hall, 1987.

———. "Jorge Luis Borges y el Islam." In *El legado de Borges*, edited by Rafael Olea Franco, 179–97. México: El Colegio de México, 2015.

———. "Lo que había del otro lado del Zahir de Jorge Luis Borges." *Numen* 8, no. 1 (2005): 71–119.

———. "*Ultra Auroram et Gangem*: Los laberintos islámicos de Jorge Luis Borges." In *La fe en el universo literario de Borges*, edited by Ruth Fine and Daniel Blaustein, 111–36. Hildesheim: Georg Olms Verlag, 2012.

Lucian, John B., W. Willson, and A. P. Garnett. *Lucian's Wonderland: Being a Translation of the "Vera Historia."* Edinburgh: William Blackwood and Sons, 1899.

Ludmer, Josefina. "Las justicias de Emma." *Cuadernos Hispanoamericanos* 505–7 (1992): 473–80.

Magnavacca, Silvia. *Filósofos medievales en la obra de Borges*. Madrid: Miño y Dávila, 2009.

Makki, Mahmoud. "The Political History of Al-Andalus." In *The Legacy of Muslim Spain*, edited by Salma K. Jayyusi, Leiden: E.J. Brill, 2010.

Martínez, Guillermo. *Borges and Mathematics: Lectures at Malba*. West Lafayette: Purdue University Press, 2012.

Masiello, Francine. "Lenguaje e ideología." In *Museo de la Novela de la Eterna*, edited by Ana Camblong and Adolfo de Obieta, 520–35. Madrid: ALLCA XX, 1996.

Molloy, Sylvia, and Oscar Montero. *Signs of Borges*. Durham: Duke University Press, 1994.

Montes, Gregorio Santiago. "La intrusa en la vida de Borges." *Proa* 42 (1999).

Novillo-Corvalán, Patricia. *Borges and Joyce: An Infinite Conversation*. Oxford: Legenda, 2011.

Núñez-Faraco, Humberto. *Borges and Dante: Echoes of a Literary Friendship*. Oxford: Peter Lang, 2006.

———. "In Search of the Aleph: Memory, Truth, and Falsehood in Borges's Poetics." *Modern Language Review* 92, no. 3 (1997): 613–29.

Ortega, Julio. "El Aleph y el lenguaje epifánico." *Hispanic Review* 67, no. 4 (1999): 453–66.

Ortega, Julio, Elena del Río Parra, and Jorge L. Borges. *"El Aleph" de Jorge Luis Borges*. México: El Colegio de México, Centro de Estudios Lingüísticos y Literarios, 2008.

Ortega y Gasset, José. "La deshumanización del arte." In *Obras Completas*, 3:353–86. Madrid: Revista de Occidente, 1957.

Petersen, Alice. "Borges's 'Ulrike'—Signature of a Literary Life." *Studies in Short Fiction* 33, no. 3 (1996): 325–32.

Podlubne, Judith. "Borges contra Ortega: Un episodio en su polémica con Mallea." *Variaciones Borges* 19 (2005): 169–81.

Rice, Thomas J. "Subtle Reflections of/upon Joyce in/by Borges." *Journal of Modern Literature* 24, no. 1 (2000): 47–62.

Ríos Patrón, José. *Jorge Luis Borges.* Buenos Aires: Editorial La Mandrágora, 1955.

Rivera-Taupier, Miguel. "Emma Zunz y sus precursoras." *Hispanófila* 164, no. 1 (2012): 69–80.

Rodríguez Monegal, Emir. "In the Labyrinth." In *The Cardinal Points of Borges: A Symposium*, edited by Lowell Dunham and Ivar Ivask, 17–23. Norman: University of Oklahoma Press, 1971.

———. *Jorge Luis Borges: A Literary Biography.* New York: E. P. Dutton, 1978.

———. *Obra selecta.* Caracas: Biblioteca Ayacucho, 2003.

Rojo, Grínor. "Sobre 'Emma Zunz.'" *Revista chilena de literatura* 45 (1994): 87–106.

Rosato, Laura, and Germán Álvarez. *Borges, libros y lecturas.* Biblioteca Nacional, 2017.

Roux, Dominique de, and Jean de Milleret. *Jorge Luis Borges.* Paris: L'Herne, 1964.

Said, Edward. *Orientalism.* New York: Vintage Books Edition, 1994.

Sarlo, Beatriz. "El saber del cuerpo: A propósito de 'Emma Zunz.'" *Variaciones Borges* 7 (1999): 231–47.

Sasso, Eleonora. *The Pre-Raphaelites and Orientalism: Language and Cognition in Remediations of the East.* Edinburgh: Edinburgh University Press, 2018.

Sasson-Henry, Perla. *Borges 2.0: From Text to Virtual Worlds.* Latin America 13. New York: Peter Lang, 2007.

Sosnowski, Saúl. *Borges y la Cábala: La búsqueda del verbo.* Buenos Aires: Hispamerica, 1976.

Spivakovsky, Erika. "In Search of Arabic Influences on Borges." *Hispania* 51, no. 2 (1968): 223–31.

Spraggon, Julie. *Puritan Iconoclasm During the English Civil War.* Woodbridge, UK: Boydell Press, 2003.

Stavans, Ilán. *Borges, the Jew.* Albany: State University of New York Press, 2016.

Sturrock, John. *Paper Tigers: The Ideal Fictions of Jorge Luis Borges.* Oxford: Clarendon Press, 1977.

Tapscott, Stephen. *Twentieth-Century Latin American Poetry: A Bilingual Anthology.* Austin: University of Texas Press, 2000.

Vázquez, María Esther. *Borges: Imágenes, memorias, diálogos.* Caracas: Monte Avila, 1977.

Whelan, Estelle. "The Origins of the Miḥrāb Mujawwaf: A Reinterpretation." *International Journal of Middle East Studies* 18, no. 2 (1986): 205–23.

White, Alan. "An Appalling or Banal Reality." *Variaciones Borges* 15 (2003): 47–91.

Williamson, Edwin. *Borges: The Biography.* London: Viking, 2004.

Zamora, Lois P. *The Usable Past: The Imagination of History in Recent Fiction of the Americas.* Cambridge: Cambridge University Press, 1997.

Index